The
Male Dilemma

The Male Dilemma

How to Survive the Sexual Revolution

Anne Steinmann

David J. Fox

Jason Aronson, New York

HQ
31
.S79
1974
apr 1995

Copyright © 1974 by Jason Aronson, Inc.

LIBRARY OF CONGRESS CATALOGING IN PUBLICATION DATA

Steinmann, Anne.
    The male dilemma.

    Includes bibliographical references.
    1. Sexual ethics.   2. Women's Liberation Movement
3. Men—Sexual behavior.   4. Sex roles. I. Fox,
David J., joint author.   II.   Title.
HQ31.S79   301.41   73-81213
ISBN 0-87668-094-5

Designed by Sidney Solomon

Manufactured in the United States of America

To Herbert and to Louise, with love

Contents

Preface

The United States in the 1960's saw the beginning of a profound and sweeping sexual revolution and, in the 1970's, that revolution shows no signs of slowing down or reversing its direction. Instead, with the proliferation of women's liberation groups and the iconoclastic behavior of the young, changes in the laws governing divorce and abortion, the advent of the Pill and the new biology, the revolution promises to accelerate. Sexual relationships and roles as we have known them in this country, including marriage and child-raising, seem to be shaken to their very roots.

Just what this revolution is doing to the average American man and woman is the subject of *The Male Dilemma.* Long the "second sex," the American woman is speaking up for an equal share of freedom, opportunity, and responsibility. But, for every gain she makes, there is a corresponding loss of male power and prestige. The age-old battle of the sexes has taken on new and potentially disastrous dimensions. Men and women are at each others' throats with an intensity that is new in our history. The statistics on divorce, illegitimacy, and the incidence of venereal disease, along with less tangible but nonetheless troublesome indications of object love, increasing promiscuity, and more overt homosexuality, reinforce our view that American men and women stand at a sexual crossroads. The traditional standards of masculine and feminine behavior are breaking down, and as yet no new patterns have evolved to take their place.

There has been, and continues to be, a rash of books about the woman's side of the sexual revolution and about her roles and rights. But what about the male side; what about his roles and rights? We believe *The Male Dilemma* presents the first balanced view of the contemporary conflict between the sexes. Men and women alike share the responsibility for their present sexual bind; together they must search for a viable solution to their problems. This book investigates both sexes in detail, along with the psychological and social forces—past and present—that have shaped their behavior and led to the current impasse. The work is based on twenty years of clinical experience and comprehensive research into sexual roles and relationships, research that has provided incontrovertible evidence that both men and women share a deep-rooted ambivalence, within themselves and toward each other, about their sexual roles. They are no longer sure what it means to be masculine or feminine; they are not certain what their roles should be in work, in sexual intercourse, in marriage, and in child-raising. Their sexual ambivalence is reflected, we have found, in their social behavior and attitudes, in their political beliefs, in the generation gap, and in the new "permissiveness" of contemporary culture.

How did it begin and where will it all end? *The Male Dilemma* has been written for the general reader, male and female alike, and it is hoped that each reader will respond on a personal level. It also includes questionnaires and surveys that we used in our research, so that each reader can measure his or her own sexual attitudes and behavior.

We believe that the next few years are crucial in the search for a resolution to our sexual conflicts. They are crucial for adults of the present generation groping for some means to adapt traditional patterns of behavior to a society in rapid transition, as well as for the younger generation, which must also find a way to adjust to new freedoms. We will offer our own solutions to these problems after we have described their origins and effects. We present, we feel, a rational and realistic view of issues that are too often clouded by emotionalism.

The Male Dilemma calls on men and women and upon the society they have made to revise anachronistic and unworkable patterns of sexual behavior. This must be done if they hope to salvage the relationships they already have, and achieve psychological and social stability and mutual sexual satisfaction in the future.

Acknowledgments

This book represents two decades of research into the area of sex roles and perceptions, and obviously reflects not only our own thoughts and analyses, but our interactions with our colleagues.

Among the many professional colleagues who have helped, we particularly wish to thank Alexandra Botwin, Ph.D., who devised the original Inventories and who, over the years, has encouraged us in our research, and Professors Ethel Alpenfels and Georgene Seward, Dr. Joseph Levi and Dr. Emanuel K. Schwartz for their encouragement, and "B," who believed in the book from the beginning. We are grateful, too, to Dr. Bernard F. Riess and the Research Department of the Postgraduate Center for Mental Health, Barbara B. Fox and Dr. Lewis R. Wolberg, Chairman of the Board of the Postgraduate Center for Mental Health, Dr. Lawrence Hatterer, A. Morton Baliba, Philip Robbins, and Tom and Joye Hartzog, who, through their help to Maferr Foundation, Inc., have assisted the research immeasurably.

We wish to acknowledge with a special "thank you" the stimulation and pleasure of our professional collaboration with Dr. Ruth L. Farkas, who during her years on the Board of the Maferr Foundation, has aided us in every way.

In developing the manuscript, the innumberable critical readings and suggestions of Louise Fox and Herbert Steinmann were invaluable, and we appreciate their willingness to read and reread and their ability to be the candidly critical, insightful reactors we needed.

Finally, the research on which this book is based, involving thousands of respondents throughout the world obviously represents the efforts and work of many people, and we acknowledge with thanks the professional contributions of the colleagues listed on the following pages.

Thanks are due to the current staff of Maferr Foundation, Inc.: Eileen M. Breslin, Mary Cosme, and Raymond Sheehan; to Joanne Goldberg, Pearl Knie, Dr. Alan Rappaport, Freada and Max Weiss, and Sophie Colten for their contributions to data analysis; to Lillian Steinman and Anne Goldstein, who typed the final manuscript; and to Eretha Scott, who managed the Steinmann household so effectively.

We are grateful to our publisher, Dr. Jason Aronson and to the editors of *The Male Dilemma*, Nancy Binns, Warren Paul, Jane Murray, and especially to Burton Beals whose creative editing was of inestimable help.

While the professional colleagues and staff noted made the substance of the research possible, the spirit of the research and the essence of the book were made possible by the support and encouragement and patience of our spouses, Louise Fox and Herbert Steinmann, our children, Amy, Mara, Heather, and Erica Fox, Shelley List, Peter, Daniel, and Paula Steinmann, and grandchildren Julie, Abagail, and Robert who proved there is no generation gap in encouragement. They all proved, too, that the richest parts of the human experience continue to lie within the family.

The idea that if you're not part of the solution you're part of the problem, has no greater application than to the spouses involved when you write about sexual role conflicts and the male dilemma. We have both been fortunate in having spouses who not only were part of the solution, but who by their actions and feelings showed that "solutions" were possible, and provided us with models of the behaviors needed for those solutions: Herbert Steinmann showed us a man married to a woman with a busy, complex professional life can live a secure and solidly masculine life with rich family interactions, and Louise Fox demonstrated that a woman can combine a full professional career, with varied social service activities, without diminishing the quality of her life with her children and husband. Without them there would have been no book.

Colleagues Who Participated in Data Collection

IN THE UNITED STATES

Dr. Robert Amundson, Loretto Heights College, Colorado

Rabbi Charles Davidson, Bridgeport Temple, Connecticut

James Debeneure, Johnson C. Smith University, North Carolina

Sister M. Austin Doharty, Alverno College, Wisconsin

Miriam Erb, California

Dr. Ruth L. Farkas, New York

Dr. Louise W. Fox, Hunter College, New York

Linda Garcia, New York and Philippines

Dr. Herman Goldberg, Hofstra University, New York

Dr. Ralph Gundlach, New York

Dr. Laurence Hatterer, New York Hospital, New York

Margaret Karlin, Attorney, New York University, New York

Mrs. Philip Karp, New York

Dr. Rayleh Krevere, Adelphi University, New York

Dr. Joseph Levi, New York

Dr. Lucille Loseke, American Medical Women's Association, New York

Dr. Stuart Losen, New Canaan Public Schools, Connecticut

Kathleen Malone, Clarke College, Nebraska

Marguerite Massa, American Medical Women's Association, New York

Annamarie V. Miller, League of Business and Professional Women, New York

Professor Gerhard Neubeck, University of Minnesota, Minnesota

Peter Pollack, American Federation of Artists, New York

Ersa Poston, School of Education, New York University, New York

Dr. Alan Rappaport, Montclair University, New Jersey

Dr. Bernard F. Riess, Postgraduate Center for Mental Health, New York

Florence and Philip Robbins, New York

William Robbins, New York University, New York

Ferdinand Schomberg, Department of Social Services, New York

Dr. Nola Stark, University of California, California

Danny Steinmann, New York
Dr. Mary Stewart, Northwestern University, Illinois
Dr. Margaret Tobin, University of Wyoming, Wyoming
Dr. Richard B. Tucker, Veteran's Administration, Kentucky
Johnsie Young, North Carolina
Toba Zigmund, New York

IN COUNTRIES OTHER
THAN THE UNITED STATES

Dr. Reynaldo Alarcon, Universidade Nacional Magor de San
    Marcos de Lima, Lima, Peru
Dr. Nezehat Arkun, Istanbul, Turkey
Dr. Iraj Ayman, Iran National Institute of Psychology, Teheran,
    Iran
Z. Behbahani, Iran National Institute of Psychology, Teheran,
    Iran
Dr. Vera Campo, Buenos Aires, Argentina
Dr. A. S. Dalal, New Delhi, India
Professor Eleanor Elequin, University of the Philippines, Quezon
    City, Philippines
Dr. Jurgen Friedricks, Freie und Hansestadt, Hamburg, Germany
Dr. Wolfgang Gieselbrecht, Freie University, Berlin, Germany
Dr. Elina Haavio-Mannila, University of Helsinki, Finland
Jane Hilowitz, Somerville College, Oxford, England
Dr. Viola Klein, University of Reading, Berkshire, England
Dr. Sol Kugelmass, Beer Sheba College, Hebrew University,
    Jerusalem, Israel
Madeleine Lavoegie, Centre d'Application Psychologie dans
    L'Industrie et le Commerance, Paris, France
Dr. Rafael Nuñez, University of the Americas, Mexico City,
    Mexico
Dr. Karl Pech, Charles University, Prague, Czechoslavakia
Professor Elizabeth Pfiel, Freie und Handsestadt, Hamburg,
    Germany
Professor Edith Ramos, Universiade Federal Rural do Rio de
    Janeiro, Rio de Janeiro, Brazil
Dr. Josephine Rolla, Buenos Aires, Argentina
Dr. Kojo Sato, Kyoto University, Kyoto, Japan

Mrs. Christina Schollin, Stockholm, Sweden

Marie-Louise Schwartz-Schilling, Büdingen/Hessen, Germany

K. Tabari, Iran National Institute of Psychology, Teheran, Iran

Drs. George and Vasso Vassilou, Athenian Institute of Anthropology, Athens, Greece

Dr. Yael Vered, Beer Sheba College, Hebrew University, Jerusalem, Israel

The
Male Dilemma

CHAPTER 1

The Pain of Transition

What is it like to be a man in a society that no longer has need of his physical strength, his agility, his adroitness, or his speed; a society which finds less need each day for his intelligence and intellect; a society in which the simple machine, once a symbol of man's ingenuity, has evolved into the complex computer, a symbol of his loss of individuality and personal prestige, a society in which a cruel disortion of technological know-how has resulted in the discontent of a majority of Americans with their work? What is it like to be a man in a society which faces him with a loss of identity because of the pressure to conform to the "democratic group"; which demands that he be a "good Joe," a good citizen, a good worker and provider, and last but not least, a good son, father, husband and lover?

What is it like to be a man in a society undergoing nothing short of a sexual revolution, in which every major change in the relative status of men and women during the last fifty years has brought women freedom and power undreamed of even by the early crusaders for women's rights? What is it like to be a man at a time when, with the advent of the Pill, women have the sexual freedom formerly practiced only by men and known to women only in fantasy; a time when every gain for women is paralleled by a corresponding loss of male freedom, job and status? What is it like to be a man in a society in which these changes occur at an ever-accelerating pace and in which every book written about the period ponders the problem of . . . women?

To find the answers to these questions, we have asked thousands of men for their feelings, opinions, and reactions, and we believe we have learned what it is like to be a man in such a world. We are troubled by what we have learned, for the male world we see is a confused one, a world in which men express contradictory ideas about who and what they are, and agree only

3

that they are not the kind of men they think women want them to be. They are confused about themselves and about the twentieth-century woman with whom they will live, or with whom they are presently living. How, they ask themselves, are they to relate to her, much less live with her, if they decide to live with her at all?

Consider what we have learned about the mid-century American male. Men feel themselves pulled in two directions, held to two different standards of masculine behavior. On one hand, they express a need for the aggressive, outgoing, individualistic, and creative activities which have always been associated with men. On the other hand, they are more than aware of social and psychological pressures which demand an opposite behavior, pressures which inhibit aggression, and encourage group participation and the derivation of at least some satisfaction from other people's achievements. In our extensive research with educated American men, we have found that they express strong components of both individual and group drives and needs. They see themselves as slightly more aggressive than inhibited, and more individualistic than groupish. And consistently men have told us that they would like to be *more* aggressive, *more* individual, and *more* outgoing than they are. In sharp contrast, when we asked them what kind of man they thought women preferred, they were also consistent: women, they told us, want a man who is not at all aggressive, whose life centers around the family group, and whose satisfactions derive from the activities of its members.

Obviously, there is a wide gap between these two concepts of the male role and appropriate masculine behavior, and we believe that man's efforts to resolve these different concepts add up to nothing short of a dilemma, which, in its dictionary definition, is simply a situation that involves making a choice between two unsatisfactory alternatives. The dilemma for the modern American man is this: as he moves and develops in ways which bring him closer to his own ideals, he moves further away from what he thinks women want him to be; as he lives and behaves as he thinks women want, he moves further and further away from what he wants to be, and suffers the conflict and confusion that inevitably result from living a secondhand life. In our research, we have found distressing evidence of this conflict and confusion, not only in men's personal lives and their relationships with women, but also in their roles as fathers, in their jobs, and as members of the social community outside the home.

Not too many years ago, before our country evolved into the highly mechanized, highly specialized society of the mid-twentieth century, man's sheer physical strength was a basic requirement for his survival. The pioneer men were rugged souls who waged backbreaking battle with a hostile environment. Farmers, miners, and construction and factory workers contributed brawn as well as brains in building a new nation. The folk heroes, Paul Bunyan, John Henry, were men of muscle. It is a far cry from guiding a plow across the Great Plains to mowing a suburban lawn, from stoking a blast furnace to lighting a backyard barbecue. Once much of the work of society was hard work, performed often by men, women, and children alike. The men, however, led the way, and the ideal man was strong, brave, aggressive, and "rough and ready."

No less important than the workingmen were the intellectuals, the scientists and inventors, the political and industrial leaders—men like Jefferson, Franklin, Lincoln, Thoreau, Twain, Rockefeller, Ford—individual men, who played such vital roles in the history of our country. The American ideal, the fulfillment of the Horatio Alger dream, is perhaps best illustrated by a man like Thomas Edison, a poor boy who combined hard work, genius, and native cunning to win fame and fortune, and to leave an indelible mark on the world. But once again, it is a big step from Edison experimenting in his makeshift Menlo Park laboratory to the anonymous research and development teams at General Electric, from a John D. Rockefeller or a Henry Ford to the faceless, gray men in executive suites, from the daring, singlehanded adventure of Lindbergh to the computerized, insulated efforts of the astronauts and NASA's mission control, from Thoreau to a California "think tank," from Thomas Jefferson to Richard Nixon. Intelligence and creativity are no less highly prized as masculine traits in our generation, but opportunities for individual expression in any field are hard to come by in a complicated society geared to mass production, mass communication, and mass consumption.

Even the concept of the "good man" has undergone subtle change in our age, for, apart from his strength and intelligence, the ideal man was once also a moral man. In centuries past, he stood alone with God; his conscience was his guide. With the eighteenth century, the cult of reason shifted the emphasis from duty to God to man's moral obligations to himself and his society. A good man was a rational man. But today neither religion nor reason seem adequate to govern, or even explain, the complex range of human behavior. In our society, to be a good man somehow seems less desirable, and much less rewarding, than to be a successful one.

There has perhaps always been a discrepancy between the masculine ideal and the human reality, but traditionally a man had concrete, clearly defined obligations and privileges. He was, in the old phrase, "his own man," free to seek satisfaction for his own needs, free to explore the limits of his own abilities. He honored his father and mother and loved and supported his wife and children. He employed his physical or mental powers, or both, in useful work, and, apart from his duty to himself and his family, made his way in a society that needed all the raw ingredients of his being. Traditionally, to be male was to be active, to be a good provider, to possess authority, and to make decisions at home and abroad. Sexually, man was master. It was he who decided when and where and even whom to impregnate. Man was the doer, the thinker, the axis on which the rest of the world revolved.

All that has changed, chiefly because the society which engendered and utilized that kind of masculine behavior has changed. And surely the most significant change is the sudden emergence of the female to challenge the age-old tradition of male superiority. Scarcely a generation ago woman, too, had clearly defined obligations, if far fewer privileges, than the male. She was a dutiful daughter, a respectful, submissive wife, and a loving mother. She tended house, cared for her family, and possibly was concerned with her neighbors and community, although her influence rarely extended much further than that. Woman was the keeper of morals. She represented ethical stability and cultural continuity. Her mind, like her body, was subservient to man. Seldom was she considered apart from her husband and family. If she functioned outside her home, it was for them, not for herself. To be feminine traditionally meant to be passive, obedient, and, if possible, pretty.

The sexual revolution, with its battlecry, "Women are people, too!" has forced many women to take a new look at themselves and their traditional roles. Barraged with conflicting advice, they have been told, on one hand, that they are in fact inferior beings, and that true feminine fulfillment can only be found in housewifery and child-raising. But on the other, they are told that they are the equal of any man and that they must seek fulfillment for themselves in addition to, or even apart from, the other vicarious satisfactions of marriage and motherhood. Thus the American female of the 1970's finds herself in a quandry no less perplexing than the dilemma faced by her male counterpart. Which voice is she to heed; in which direction is she to move? If she strikes out for herself, will she have to sacrifice the security and undeniable pleasures of the traditionally feminine role? Must she neglect her children and alienate her husband in the pursuit of her own fulfillment? Or, if she settles for the wife-and-mother role, must she forever feel that she has wasted her real abilities? Just as the man may fear that his masculinity is threatened by the encroachments and restrictions of contemporary life, so the woman fears that she will no longer be considered feminine if she tampers with tradition.

Where does this leave the contemporary American woman? To find out we asked thousands of women themselves and we discovered that, like the men, they express contradictory ideas about who and what they are, who and what they would like to be, and who and what they think men would like them to be. Women, too, feel themselves pulled in two directions. The tug toward traditional feminine roles is a strong one, even for the very young woman, but equally strong is the attraction of expanding those roles to include participation in activities that were once considered exclusively masculine. The quandary for the woman, then, is simply this: if she does take advantage of the new freedoms and opportunities available to her, she may find herself in direct competition with men, particularly her husband; but if she does not, she may suffer the inner conflicts and frustrations that result from living only half a life.

If men and women lived in separate vacuums in our society, perhaps these inner conflicts could be worked out with less anger and strife. But they do not: they live together as husbands and wives, fathers and mothers. The decisions they make inevitably affect not only themselves but each other; their indecision has had, and continues to have, profound repercussions in male–female relationships, in the family, and in society itself. Clearly we are going through a period of dramatic and far-reaching transition. Our generation has seen the destruction or drastic revision of any number of cherished customs and beliefs, chief among them the traditional patterns of masculine and feminine behavior. Just what does it mean to be a man or a woman in today's world: what does it mean to be masculine or femimine? Our extensive research indicates that there are no longer any positive answers to these questions. The once clear-cut distinctions that separated men from women in their sexual and social roles have begun to blur and break down, and no new patterns have as yet emerged to take their place. The familiar landmarks are fading, and both men and women, adrift in the same boat, are uncertain as to which course to steer.

Eventually they may reach safe harbor, but in the interim, the price men and women are paying while they wait for time to restructure roles and resolve conflicts is staggering. A soaring divorce rate, now dissolving one marriage in three, is only one of those prices. Another is an illegitimacy rate that has increased so dramatically that even junior high schools have developed programs for unwed girls returning to school after giving birth. And venereal disease is described by public health sources as having reached epidemic proportions. Behind these statistics lies the less easily identifiable atmosphere of object love, of sex for sex's sake, that seems to pervade our culture. Traditional moral values are too often sacrificed to ephemeral "kicks"; social, and even sexual, realities are distorted by the ever-increasing use of alcohol, drugs, and narcotics.

Less obvious but no less dramatic is the confusion and anguish of thousands of couples trying to develop a life pattern in which both husband and wife recognize and meet their marital responsibilities, and at the same time have equal freedom and opportunity to develop and utilize their individual abilities. For these couples the dilemma of which we write is not a statistic showing abortions on the rise, but indecision about who stays home when one of the children is sick and both husband and wife have important work schedules. It is not the divorce rate of the 1960's, but a husband doing dishes with internal surges of anger and resentment, while his teacher wife works on her lessons for tomorrow with equally powerful surges of guilt and feelings of failure. It is not so much the data on illegitimacy as it is a man sulking through a party of his wife's friends and associates in the League of Women Voters, experiencing what it is like to be Mrs. Smith's husband, not an individual in his own right; or the secret fury of Mrs. Jones when she is introduced to her husband's friends and associates as "the little woman." For couples like these, the upheaval in traditional values has resulted in an immediate and day-to-day confusion of sex roles along with the marital conflict that is the inevitable result.

During this transitional period, the emphasis has been on trying to understand the contemporary female and how the changes in traditional sex roles have affected her, although it is obvious that men as well as women are facing tremendous problems of adjustment and adaptation. But this is not surprising. Whenever there is a major revolution or change in the power structure of some aspect of society, the outs, the insurgents, the underdogs always become the center of attention and receive the major share of publicity. Thus, in the United States, the activities of racial minorities and youthful rebels are given center stage, while their adversaries, the white, middle-class, middle-age establishment, sink into the shadows.

In the sexual revolution, the male has been cast as the adversary, the "enemy." He is held responsible for society's sexual ills and inequalities. He must recognize that the power structure of the male-female relationship has begun to change. He must revise his attitudes, alter his behavior, yield and divide his power. The leaders in the "liberation" of women have become increasingly numerous and increasingly vocal. Book after book has been written about women and their problems, their search for identity, their determination to claim their fair share of equality and opportunity. The publicity surrounding the "women's lib" movement has been formidable, but rarely, if ever, in the avalanche of words by or about women, has man been mentioned at all. He is told he must move over, but no one has bothered to tell him where or how. Like the establishment, he has become a symbol, a shadow.

Yet it is only common sense to realize that no significant change can be made in women's roles without having an im-

mediate effect on men and their roles. In fact, we believe that the
sexual revolution, the changes and shifts in the relationships of
men and women, has posed a more severe problem for the man
than for the woman. Women have moved out *beyond* the traditional roles and patterns established for them over the years, and
the basic problem they face is how to incorporate new opportunities and freedoms into their repertoire of behavior, while at
the same time retaining those traditional rights and duties they
wish to retain. In contrast, men are faced with the necessity of
adapting to a new concept of the male role, a role in many cases of
diminished opportunities and freedoms which were previously
theirs simply because they were "male."

It is difficult to say just where the sexual revolution began and
where it will end. But in the recent past, and particularly in the
present generation, it has been characterized by pressures of all
sorts from all sides on men, pressures that have forced sweeping
changes in the traditional relationships between men and wom-
en. The notion of a natural inequality between the sexes, a notion
perhaps as old as the institution of human society itself, has been
effectively attacked and considerably altered. The myth
of the physical and mental inferiority of women has been completely discredited. Social pressures have forced revisions in concepts of personal and property rights, upsetting man's once-
privileged position before the law. Sexual pressures have virtually destroyed the nineteenth-century pattern of the male-female
relationship—a pattern in which men enjoyed and women en-
dured sexual acts—and replaced it with the twentieth-century
model of sexual compatibility and shared pleasure. Economic
pressures, along with increased educational opportunities for
women, have resulted in expanding roles for women outside the
home. A long list of occupations and professions, once exclusive
male preserves, are now open to women. And finally, all of these
pressures, at home, at work, and in the world at large, have
combined with a massive personal pressure from within men
themselves to act or somehow react to the changes occurring all
around them.

The changes in the rules governing relationships between the
sexes represent for contemporary man a narrowing of his world,
a world which at the beginning of the twentieth century was
exclusively male. They also represent a loss of status, of privilege,

and of opportunity automatically available by reason of sex. Taken all together, they have culminated, to some degree, in a loss of sexual identity. The traditional definitions of masculinity have blurred: a man is no longer masculine simply because he fights, works, or makes love. The traditional ways in which he could express his masculinity have been gradually chipped away. And if, as it would appear, mind has finally triumphed over matter and we now live in a world of the intellect, man must share that world with women whose intelligence is in no way inferior to his own. But that is not all, for the modern world is a strangely complex and impersonal one. Thus, in addition to the real loss of masculine privilege and the symbolic loss of avenues of masculine expression, today's man is also subjected to feelings of isolation and depersonalization. And small wonder in a society which sees him as a faceless unit, identified not by his name but by his social security number, a society whose most profound thinkers are not humanists concerned with the whole man, but scientists and technicians who see him as a collection of replaceable parts.

Pressure, pressure on the American man. With the old definitions of masculinity disappearing fast, he has to be all things to himself, all things to other men, all things to the women and children in his life. Somehow he must fit into a world he has helped shape, and that in turn has shaped him, a world of change, conflict, and contradiction. Just what kind of man is he supposed to be: a man's man in the traditional sense, the kind of man his father was, the kind he was brought up to be, the kind he himself thinks he would *like* to be? Or should he be the kind of man he thinks his wife wants him to be? His children, too, exposed to different traditions and changing concepts of masculinity, make their own demands. Assailed from every direction, how can he relate to them all, reconcile their wants and needs, and still be true to himself? Thus the male dilemma becomes clear. Just what is the American male, living in a period of revolutionary change as to the concept of the roles of the sexes, supposed to do? How to react? What to think? What to say?

One alternative for the man is to fight the sexual revolution tooth-and-nail, to insist upon the traditional definitions and concepts, at least within his own family and wherever else he may exercise sufficient influence and authority. But most men realize that resisting sexual and social equality for women brands them as old-fashioned and undemocratic, possibly even bullheaded and reactionary. A man who does so risks alienating his more enlightened friends, and, above all, his wife.

Another even less desirable alternative is to accept all of the gains women have made, along with the concomitant loss of his own power and male preserves. In other words, peace at any price. But here he risks sacrificing his "masculinity," and with such sacrifice comes self-pity and the awareness that he may become an object of contempt among his friends and even his wife and family.

A third alternative is for the man to talk as if he accepts women's new sexual freedoms and social opportunities, but subtly and indirectly to communicate to the women in his own life that he yearns for the good old days when man was supreme—a tactic involving neither all-out battle nor abject surrender, but a series of small, limited engagements, giving up territory when necessary, and reclaiming it when the opportunity arises. This, too, is conclusive against the man, for it brings, in the name of compromise, a measure of confusion, double-talk, hypocrisy and guilt which soon proves intolerable to man and woman alike.

But must compromise always be unsatisfactory? Surely a fourth alternative is possible: a sane and workable agreement reached through love, understanding, accommodation and mutual recognition and acceptance of the needs of both the man and the woman. Unfortunately, again it does not appear to be simple. Men and women, like nations, are slow to learn the secrets of successful compromise, and the chief reason for it is a pervasive and clear lack of communication between the sexes, a lack we have noted time and time again in our research, one that deepens the conflict and ambivalence between men and women, and is directly responsible for man's inconclusive vacillation among the alternatives in the male dilemma.

The dilemma is even further compounded by the variety of alternatives now open to women, and there is ample evidence to show that women are just as uncertain in coping with their expanding freedoms as men are in adjusting to their diminished status. Should woman simply ignore the sexual revolution and content herself with the traditional feminine roles of wife and mother, even though she may suffer the derision of her more enlightened sisters as a result? Should she renounce these roles entirely and set out on a single-minded pursuit of her own fulfillment? If she does so, will she be accused of being unfeminine and suffer the sexual and social handicaps that accrue from that blanket condemnation? Or should she somehow try to combine her role as wife and mother with a career outside the home, perhaps the most difficult alternative of all, for there is the very real risk that she may spread herself too thin and give an unsatisfactory performance in both areas? If she receives contradictory or hypocritical cues from her husband, again because of a lack of open and honest communication, her ambivalence can be formidable and the resulting conflict, both within herself and with her husband, can seriously undermine their relationship.

At any age, men and women seldom feel free to express feelings of doubt, resentment or guilt about their sexual roles. It is an extremely sensitive area, one that touches the very core of their concept of self. Hung up on the traditional definitions of masculinity and femininity, many men and women fail to recognize or refuse to tolerate personality traits thought to be characteristic of the opposite sex in their own behavior or in the behavior of others of their sex. In the popular view, a man is somehow less a man if he displays tenderness and sensitivity, so-called feminine qualities, and a woman less a woman if she exhibits the active, achieving drives that are supposed to be the exclusive province of the male. Men, in particular, uncertain of their own masculinity in this transitional age, feel threatened by the strong, domineering woman, whether she exercises her domination in aggressive behavior or in the tyranny of utter dependence. Women are equally uncertain of their femininity because traditional definitions fall far short of present-day possibilities. With such uncertainty, it is no wonder that both men and women are insecure in their concepts of self and have only the vaguest notions of their relative roles in marriage; it is no wonder that they are unable or unwilling to talk about them.

Psychologically, the present age is fertile ground for this kind of ambivalence. The man is guilty about his traditional feelings that women should be passive and submissive; he is guilty about the "feminine" side of his own nature; he is unable to live up to the old standards and reluctant to accept the new. The woman, for her part, is no longer content with her traditional roles and is resentful of those who attempt to enforce them. Yet she, too, is guilty about the "masculine" side of her nature and reluctant to abandon the security of the old values. Just where this ambivalence will lead is impossible to predict, for the sexual revolution that spawned it has only just begun. So far, it has succeeded only in forcing men into the untenable position of having to cope with a movement to which no one can object, but which places upon them almost unbearable pressures and demands. How can they seek to satisfy their psychological needs and resolve their insecurities in a world of changing sexual roles and diminished male power without appearing to impede the progress of women? How can women meet the new demands and pressures placed upon them without intimidating and alienating men?

These are difficult questions, but we must search for possible answers before sexual confusion and conflict become a major social catastrophe. The sexual revolution has begun to free both men and women to enjoy relationships rooted in mutual love and respect, in equality of opportunity and responsibility, in a deeper knowledge of who they are and what they hope to achieve as individuals and as husbands and wives. That is the goal, at least, but it will not be easy to attain.

CHAPTER 2

A Brief History of Sexual Roles

How did we reach the point where confusion, suspicion, guilt, and anxiety seem to typify relationships between the sexes? Is it due to characteristics inherent in all men and women, or just the modern American male and female? Has it been true of every society and culture, or is it true just of our own?

In more primitive and less complex cultures, the roles of each sex and their relationships were also less complex. Consider earliest man in any social sense. Whether it be protoman that Louis and Eleanor Leakey claim to have discovered in central Africa, or Peking man which other anthropologists believe to be the earliest known individual man, his primary mission was simple survival in a hostile and dangerous environment. Whoever he was, however elementary his thinking processes, and however simple his society, we can be certain of two things: men and women were *different*, and roles, responsibilities, and functions were allocated on the basis of that difference. This holds true for all primitive human cultures which have been studied, and for higher forms of animal life. Every society distinguishes male from female: all mammals do, and so do birds and fish.

Sexual roles and relationships in early societies were strictly functional. They served a specific purpose in the total society; in most cases it was simple survival. It is probable that these functional roles were rigidly adhered to, just as they are today in primitive societies. Roles were elementary and based on an immutable fact, the sex of the individual.

Restrictions were also elementary and rigid. Expressing desires contrary to the role imposed by the fact of sex was a threat to the entire primitive social structure. The system could work only if everyone accepted the basic rationale under which it operated, a rationale which might be stated as "anatomy is destiny." When deviations or desires contrary to those appropriate for the individual did occur, they could not be tolerated and were the basis of taboos, restrictions, punishments, and sometimes even death. The taboos focused on deviation in sexual practices, specifically homosexuality. In fact, the surviving records of primitive societies are richest in their documentation of this type of deviation. But in all probability the prohibitions extended beyond physical sexual relationships to the deviant in other functional roles as well.

The very existence of these restrictions and taboos reveals an important fact about early man and woman: from the first there were individuals unsuited to the assignment of a functional role on the simple basis of sex. There *were* women who would have preferred to hunt and men who would have preferred to weave, just as there were women who preferred sexual relationships with other women, and men who preferred sexual relationships with other men. A taboo is unnecessary unless deviant behavior exists or is real enough to be understood as a threat. No society prohibits activities it does not know or cannot contemplate, and so prohibitions of deviations from the rigid sex-based functional roles suggest that from earliest times there were individuals who found their specific sex roles intolerable.

There has always been considerable variety in the functional roles assigned to members of primitive societies apart from their immutable roles in procreation. Most often, men were assigned the physically taxing chores demanding strength, endurance, and agility. Women were assigned family care and child-rearing. But as soon as mankind evolved more complex patterns of socialization, these assignments, too, became more varied and complex. Depending on the locality, women as well as men could have a food-gathering responsibility. Similarly, depending on the society, either women or men could make pottery, weave cloth or perform various roles, and responsibility was given to only one of the sexes. This is still true in primitive societies. Among the Hopi, the men are the weavers and among the Navajo, the women are, but in each case weaving is the function of one of the sexes.

Once you were old enough to know and be aware of your sex and your functional role, you would also be aware of your future.

It was there to see by watching what the adults of your sex did or did not do. For most people a choice of an occupational or recreational role would have been an impossibility. There was no question of whether or not you *wanted* to be a hunter or a potter or a dancer. If you were a man you were going to be a hunter, and if you were a woman you were going to be a potter, and it was unheard of for a woman to become a dancer.

If anyone faced a dilemma in those early societies, it could only have been the deviant. The man who hated hunting and longed to sit by the potter's wheel in a society where women made pottery faced a true dilemma. One unpleasant choice open to him was to live his prescribed sex role and hunt despite his aversion to it. The other choice was to attempt to flaunt the assigned sex role and abandon hunting for pottery. But this choice, too, was unpleasant, for typically it meant social ostracism at best and exile or death at worst. Thus, in early societies, the dilemma associated with sex roles had two characteristics. First, it was faced only by the deviant, and one extreme enough to contemplate a choice involving severe social retribution. Second, it was a dilemma that involved accepting or rejecting the socially prescribed role, as opposed to the modern dilemma, which involves, in part, choosing between various socially acceptable roles.

Originally it was hard to question the allocation of roles based on the obvious differences between the sexes. The men were larger, stronger, and had more endurance. The women were smaller, weaker, and were subjected to mysterious periodic attacks of bleeding. The women also bore children and had to nurse them. There were long months when they were semi-restricted both in the kind of work they could perform and in their mobility. Thus, the men, physically stronger, free of periodic bleeding, free of any role in the bearing and nurturing of children, took on the chores involving strength, mobility, and often absence from home for long periods of time, while the women took on those activities centered in and around the home. The logic of this arrangement was such that even the most ardent feminist cavewomen would hesitate in taking issue with it.

If not logic, then simple experience led primitive man to conclude that such an arrangement best met his needs. Allocating to each sex the roles most appropriate to its overt physiological characteristics must have made sense even to the simple level of thinking we generally attribute to early man. In fact, physical differences are so obvious that they could have been the basis of role distinctions even before language and socialization took place. Anyone who has been, or has seen, a pregnant woman in her eighth month attempting to catch a bus can imagine the liability she would be in a group out to catch a wild boar for dinner. One or two such fiascoes and the most primitive mind would decide it would be better if she stayed home. Enough specific experiences would lead to the conclusion that the pregnant woman, the menstruating woman, and the nursing woman should stay home. Perhaps even the most primitive mind finally came to the general conclusion that *all* women should stay home.

There is one other difference which was obvious to early man, the different roles of the sexes in intercourse, which eventually became the foundation of the value judgments or qualitative distinctions which mankind attached to the two sexes. The physiological fact of women being the sexual receptor became confounded with the social or psychological qualities of passivity and submissiveness. Similarly, the physiological fact of the male being the introjector became associated with activity and aggression. It is not a very big step from passivity to dependence, and from dependence to inferiority. Thus women came to be seen as inferior, or at least secondary, while men, in contrast, were seen as primary in their sexual and social roles.

This primitive set of distinctions and value judgments persisted essentially unchallenged throughout much of the history of mankind, and indeed, to varying extents, still persists. In fact, if one were to make up a wall chart showing the history of mankind, and place on this chart various significant changes contributing to the male dilemma, the chart might run across a 15-foot wall with all of the significant events crowded together in the last few inches on the far right. For centuries the functional perceptions of appropriate sex roles have persisted unchallenged. Not only did they remain unchallenged, but forces emerged which made them extremely difficult to alter even after the original primitive conditions which led to them had long since disappeared. First, as human beings moved through the early stages of the evolution of societies, practice became custom and custom tradition. The differences between the sexes were eventually formalized and even institutionalized. With women seen as dependent and inferior, it was a relatively short step to social structures which viewed the woman as little more than chattel, or the personal property of men. Chief among them were the ceremonial beliefs and practices that eventually evolved into formal religions. These early religions not only incorporated, but often sought to explain the distinctions between the sexes as divinely inspired and ordained. It is no surprise that later and more complex religions did the same thing. In this way theologies were formulated to perpetuate early functional distinctions.

Those religious beliefs which have influenced our western culture are no exception. Originally, Jews and Christians alike held that woman was merely a physical off-shoot of man, created as an afterthought, primarily because of man's loneliness and man's need. The Old Testament codifies woman's physical and social inferiority, and even today, women play a minor role in the orthodox Jewish religion. Until recently, all Jewish liturgy included a prayer in which the man thanks God for not having made him a woman. The strength of the Jewish religious feeling about women is also reflected in such basic practices as considering only men when determining if sufficient persons are available for a religious service, or in the separate seating of the sexes in the synagogue. Christianity strengthened and reinforced the concept of male superiority as, for example, in Catholicism where the priesthood was established exclusively for men, a practice only now beginning to be questioned.

The Biblical story of Adam and Eve, common to both the Jewish and Christian traditions, adds another dimension to the psychological differentiation between the sexes. It is Eve who is devious, not Adam. It is Eve who disobeys the injunction, not Adam. Passive, dependent and inferior she may be, but she uses her sexual attractiveness to manipulate Adam. And so, in this first interaction of male and female, women's sexual characteristics become the mechanism to achieve an evil end. Eventually sex itself was considered evil, and woman, the sexual object, bad and wicked. Seen another way, the story illustrates one of the most intriguing paradoxes in the area of sexual roles and relative power. For in the Adam and Eve saga, it is actually Eve who becomes the prime mover in the sense that the final significant action taken is the action she wishes to take.

There is ample evidence from recorded history to show that this is a frequent pattern; man holds the overt power while the woman often exerts what might be called hidden power by manipulating the man in social, and particularly, sexual relationships. Thus, other personality characteristics, such as deviousness, disobedience and the ability to manipulate man, were added to the stereotyped notions of what woman was like through the ages. Even in the United States today, this distinction between overt male and hidden female is recognized. If women accepted this stereotype, at least until quite recently, it was perhaps because they felt they had no alternative, or were content to exert what influence they could from behind the scenes. Denied overt power through the ages, they exercised their hidden power with considerable, but not always constructive, effect.

Both Catholic and later Protestant traditions reinforced the inferiority of women. The writings of St. Paul in particular dwell heavily on woman's role as temptress, as the wordly seductress who lures man to the pleasures of the flesh. And as recently as the 1930's a Papal encyclical[1] made clear the Catholic Church's perception of male superiority in the relative roles and importance of the sexes by noting:

> Domestic society being confirmed, therefore, by this bond of love, there should flourish in it that "order of love," as St. Augustine calls it. This order includes both the privacy of the husband with regard to the wife and her willing obedience, which the Apostle commends in these words: "Let women be subject to their husbands as to the Lord, because the husband is the head of the wife, as Christ is the head of the Church."

After the Reformation, the Protestant denominations which emerged moved even further in the direction forecast by the connotation of sex as evil in the story of Adam and Eve. For now sexual pleasure was overlaid by sexual guilt. The Reformation had as one of its prime motivations a reaction to what was seen as an excess of concern with worldly activities and the pleasure orientation of the hierarchy of the Catholic Church. This reaction led to the development of a series of Protestant sects which became more and more repressive of those aspects of human life which they considered pleasurable, with particular emphasis on sexual pleasure.

Of special relevance in understanding the social and psychological climate of the United States is the fact that Puritanism was a dominant influence in the development of our moral and philosophical systems. Emerging during the reign of Queen Elizabeth, the Puritans banded together to oppose the pomp, politics and wordly orientation of the English Church. They viewed man as wholly sinful by nature, and like the Calvinists, they distinguished between the damned and the elect who belonged to the church, a membership the elect could maintain only through hard work, discipline, and constant self-examination. The man or woman in the stocks has become a cartoon cliché of American history. Even so, the behavioral code of the Puritans did strongly repress a wide variety of social interactions and infractions of their moral standards, including drunkenness, games of chance, theatrical performances, blasphemy, indolence and, of course, fornication.

Their prohibitions did not stop these practices either when New England was first settled or later when the original Puritan doctrine was revised and the prohibitions modified. But it did manage to make those who did drink, or did play games of chance, or did fornicate, do so with the guilt which comes from behaving in contradiction to a dominant belief system. So the realistic Puritan heritage which comes down through the eighteenth and nineteenth centuries to the twentieth is not that you cannot "enjoy, enjoy," but that you shouldn't. If you do, your pleasure is "guilt plated."

Nowhere is this attitude stronger than in sexual behavior. For here it is not just the Puritan heritage which grudgingly accepts sexual relations only because they are necessary to the survival of the species, but all of the Christian religions. The perception of sex as intrinsically evil leads to the prohibition of sexual relations for any reason other than procreation and, equally important, it leads to a belief that pleasure from sexual relationships is illicit and wicked. And so it is wrong for any but married couples to have sexual intercourse, wrong even for them to engage in it except to have children, and perhaps worst of all, wrong for them to enjoy it when they do.

Still another force, the law,[2] added to the weight of social and religious practices to formalize male superiority and female inferiority. The legal statements of those early societies, complex enough to develop codes of law, clearly described a male world. With the exception of the Code of Hammurabi, under which both men and women enjoyed freedom and dignity, early societies gave men all the rights and prerogatives in two important areas: the sexual relationship, including marriage; and the ownership of property. Thus, in the Mosaic tradition, a man had social freedom, while the woman's social position was that of captive, first to her father, then to her husband. The husband could divorce his wife, but she could not divorce him. The men alone inherited property; it passed into a woman's hands only in the absence of male heirs.

Roman law continued this orientation, for a husband acquired a woman's property when he married her, and a father's control of a daughter continued into her adult life if she did not marry. Rome typified the more complex societies which developed, and which, in a logical extension of male privilege, limited all public officeholding to men. Although later Roman law, particularly during the reign of Justinian, began to take some of the exclusive legal privileges away from men, canon law later returned to earlier social and legal traditions, and this regression was heightened and highly institutionalized during the feudal period.

Here the orientation to male superiority became intimately connected to the need of the times for constant armed protection. The complex social hierarchy of the period was tied to the ability to serve under arms, a privilege extended only to males. Similarly, the right to hold land was tied to the ability to defend it militarily, and so landowning became a male prerogative. The landholder passed on the ownership of his land after his death to his male heirs, for once again it was only the sons who could meet the military obligations which accompanied landowning.

Male control continued in the English legal tradition; for while the single woman had rights as an individual before the law, nearly approaching those of males, the married woman lost most of these rights to her husband. Just as in earliest Jewish and Roman times, her property became his upon marriage; the profit from any business she had was his, and he was free to dispose of her personal property in any way he wished. Not until the eighteenth century was there any significant modification of male control and power within the law. Women gradually achieved the right to retain certain property and to acquire and own property. While this was a significant break in the totality of male control of society, it was, in fact, only a slight alteration in the relative power structure. Until the twentieth century, under English law, if there was no will, female heirs could not inherit real estate unless there were no male heirs.

American law, descending from the English common law, continued the basic orientation to male power and male control until the nineteenth century. Then, within the framework of other social reform movements, the law was modified to permit married women the same property rights as those extended to single women in eighteenth century England. The first American state to institute the reform was Mississippi, in 1839, followed by Maine in 1844. Once begun, a series of legal reforms gradually took effect, giving a married woman the right to enter into contracts, to control the expenditure of her own earnings, to bring suit in her own name, to establish a separate domicile (whether or not her husband agreed), and to make her own will.

Thus, men have lost control over their wives as property, and over their wives' property. Put another way, men no longer have the exclusive right to own property, a substantial loss to incur in less than two centuries. But the relative power of men and women before the law has depended in recent times upon the marital status of the woman. Marriage is therefore the sexual-social-legal institution of greatest importance to the concerns of this book.

Marriage is possibly the most ubiquitous of social institutions if it is considered in general terms, for all known societies have some rationale for regulating the mating relationship between men and women. Anthropologists differ as to whether, even in earliest prehistoric times, there was a period of indiscriminate mating, or whether man and woman have always lived under some system for regulating sexual interactions and relationships. But all agree that those societies about which enough is known to categorize their social behavior have evolved some rules or regulations to control mating. Even the smallest and most primitive group defined the limits within which a man and woman might seek a mate, sometimes permitting mating only within the group, sometimes doing exactly the opposite by demanding that a mate be sought beyond the group. This kind of regulation is also indicative of how marriage, as an institution, was used for social as well as sexual purposes from the beginning, for whether or not marriage was permitted beyond the group seems to have been determined by the needs of the group for establishing contacts with its neighbors.

Marriage serves other purposes for primitive societies for, through the customs which developed around it, decisions were automatically made about where people lived, who counted as whose descendants, and subsequently whom a child was named after. Historically, there have been all possible combinations in reckoning descent through the male (patrilineal) and the female (matrilineal), as well as deciding whether a newly formed family should live with the family of the male (patrilocal) or that of the female (matrilocal). Societies have existed (and still do) in which the male goes to live with the wife's group, but descent is nevertheless figured through the male line. There are examples of other possibilities as well.

Once descent and location are institutionalized, man develops some procedures for allocating responsibility for the support of children and governance of the family. Once again there are historical examples of societies in which this was a male responsibility (patriarchal societies) and also those in which it was a female responsibility (matriarchal societies). In fact, during the 1960's, one of the popular explanations for the socioeconomic difficulties of black Americans was the fact that in a major culture which was patriarchal, the black subculture was matriarchal, leading to (or because of) the high incidence of broken homes, a weakened male image, and the difficulty for black males to earn income sufficient to support a family.

Looking back into time and wondering what individual as well as social forces were involved as marriage began and was formalized, anthropologists have considered two different approaches. One sees the man as the primary mover toward some structure, motivated by his wish to have exclusive access to the woman he has selected. In recent years the notion of an almost instinctual possessiveness by the male of many species toward the females in his life space, and even toward that space itself, has been developed by Ardrey;[3] and it is a feeling much like this that some consider was the individual push toward control of the relationship between men and women. Others see it beginning differently, as the result of the woman's desire for protection of herself and her children, and for support during her child-bearing years. Of course, these two hypotheses are not mutually exclusive. Marriage probably would not have developed as easily if the male seeking exclusivity had met the modern woman seeking equal rights and power, but the woman of early societies apparently had no such concerns. It is interesting that once early man and woman developed rules and customs to govern where they lived, how to reckon descent, and the responsibilities for child-rearing, they had the institutional essentials of marriage for all future societies up to the present.

Societies have grown more complex, and the rites and ceremonies attached to marriage have become more elaborate, but the essentials of the relationship are the same, with nothing having been added until the middle of the nineteenth century, when romance and love became new elements in marriage. They had been there before, obviously, but not as a consistent and critical force within the institution. Through the nineteenth century, marriages were arranged, as they had always been arranged, according to the society's rules for selecting mates, and from the groups with which it made social and political sense to have such relationships. History and literature have notable examples of couples who tried, usually without success, to substitute love as the motivation for marriage and break the rules which prevented marriage across the lines drawn by position and/or social class (Edward VIII and Wallis Warfield Simpson), or tribal affiliation (*Romeo and Juliet*). But with the general flowering of freedom, individualism, and reform which marked many of the social movements of the nineteenth century came freedom to choose a mate by the criterion of love. This new element did not change the basic functions of marriage, nor did the addition of romantic love, as a more or less essential prerequisite for marriage, remove the boundaries from within which one could select a mate. They still exist and, while in some societies, such as the United States, they have slowly been extended in terms of national origin and social class, they are almost as solid as ever in terms of the tribal lines drawn between race and religion.

Indicative of the survival of this last taboo is the thematic change in the recent literature of ill-fated lovers. In the twentieth century, it is not the fact that a couple wants to marry for love which provides the source of the drama; that is now taken for granted. Instead, the conflict comes from the lovers' desire to marry across one of the still-forbidden boundaries of religion (*Herzog*) or race (*Guess Who's Coming to Dinner?*).

The basic stability through the centuries of almost all the facets of marriage as an institution, and its essential role in maintaining the stability of society, is the reason why revolutionary movements so often focus attacks on it. During the 1930's in the United States, radical movements attacked both the notions of sexual sanctity and marriage with their talk of free love and trial marriages. And today, in the 1970's, marriage, in traditional form, has become one of the institutions most openly flouted. The phenomena of couples, trios, or quartets openly living together without pretending to be married, and moreover proclaiming their total disinterest in marriage, have become sufficiently widespread so that even some public figures are able to flout the old morality. And that most basic rule, common to all tribes, that whatever other boundaries are ignored, a mate must be selected from the opposite sex, has been challenged in innumerable instances, not only in practice, but also in principle.

The Reverend Robert Weeks, an Episcopal priest quoted in *Time* magazine, referred to "an acquaintance of mine who has been 'married' to another homosexual for fifteen years. Both of them are very happy and very much in love. They asked me to bless their marriage and I am going to do it."[4]

The critical social importance of the rules governing mating and then marriage makes it clear why this was one of the earliest areas into which religion moved. In Jewish tradition, marriage was firmly founded on the command of the Old Testament to be fruitful and multiply, which from earliest times among the Jews meant first marriage and then children. It also meant divorce, for the Torah granted the husband the right to divorce his wife. Grounds for divorce varied through the centuries, beginning with infidelity, moving on to barrenness and other reasons. Although the early rights to divorce were clearly vested in the male, about 1000 B.C., the law was interpreted to mean that divorce could not be granted without the consent of the woman, and soon thereafter she too could sue for and be granted a divorce if the husband kept her from participating in "joyous functions" or if she found him repulsive.

With Catholicism came the notion of the permanence of marriage, the view that the husband and wife become one flesh in the eyes of God, expressed in the phrase from Mark (10:9), "what therefore God hath joined together, let no man put asunder," and ultimately in the idea of marriage as a sacrament enunciated by St. Paul. Thus the traditional foundation of marriage which comes down to recent times is a religious rite signifying a permanent bond, established by a ceremony commemorating the union before God of a man and woman, in which the woman pledges to "obey." That marriage is also a civil contract in all Western countries was less significant until the nineteenth century, when the push for legal equality by women focused on achieving equal rights for the married woman.

To sum up, role differences developed between the sexes which originally stemmed from physiological differences relating to strength, menstruation, and pregnancy. Then, as social systems developed, these physiological differences and the functional roles that proceeded from them, combined with the actual postures of the two sexes during intercourse, led to a value judgment concerning the dissimilarity of the two sexes, with man seen as superior and woman inferior. In recent centuries, as written language and complex societies came into being, these differences were codified and institutionalized in religion and law, the warp and woof of any social fabric, and if these differences were questioned, the basic fabric of the social system itself became vulnerable.

The first strand in the fabric to weaken was religious belief. The divine assumptions underlying the relative status of the sexes were questioned by the physical sciences. Through the work of men like Copernicus and Darwin, and others who began to investigate the nature of the universe and the human organism that inhabits it, many of the traditional theological explanations of human life and the schema of human existence were seriously undermined. Copernicus challenged the idea that the earth was the center of the universe, and showed it to be false. If the earth was just one of several planets revolving around the sun, rather than the center of the universe, and, as Darwin maintained, if the human species gradually evolved over aeons from lower species rather than having been created at one moment in time by divine command, then Eve was not made of Adam's rib and did not bring about the expulsion of mankind from Eden. It gradually became apparent, in the view of science at least, that the superiority of the male was no more divinely ordained than the earth was the center of the universe.

One direct offshoot of the developing sciences and technology, and a serious blow to the traditional concepts of the sexes, was the century or so of dramatic social change which historians lump together under the phrase, the Industrial Revolution. With it came the emergence of the factory, of centers of production outside the home. The clearly defined roles and responsibilities of family members began to blur as father, mother, son, and daughter alike left home to work. Work itself lost its purely masculine connotations; the mass occupational classification "factory worker" had no clear-cut sexual identification. Moreover, with the urbanization which inevitably accompanied industrialization, the family began to lose its unique character as a socially and economically self-sufficient unit. Food was purchased rather than grown, and living space was rented rather than built and owned. Working hours and conditions were set by the factory owner rather than by the demands of nature or the desires of the individual.

Several aspects of this change in the life style of a large segment of the population hit directly at the role of the father. Under urban conditions, he was no longer the dominant figure about which work revolved. When the whole family worked on the farm, they generally worked for, and under the supervision of, the father. In the urban factory they all worked too, but the father became one among many faceless workers, not the center of the work force, not a supervisor, but a follower of orders. In the mass poverty which accompanied these initial stages of urbanization, he was not even a totally adequate provider.

Disintegration of traditional roles continued as the closely woven web of family enterprise physically centered about the home and surrounding land was broken. The social life which once revolved almost totally about the family was broadened by the move to the factory town. The occasional neighbor who visited on foot or horseback was replaced by the hundreds of neighbors living within a yell or sometimes even a whisper away. Social mobility increased immensely to pull the young away from the family group and further break down the central authoritative role of the father.

The combination of these economic and social forces created a new reality for the family, with a less central role for the father and a less functional one for the mother. Yet the psychological balance of social and familial power was largely unaffected until women attacked it directly.

The first feminist movements of any scope began at the end of the eighteenth century. They arose both as a consequence of the changing roles within the family, as a reaction to the social horrors of the Industrial Revolution, and were expedited by changing belief systems and the politically revolutionary climate of the turn of the century.

The failure of the belief that all things exist as they do because that is how God wills them had an immediate impact on legal and political systems, particularly on the kings who were pleased to claim divine right as the basis for their rule. The end of the eighteenth century saw two major revolutions, in France and in the American colonies, with each revolution claiming the rights of man to be free and equal to determine his own destiny. While the men who voiced these sentiments meant "men" (or even more specifically, "white men"), the climate of revolution and freedom was sufficiently contagious for the last decade of the eighteenth century to see the beginning of the feminist movement, when for the first time women began to attack directly the social practices giving men superior and dominant social and legal status. Although there were earlier efforts, *A Vindication of the Rights of Women*,[6] published in 1792 by Mary Wollstonecraft, was the first major book to argue that "Marriage will never be held sacred until women, by being brought up with men, are prepared to be companions rather than their mistresses." But she advocated no mechanical equality between the sexes: "Whatever tends to incapacitate the maternal character takes woman out of her sphere."

The feminist movement was integrated with the two great revolutions of the eighteenth century, and in both the feminist leaders actively agitated for change. For a time, in France, their demands that liberty, equality, and fraternity apply to both men and women made some headway, until the Napoleonic Code ended the possibility. In the United States, as well, there was pressure to codify equal status for women, but the Constitution made no reference to women's rights, and no dramatic progress for the movement occurred until the Women's Rights Convention of 1848, which met in Seneca Falls, New York, under the leadership of Elizabeth Cady Stanton. Mrs. Stanton, who had been educated in a female seminary, was the wife of the abolitionist, Henry Stanton. Their honeymoon had been spent attending the worldwide antislavery convention in London, which, reflecting the limited social orientation of its organizers, who considered emancipation a specific and not a general principle, barred female delegates. One of those barred was Mrs. Lucretia Mott, who met and joined forces with Mrs. Stanton to work for the cause of women's rights, and who, with her, organized the Women's Rights Convention in Mrs. Stanton's hometown of Seneca Falls.

Even before this first organizational step was taken, the cause had gained a few victories. We noted earlier that Mississippi in 1839, and Maine in 1844, granted property rights to women, and in 1848 Mrs. Stanton was instrumental in securing the passage of a similar law in New York. With the organization of the movement, the pressure for change became constant. Mrs. Stanton, for example, addressed the Congress annually, seeking a constitutional amendment to grant women's rights. The Woman's Suffrage Association was founded and fought specifically for the right to vote. Pressures on education institutions to provide for women's higher education and the education of women for the professions led to the first admission of women to medical college in 1847 and the first woman to enter law school in 1869. Finally, what had not happened in thousands of years happened in 1920. Women added the right to vote to the legal, educational, and social gains acquired since 1839. Yet a realistic assessment of these fourscore years reveals that despite these changes, the basic balance of power between the sexes had not significantly altered. Only a few women took advantage of their new opportunities, and these few were seen by men and women alike as deviants. The psychological climate of the 1920's continued to be male-centered and -dominated. It took another revolution to challenge that domination.

That revolution was the development of the social sciences as separate and recognized disciplines. Sociology, the formal study of societies and the ways they function, began in 1838; cultural anthropology, the study of man and his cultures, in 1871; and psychology, the study of the individual, in 1879. It was inevitable that these social disciplines would look critically at many of the assumptions, customs, and traditions that man had accepted for generations. Anthropologists found, for example, that the roles, functions, rights, and responsibilities of each sex were cultural phenomena and not the result of some divinely ordained or natural law. Sociology emphasized cultural relativity and focused on society as a functioning entity, with the consequent highlighting of areas of social injustice. Psychology contributed, of course, the psychoanalytic insights of Freud, particularly the concern with sexual relationships, and later detailed observations of human development, personality and behavior.

In such a vast body of knowledge, it is hard to single out particular facts or theories that led to the overthrow of traditional concepts of sexual roles. The total impact of the social sciences was enormous, and by the mid-twentieth century, the rudiments of social scientific thought were part of the intellectual equipment of every educated man and woman. Consider, for example, the concept that society itself is a changing and changeable organism. The wide variety of social organizations that had once existed, or were still in existence, certainly suggested that a group of people, even a nation, could remake its social order, could rationally and deliberately establish new criteria for social functioning, could reallocate roles and responsibilities, and could alter some of the fundamental structural components of society. In other words, no institution was sacred.

Anthropological evidence challenged personal and social patterns of behavior which had been taken for granted in Western culture. It was shown, for example, that adolescence need not be a period of storm and strife and inner turmoil, for there were cultures in which it is not. Notions of the inviolate nature of acquired property were struck a blow by descriptions of cultures which accumulated property at great expense, only to destroy it ceremonially. Sex roles turned out to be far more variable than the limits placed on them by Western culture suggested. And sexual relationships could be conducted under freer conditions and with fewer inhibitions than those that characterized American culture in the early years of the twentieth century. Perhaps the most fundamental contribution of the cultural anthropologist was to make clear that all basic human interrelationships lend themselves to observation and serious systematic study. It is a large step from the abstract and theoretical notions of culture outlined in *The Golden Bough*[7] to the detailed descriptions of modern anthropology. However, once this first step has been taken, it becomes a series of increasingly shorter steps to get from Margaret Mead studying sex in Samoa[8] to William Masters and Virginia Johnson photographing American men and women in acts of sexual intercourse.[9]

Anthropological candor in considering sexual matters was, of course, directly related to Sigmund Freud's work in psychology, for he offered a theory of human behavior which was based on stages of sexual development. As has often been said, he saw sex everywhere, and it was not long before everyone else was seeing it too. But perhaps the single theory of Freud's which had the greatest impact in the area of sexual roles was the Oedipus complex, the concept that male children face deep internal conflicts involving their sexual feelings for their mothers and the consequent rivalry, hostility, and feeling of helplessness toward their fathers. In this sense, Freud was the first psychologist to pinpoint a male dilemma. For in Freudian terms the male child is faced with a doubly unpalatable choice. One alternative involves him in direct competition with his father for the affections of his mother, with the accompanying fears of castration and destruction. The other involves abandoning his mother to his father, with accompanying feelings of frustration and loss. Freud did not develop the Oedipal theme for women in the same detail as he did for men. The obvious parallel is of the female child competing with her mother for the affections of her father. But once that is stated, the female's problem remains vague, since the mother has not been seen in the same power position as the father, nor is there a comparable fear of castration.

Freud was vague about women in general but, however vague, it is clear that he regarded them as physically and psychologically inferior to men. In these views Freud reflected the social conditions of his time, the strongly traditional, almost medieval society of nineteenth-century Austria, as well as the ancient Jewish view of the sexes. Thus these Jewish views, among the oldest philosophical beliefs on the relative roles of the sexes, were among the shaping influences on one of the newest belief systems of the twentieth century. In his essay on female sexuality,[10] Freud noted that male superiority stems from his possession of a penis, and that there is a measure of disparagement in his attitude toward women, whom he regards as having been castrated. He went on to say, "When a little girl has sight of a male genital organ and so discovers her own deficiency, she does not accept the unwelcome knowledge without hesitation and reluctance."[11] From this he posited the concept of penis envy, the female's lifelong burden, for no effort, no success, fully compensates for her lack of a penis. Freud felt that this lack typifies the inferiority of the female and, in contrast, the superiority of the male. But somehow his affirmation of the traditional view of the superior male, primarily by virtue of his possessing a penis, did little to bolster either man's sexual or social position. This may in part have been because Freud also postulated a life of fear for men over losing the prized possession.

It is an interesting historical paradox that Freud's work, which relied so heavily on the notion of unconscious sexual impulses, contributed to the development of a period in which sexual activity became more than conscious, in fact, a central focus of the life of the educated American man and woman. As psychological knowledge and half-truth and overgeneralization filtered down from the scientific community to the schools and colleges, men and women alike became acutely aware of their own motivations, sublimations, impulses, libidinal needs and sexual drives. Awareness was followed by a veritable flood of advice; advice on how to make love, how to arouse the sexual partner, how to achieve higher and higher levels of satisfaction, even how to raise children.

While Freud's influence on twentieth-century society can be seen in many areas, two are of particular interest to our history here. First, his emphasis on understanding and analyzing one's drives and motivations quickly led to an atmosphere in which everyone appraised the extent to which his drives were acted upon and his motivations realized. Freud's influence was particularly strong in America, where educated segments of society moved into decades of self-analysis, self-appraisal, and self-evaluation of the extent to which they had fully realized their potential for development.

The practice was not limited to men. Despite Freud's orientation to male superiority and female inferiority, the psychological approach and processes he unleashed were equally applicable to both sexes. Women too could look into their psyches to search for what they really wanted, what they were sublimating, how satisfied they were, how fulfilled they were. As a result, many women began to question and express open dissatisfaction with the traditional limits on their roles and activities. Their questions came at a time when other social relationships which had remained basically stable since the Industrial Revolution, such as those between labor and management, between the city and the country, between the citizen and the government, between the majority and the minority, between black and white, were also being examined, rejected, and revised.

Freud's second significant influence came from his consistent emphasis on the central role that sexual drives, responses and feelings play in human functioning. Once his psychology achieved acceptability among the educated, the study of sex was released from many of the restraints placed on it; by the Puritan ethic and its primarily psychophilosophical position in American thought and social processes. In a sense, Freud was the necessary precursor of Kinsey, Masters, and "Oh, Calcutta!" and it was Freud's work which precipitated the sexual obsession of the mid-twentieth century.

Another intriguing aspect of Freud's influence was that it was most strongly felt in the United States, not in his native Austria, nor in Europe. His theoretical system, which sought to explain sexual repression, frustration, and guilt to encourage sexual expression, satisfaction, and fulfillment, found a particularly responsive audience in an American society still struggling with a strongly Puritanical moral value system, firmly built around guilt at any excess of pleasure, particularly sexual pleasure. For the frustrated and anxious, Freud provided an explanation of what had been troubling them all along. For those wanting to break out of the old value system, he provided a scientifically based justification for trying the sexual activities they wanted to try. For still others, he provided a scientific rationale for talking endlessly about sex, love, and fulfillment.

The synthesis of all of these influences resulted in a period, beginning in the late 1930's, during which educated Americans were preoccupied with self-analysis and self-evaluation, and sexual criteria dominated all others. It was a period in which "satisfaction" and "climax" became the most important considerations in sexual encounters, in which making love became an objective skill taught in a book, and fulfillment became the goal of marriage. How good a lover is each husband, how well and how often has each wife been satisfied? Questions such as these were soon to represent the dominant dimension of marriage. It was no longer enough that the husband was able to provide the material components of marriage such as shelter and clothes and food. Nor was it enough that the wife kept the house functioning, got the children off to school and the clothes back from the cleaner. Nor was the marriage evaluated on the basis of whether or not they got along, or whether or not they liked each other. Success or failure was measured in bed. How satisfying was the love-play period? Did they both achieve orgasm? Did the orgasms coincide?

But these were criteria applied by adults who grew up when repression rather than expression of sexual thought, feelings, and actions was the rule. So it was not surprising that many couples found themselves inadequate by these superimposed standards, and that many marriages began to fall apart at increasing rates when the glue of economic dependence which might have held them together in earlier decades also dissolved. Women were no longer economically captive to marriage in the 1940's, and if they could not find fulfillment and satisfaction, they wanted out.

This added a significant new dimension to the relationships between the sexes; for the first time it was women who initiated a significant proportion of divorces. Gone was male domination in marriage, the idea that wedlock revolved about the male and that as long as he was satisfied, the union would be maintained. Now, in addition to seeking his own satisfactions, he found he must also satisfy his wife, and for many men this was a pressure they could not meet, a demand for which their entire psychic structure was unprepared.

An additional by-product of this preoccupation with sex was the objectification of sexual processes and their consequent depersonalization. In the 1940's, dozens of books designed to be marriage manuals or guides to the ideal marriage suggested that there were finite, step-by-step approaches to affection and love which were equally appropriate for everyone. Forgotten, it seemed, was the individuality of each husband and wife and the unique experience of each marriage. This curious ability to depersonalize sex was best seen in the publication of Dr. Kinsey's data.[12,13] This once-intimate area of human behavior was reduced to a set of contingency tables relating how often, how many did what, to whom, and at what age. Kinsey, an entymologist, studied sexual patterns of both sexes through extensive retrospective interviews. He generally ignored psychological, sociological, and anthropological backgrounds in his research; not only that, but he and his staff "applied to the human female, the data derived from the study of laboratory animals."[14]

But if Kinsey and his associates' research on sexual intercourse seemed to consider humans as if they were laboratory animals, the research reported by Masters and Johnson actually treated them as such. They observed and photographed 300 couples in the act of intercourse in their laboratory, with each participant wired to a variety of machines recording physiological indices of response. Their findings were discussed later in a book,[9] and their research continues, with the prospect of future publications. But interestingly, their focus in the book was on woman's sexuality and the investigation of female physiological and psychological responses. Perhaps their most widely discussed finding was that the female is frequently more capable of physiologically profound sexual response than the male, and this all but completed the reversal of concern, for where at the beginning of the century a satisfactory sexual relationship was defined in terms of male satisfaction, the emphasis now is on female response, after only one or two decades of definition in terms of joint response.

The final developments which led to current sex roles and role conflicts in the United States were precipitated by World War II. The immense demands for personnel by the Army, Navy, and Air Force forced a major change; women began to enter the Armed Forces as well as industry and other previously "male only" fields. In the Armed Forces women in two decades recapitulated the centuries of role development. They were admitted first only to service in the continental United States in limited subservient roles as clerks and typists, with the highest rank to which they could be promoted as well below that available to men. Their responsibilities gradually expanded, as did their field of service, until they could serve overseas, on board ship in the Navy, and then, in the 1960's, see one of their number named the first female General. However, women are still not fully used in the military, for unlike Vietnamese and Israeli women, they are not drafted and do not serve in combat units, two dubious privileges still exclusive to men in the event of war.

In industry, Rosie the Riveter proved to be a short-term war phenomenon, but a decade or so later, when industry began to automate and the need for brawn was gradually replaced by the need for precision and reliability, Rosie and her daughters started to move into the job market in increasing numbers.

The postwar period also saw the renewal of agitation in the United States for improved social status for women. Many forces contributed to this renewal, among them the social mobility and economic independence women had achieved during the war and the large number of women, of the middle class at least, who had received educations comparable to many men. It was unreal to expect the women who had worked at jobs outside the home which demanded a high level of physical and intellectual competence to retreat back to the kitchen, or to expect women who themselves had been both mother and father (or who had seen others so serve) to abandon familial power once the men came back.

But this time the tactics of the new feminists were qualitatively different from the decades previous and even from the violent agitation of the suffragettes. For now they were not agitating for specific privileges, but rather for a basic change in social and psychological status. They still sought admission to the last of the exclusive male jobs and professions, and to the last of the male preserves; but more important they asked for a restructuring of society and its attitudes to end what they saw as the exploitation of women. Initially gaining public attention through the activities of the bra burners and women who picketed the Miss America contest, the movement soon achieved serious proportions with the establishment of the National Organization for Women (NOW) in 1966 and the Women's Liberation Front, which held its first national convention in 1968 attended by 200 women from 20 states and Canada. The political and social pressures generated by these organizations resulted in a mass of legislatively supported social changes ranging from the end of sexually segregated want ads to abortion reform, and hitting its high point in the passage by the Congress of the Equal Rights Amendment to the Constitution and its rapid ratification by the legislatures of 29 states by mid-1973.

But at that point a reaction became openly vocal. This was led by Phyllis Schlafly, who formed a Stop ERA movement to pressure legislatures not to ratify the Amendment and also succeeded in having the legislature of Nebraska rescind their earlier ratification.

Moreover, conflict within the movement came out into the open as Betty Friedan, and other feminists used the pages of the Sunday Times Magazine[14] to attack each other's devotion to the cause. Whether this internal strife is the sign of the socio-political immaturity or as is more likely, socio-political maturity, there is little doubt that the movement has gone on long enough and achieved enough success for leadership to be bitterly fought for.

The whole language of the feminine liberation movement became part of the American culture of the 1970's, with male chauvinist pig an epithet as vivid in Dubuque as in Los Angeles and Ms. as clear an address in Nashua as in New York.

As so often happens historically, social and scientific developments interact, for as the female social and sexual roles began to change, the health sciences produced a reliable pill to prevent conception. Now simply and easily women have the ability to decide whether their sexual relationships will be concerned only with sexual responses or directed to conception as well. The implications of the Pill on male-female relationships will be discussed in a later chapter; here we need only note that it is an intermediate step along the way to the much more profound point of controlling the process of childbirth, for the logical sequence in achieving full sexual parity for women is to move from sex without conception to maternity without childbirth. This is discussed at length in *The Second Genesis* by Albert Rosenfeld, who notes that "Children may be routinely born of geographically separated or even long-dead parents, virgin births may become relatively common, women may give birth to other women's children..." or that in addition to "...artificially assisted fertilization there could be (and has been, experimentally) fertilization in vitro...Furthermore, it might well be possible eventually to grow babies entirely in vitro with the protective and nourishing presence of a human mother nowhere in evidence."[15]

And while many will debate the pros and cons of the coming world of the test-tube baby, with an enzyme father and a protein mother, the militant feminist does not, as noted in the view expressed below by the woman who wrote Time magazine in reference to an article on bottle versus breast feeding:

> Sir: Not only should we women take advantage of scientific bottle feeding, but we should encourage research on test-tube reproduction to free us from the animal miseries of childbearing, so that we would have the time and energy to utilize our brainpower for a better society.[16]

The question that now must be asked, of course, is what have all these changes, and the agitation for further change, done to man. Man is left, it appears, only with what his prehistoric ancestors started out with; superior physical strength. Paradoxically, he has been the prime mover in the social, scientific, psychological, and sexual revolutions that have enveloped him; and to his credit, he has, so far, been able to keep up with them. But today the pace of challenge and change has accelerated enormously. It is no longer a matter of simply keeping up, some much more basic accommodation is required. Every year brings a new discovery, another demand. The old order and the certainties of the past are crumbling; future prospects are uncertain.

Change and uncertainty are inevitably accompanied by conflict; conflict between man and his society, between man and himself, and, in the sensitive area of sexual roles and interrelationships, between man and woman. And it is to this conflict that we will turn.

NOTES

1. Pius XII, Encyclical, *Summi Pontificatus*, Official English Version, Vatican Polygot Press, October 20, 1939.

2. This section is based on the articles on Women, in the *Encyclopedia Brittanica*, Eleventh Edition, Volume XXVIII, pp. 782-790.

3. Robert Ardrey, *The Territorial Imperative*, New York: Atheneum, 1966, 390 pp.

4. *Time*, October 31, 1969, p. 66.

5. *The Standard Jewish Encyclopedia*, Cecil Roth, Ed., New York: Doubleday & Co., 1966, p. 567.

6. Mary Wollstonecraft, *A Vindication of the Rights of Women*, republished by T.F. Unwin: London, 1891.

7. Sir James George Frazer, *The Golden Bough*, New York: Macmillan, 1951, 864 pp.

8. Margaret Mead, *Coming of Age in Samoa*,

9. William H. Masters and Virginia E. Johnson, *Human Sexual Inadequacy*, Boston: Little, Brown, 1970, 467 pp.

10. Sigmund Freud, *Female Sexuality*, London: Hogarth Press, 1931.

11. *Ibid.*, Volume XXI, pp. 225-243.

12. Alfred C. Kinsey, W.B. Martin and Clyde E. Martin, *Sexual Behavior in the Human Male*, Philadelphia and London: W.B. Saunders Co., 1948.

13. Alfred C. Kinsey, W.B. Martin, C.E. Pomeroy and P.M. Gebhard, *Sexual Behavior in the Human Female*, Philadelphia: W.B. Saunders Co., 1953.

14. Lawrence Kubie, "Dr. Kinsey and the Medical Profession," a Review of Sexual Behavior in the Human Female, *Psychosomatic Medicine*, Vol. XVII, No. 3(May-June, 1955), pp. 172-184.

15. Betty Friedan, "Up from the Kitchen Floor," *New York Sunday Times Magazine*, March 4, 1973.

16. Alfred Rosenfeld, *The Second Genesis*, Englewood Cliffs, N.J., Prentice Hall: 1969, p. 108.

17. *Time*, August 2, 1968, p. 8.

CHAPTER 3

Studies in Conflict and Confusion

Like many other behavioral scientists in the late fifties and sixties, we became concerned about the growing sexual conflict which seemed to typify the relationships between men and women. The "battle of the sexes" is nothing new in history, but suddenly during the postwar years in America it became much more than the subject for jokes and cartoons. Evidence everywhere indicated that it was being fought in dead earnest, not only in the comparative privacy of bedrooms and divorce courts, the traditional arenas, but, with the gathering momentum of the sexual revolution, in business offices and even on the streets in the full glare of front-page publicity.

One of us, a therapist-psychologist, came into almost daily contact with problems in male-female relationships that were tearing apart so many marriages. Just what was going wrong? The other, a research psychologist, revealed that there was little or no valid information about these problems—why they were occurring with increasing frequency or what could be done to solve them. In general terms, the lines of battle seemed clear enough. Within the space of only a few short years, man had been toppled from his pedestal of unquestioned superiority in what used to be called a "man's world" to a rather anomalous and ill-defined role in a world that seemed to have slipped beyond everyone's grasp. Gone, or going fast, was his favored position in religion and the law; gone his complete authority in marriage and the family; gone his superiority in the social and economic spheres outside the home; gone, too, even his dominant role in sexual intercourse.

These many challenges—and defeats—seemed to stem from an accelerating spiral of circumstances, and there was no short-

age of commentators and critics to trace man's decline, whether
it was attributed to the isolation, depersonalization, or dehumanization of abstract social forces, or to such concrete encroachments as a working wife or the Pill. Nor was there any
dearth of comment about the corresponding rise of woman. Her
roles were undergoing an even more dramatic change, and because this was the most recent upheaval in male-female relationships, and because it posed the most obvious threat to the con-
ventions of marriage and family life, perhaps here were the root
causes of the new and pervasive sexual conflict.

In short, it appeared to us, as it did to many other observers,
that it was the women who were rocking the boat. Was the
soaring divorce rate caused by significant numbers of women
being frustrated within the limits of their family roles? Were
there really satisfactory alternatives to marriage and child-
raising? And what about women who tried to combine a domestic
career with a career outside the home: did the combination work
or did both careers suffer? To find out, we decided, at first, to
collect data which would enable us to talk with some precision
about women's views of their roles, activities, and behavior. And
to do that we followed an old but often ignored rule: "If you want
to know what people think, ask them." We devised a set of direct
questionnaires which eventually became known as the Maferr
Inventory of Feminine Values and administered it to thousands
of women throughout the world.[1]

The women we questioned ranged in age from seventeen to
seventy years, but most were between twenty-eight and forty-
eight. We decided to concentrate on the relatively well-educated
woman who could, if she wanted, move into an active life beyond
her family roles. The largest occupational groups were teachers,
physicians, attorneys, artists, scientists, and people in business.
There was one group composed of those who called themselves
housewives, and among the other groups many women described
themselves as "physician-housewife," "teacher-housewife," etc.
To a somewhat lesser degree, we also tried to obtain some insight
into the views of the less-educated and less-active women, including wherever possible, housewives who were not working. And
last but not least, we questioned thousands of college students
whose choice of roles, theoretically at least, was still ahead of
them. Taken all together, the Inventory has been administered

over the last twenty years to over 11,000 women in the United States and approximately 13,000 women in seventeen foreign countries.

Basically simple and straightforward in its approach, the Inventory was designed to encompass five major areas in male-female relationships and presents a series of thirty-four statements to which a woman can respond, thus revealing her attitudes about herself and her roles. (The complete Inventory of Feminine Values is contained in Appendix A.) The first group of statements consists of items such as "I am energetic in the development and expression of my ideas," or "When I am doing something with a group of people, I often seem to be drifting into a position of leadership." These and others like them are concerned with the personal and social characteristics of women. A second group of items concerns the interrelationships between husbands and wives. This group includes items such as "I would like to marry a man whom I could really look up to," or "I would rather not marry than sacrifice some of my essential beliefs and needs in order to adjust to another person." A third area is concerned with motherhood, such as the item, "I will have achieved the main goal of my life if I rear normal, well-adjusted children." The fourth group of items concerned the interrelationships of work and family responsibilities for women, including such items as "I believe the personal ambitions of a woman should be subordinated to the family as a group." The fifth area involves a woman's self-realization, i.e., "I would like to create or accomplish something which would be recognized by everybody."

We felt that a woman's responses to these statements would enable us to place her somewhere on a continuum between the extremes of feminine attitudes and behavior in all of these areas. At one extreme would be the woman who considers her role and function in life as primarily to serve her husband and children. This woman would derive her satisfactions from the achievements and accomplishments of her family, from her role in facilitating and encouraging their accomplishments and from the smooth performance of her own family responsibilities. When asked if marriage and children take precedence over everything in her life, this woman would say, "Yes, they do." And if we asked if the "main goal of her life is to rear normal well-adjusted children," she would also say yes. But if we asked whether a married woman should crave personal success or be satisfied with the accomplishments of her husband and children, her answer would be that personal success is unnecessary; she would be perfectly satisfied with the achievements of her husband and children and would not need personal success. The "others before self" pattern of this extremely family-oriented woman would carry over into her social relationships as well, so she would see herself as concerned with the feelings of others, and as a listener rather than talker, a follower rather than leader.

At the other extreme would be the woman who sees herself primarily as a fully functioning person in her own right and who believes that her needs and desires are as important as those of her husband and children. While she might accept household responsibilities, her primary satisfactions would come from the utilization of her own abilities and talents in situations beyond the family. This woman would say no, happy well-adjusted children do not represent the main goal of her life, and marriage and children do not take precedence over everything else. Moreover, she would not be satisfied with the achievements of her husband and children but would want her own personal success: she would want to "create or accomplish something" which would be recognized. At her most extreme, this "self-oriented woman" would also say that not only did she believe that, as a capable woman, she "has a duty to be active," but if she had to choose, she would prefer to be famous rather than to have the "affection of one man." This woman, too, would generalize her approach and attitude, and so when questioned about her relationships with people other than her husband, she would say that in social situations, she is a talker rather than a listener, a leader rather than a follower, and argues with people who try to assert their authority over her.

We knew, of course, that few women would place themselves at either extreme, but we were curious to know in which direction the scales would tip. In scoring, we used a system by which a woman who had identically balanced positions of family- and self-orientation would have a score of zero. Scores on the minus side of zero, ranging up to -68, would be characteristic of women who took the most extremely family-oriented position, and who said that they were extremely subservient in social situations.

Women who had more of a self- than a family-orientation would have scores on the plus side of zero, ranging up to +68, representing the woman who took the most extremely self-oriented position on every family item and who took the most aggressively active social position as well.

All of the women we tested were asked to answer the questionnaire in three ways. In the first version of the Inventory, called Woman's Self-Perception, they responded to the statements as they themselves really thought and felt. In the second version, called Woman's Ideal Woman, they were asked to think about the woman they would *like* to be, their ideal woman, and respond to the same statements in scrambled order as they believed that this woman would respond. Finally, we scrambled the statements once again and presented them a third time in a form called Man's Ideal Woman. This time we asked the women to think about a *man's* ideal woman and respond as they thought men would want such a woman to answer. (Perhaps the easiest way to understand what we did is to do as the women we studied did, that is, answer the questionnaires. They all appear in Appendix A, together with instructions for completing them and scoring and interpreting the responses.)

Administering such an Inventory to so many different women in so many different places over a period of so many years was, of course, a major undertaking, but well worth it, we felt, if we could derive from their responses something more than just a generalized impression of what women really thought of themselves, what they thought they would like to be, and what they thought men would like them to be. Far too many researchers, we had found, simply assumed certain attitudes and beliefs on the part of women, or projected their own attitudes and beliefs without sufficient evidence to back them up, or even made some sweeping claims based on a small and convenient sample of opinion. We were in search of a significant sample, to provide concrete evidence, and we believe we found it.

To our surprise, wherever we administered the Inventory, the answers were almost unbelievably consistent. From New York to Kyoto, from Brooklyn to Istanbul, we discovered essentially the same pattern, a pattern that showed little variation among different age groups, among different ethnic groups, and among different educational groups. The pattern was simply this: we had attempted to find out just where women stood between the extremes of self-orientation and home- and family-orientation, and we discovered that the great majority of them stood squarely in the middle. On the Self-Perception questionnaire, most described themselves as possessing elements of both an active, self-concerned woman and those of a family-concerned woman. The surprise did not come with our first studies in the United States, which is, after all, the birthplace of the sexual revolution and the new feminism, but rather with the responses that came from foreign countries, representing not only Western culture but Middle and Far Eastern cultures as well.

Furthermore, when these same women were asked to describe their ideal woman, we saw a similar consistency in their responses. While some of them described their ideal woman as slightly more active and outgoing than they saw themselves, most of them felt she would be more family-oriented than they themselves were. The basic quality of this ideal woman, too, was one of relative balance between the extremes of activity and passivity, with a slight tilt toward family orientation.

But a dramatic shift occurred when we asked women what man's ideal woman was like. In sample after sample, and in country after country, the same answer came back: the women believed that men wanted a woman who was strongly family-oriented, relatively passive and submissive in social and personal situations, and who clearly saw her role as wife and mother taking precedence over any possible activity as an individual outside the family. This family-oriented ideal that our female samples attributed to men's concept of the ideal woman was as true of the female physicians as of the college girls, as true of the businesswomen as of the full-time housewives. It characterized the housewife in Los Angeles as fully as it did the housewife in Peru or France. It characterized the college undergraduate in the United States and the undergraduate in Greece, Turkey, or Argentina. The implication of these responses was clear: women were saying that while they were pretty much as they would like to be, they were not at all like what they thought men wanted.

Were these women right? Did men really hold this extremely family-oriented woman as an ideal?

It was here that we realized that our studies would be completely one-dimensional, raising more questions than they answered, if we continued to question women only. For the answers women gave us pointed up a problem: the clear and consistent conflict between the woman they said they were and wanted to be, and the woman they thought men desired. Were the women right or were they simply attributing views to men which the latter did not have?

We decided that we could use the same questionnaire we had been using, and simply ask the men to answer the form called Man's Ideal Woman, and answer as they thought their ideal woman would answer. We tried to obtain male samples which were similar to the female samples as to profession, age, socioeconomic status, and nationality, and we were able to do so for six of the American and six of the foreign samples, a total of 2,000 men. We also tried to duplicate the conditions under which we asked the questions.[3] In each of these twelve samples the answer from the men came back clearly and consistently: their ideal woman was a woman who was balanced between family-orientation on the one hand and self-orientation on the other. In other words, the men's ideal woman was almost exactly the same woman that women said they actually were. She was nothing like the passive, family-oriented ideal woman which the female sample attributed to men.

Obviously there was some discrepancy here. Despite the limitations of both the questionnaire and the samples we tested, there was considerable cross-cultural agreement among men and women. But there was a great difference between the passive family-oriented woman that women believed men desired, and the well-balanced ideal woman that men actually described. How to account for it? We were faced with the necessity of explaining the results either by questioning some of the data, or by accepting all of it.

One obvious way to question the data was to argue that, when the men responded to the Inventory, they were lying. This seemed possible because the men in our samples were all reasonably well-educated and thus had been exposed to current views about equality of opportunity for the sexes. They knew very well that the enlightened man was expected to accept and even encourage activity and full self-realization of women. Thus, we could posit that they responded as if they believed in this, even if, in real life, they might not behave in accordance with that belief.

Another possibility was to accept the male responses as valid, and instead label the views women attributed to men as reflecting their own unhappiness with the level of responsibility and activity their emancipation had not only made possible, but had led their family and friends to expect of them. They were basically reluctant to move into this active new world of equal rights and responsibilities but found it difficult to say so, for generations of women had fought for just such equality. Therefore, they expressed their reluctance, and even explained and justified much of their inactivity and their lack of zeal by simply saying, "The men don't want us to do it and so to keep peace in the family, we won't do it."

A third possibility was that women were describing man's ideal in terms based on his *behavior*, and so they attributed a much more family-oriented ideal to men. Thus our discrepancy: men described their ideal woman in terms of what they considered to be the preferred and socially acceptable view of such a woman, while women described her in accordance with their perceptions of how men behaved toward her, and the conclusions they drew from that behavior as to the way men *really* felt.

Nuances such as these, however, while interesting to contemplate, are extremely difficult to prove. Assuming, then, that both men and women were telling the truth, our data revealed with vivid clarity the extent to which the sexes failed to understand each other. If men truly had come to accept a more active and self-oriented woman, and women too had come to see themselves, and to some degree their own ideal, in this way, they certainly had not communicated their basic agreement to each other. Women had no idea that men thought as they did and so neither believed nor accepted the male ideal.

It is a cliché to note that all good research raises more questions than it answers, but obviously the time had come to move into a new dimension in our survey to resolve some of these questions. We began two different approaches to seek out an explanation for the discrepancy noted between the male and female responses to the original Inventory. One approach was to meet with groups of married couples for a special version of the study. At the beginning of the evening, we asked the wives and husbands to fill out the questionnaires separately. But in evaluating them, we found exactly the same discrepancy we found when total strangers completed the questionnaires: every husband and wife, of the several in these groups, responded in approximately the same way. The wives described man's ideal woman as passive and family-oriented, and the men described her as balanced and far more active than the women predicted. To this point, these sessions simply corroborated the previous data, adding only the fact that the discrepancy occurred even with married couples. But then we told the couples what we had done, and what they had said, and asked them how it happened. "I think the men are lying," said one woman as soon as we threw open the discussion. "I agree," echoed another, and a third added, "I think they're *expected* to want women to have careers and be equal. I think they say what's expected of them but, subconsciously, down very deep, they don't want that at all."

Another of the wives went even further in spelling out why she thought the men were lying: "I've been thinking how to put it into words and I really can't find ... I think a man wants to feel that his home and his wife and children depend upon him solely and need him for their existence, and although he might not mind if a woman has an outside interest or ... he still wants to know that basically *he* is the one and he is the important factor in this."

The men, of course, said they were telling the truth, and in explaining how his ideal woman happened to be balanced between our two extremes, one of the men spelled out part of the male dilemma as well as we have heard it expressed:

In the old days, it was a pioneer setup; the man had a clear-cut role, and he either had to go out and fight the Indians or kill a bear, till the field and bring the food; otherwise the family would starve to death. And the woman had her duties in the home. Today these duties are blurred in that economically, the woman can bring home perhaps a lot more loot than the man can, and so it's not as clear-cut as it once was. So the man is in effect faced with the problem; does he want a wife, say, like Scarlett O'Hara that is always submissive to the man and thinks that the man is so smart and has all the answers? No. On the other side of the coin, does he want to marry somebody like Ethel Kennedy and play touch football all the time and get put down at family quiz games? No. So when you talk about how we react to this questionnaire, I think it's an ambivalence on our part in that we try to strike a balance between the two sides of the spectrum, but it's in large part due to the fact that the woman can't define what she wants to be. Is it Scarlett O'Hara or Ethel Kennedy? Does she want to raise kids or is she going to get bored and want to go out and be a career woman. And so I think what the men have said is valid in this context.*

Another man said emphatically, "I would greatly approve of my wife trying to seek this type of personal success." The discussion leader asked, "Which one is your wife?" Turning to the wife he asked, "Do you think he would approve?" "No," said the wife promptly. The group laughed.

This discussion again highlighted the utter lack of communication between men and women about the attitudes and behavior the former appreciate in women. Husbands and wives living together and being constantly in each other's company apparently had failed to effectively communicate on this particular issue. Similar discussion groups worked out the same way and all led to the same conclusions: the husbands and wives did not agree on how men felt about women's roles and activities.

At this point, we decided to find out if the discrepancy involving women's roles was the only role confusion. What about men's roles? Did men really know what women expected of them? What was the relationship between men's concept of themselves and their concept of what they would like to be? Were these concepts similar, as our research indicated they were for women, or was there a discrepancy between man's ideal man and how he saw himself?

All of these questions led us into a year-long period of experimentation and development during which we tried out several versions of what we came to call the Inventory of Masculine Values. The structure of the Masculine Inventory was made deliberately similar to that of the Inventory of Feminine Values. The same five general areas of research were used, so that the male version included items related to men's personal characteristics and social behavior, the interrelationships of husbands and wives, the interrelationship of work and family responsibilities for men, and men's needs for self-realization. The scor-

---

*The man obviously has his heroines confused. Scarlett O'Hara was a pretty independent young woman, and Ethel Kennedy would seem to be primarily family-oriented.

ing system and the rationale for interpreting the scores was also similar to the Feminine Inventory. (The complete Inventory of Masculine Values is found in Appendix B.)

We believed that this Inventory would make it possible for a man to choose between two clearly differentiated extremes of masculine attitudes and behavior. One extreme would be the man who sees himself as a freely functioning individual whose actions are self-motivated and oriented and who acts and reacts in terms of his individual needs and business or professional pressures. His family would play a secondary role. This is not to say that when he married he lacked interest in or affection for his wife and children, but that when there were competitive demands on his time and energy he would expect his family to understand that they must take second place. In social interactions, this man would also see himself as aggressive, forthright and firm, leading others and exerting a commanding social role in keeping with his dominant business and familial roles.

The opposite extreme would be the man whose social life centers around his family. He would see himself as part of a family unit consisting of himself and his wife as equal partners, with children having at least the same call upon his time and energy as his business and outside activities. He would also recognize that his wife had individual needs of her own and that it was, in part, his responsibility to evolve a way of life which would permit her to develop and actively participate in those activities which interested her.

We administered this Masculine Inventory over a period of six years to approximately 7,000 men, and used multiple scrambled versions, just as we did with the Feminine Inventory.[4] (Again the best way to understand what we did is to respond to the questionnaires as the men did. The questions appear in Appendix B with instructions for completing them and scoring and interpreting the responses.) First, we asked men to respond to the version called Man's Self-Perception, to tell us what kind of man they thought they actually were. The picture that came back was of a balanced man, somewhat on the active, outgoing side of the middle, but with considerable expressions of both activity and passivity, individual and group orientations, and self and family needs. In their responses to the version called Man's Ideal Man, some of this balance tipped toward the active side, for their ideal was more outgoing, more aggressive, more clearly self-oriented and involved than they believed themselves actually to be.

The third questionnaire we asked them to answer was the form we called Woman's Ideal Man. How would they respond to the questions? Once again we saw a reversal: the majority of men felt that women wanted a man who was socially restrained and family-oriented. Thus, just as women had told us that men wanted a woman more passive and family-oriented than they, the women, wanted to be, now it was the men who said that women wanted a man who was more submissive and family-oriented than they, the men, wanted to be. At this point, the data appeared exactly like a mirror image of the data from the Feminine Inventory.

To take this phase of the study to the last parallel step, we administered the Woman's Ideal Man form of the Masculine Inventory to women and asked them to answer in terms of their ideal man. And sure enough, they described a man even more active, self-oriented, and aggressive than the men were or wanted to be, and bearing no resemblance to the ideal man men attributed to women.

So now we had the other side of the picture. Our discussions, and everyone else's discussions, of problems involving women's roles had indeed been one-sided, a blind man's view of the elephant, blind because no one had asked the same kind of questions about men. We now had evidence to suggest that men had similar problems in defining their proper roles, and it appeared that men and women communicate about their respective concepts of what constitutes an "ideal man" no better than they do about what constitutes an ideal woman.

We began to ponder a parallel set of explanations. Could the women have been lying? Could it be that the emancipated woman felt she had to describe a strong, active man as an ideal to counter the argument so popular in the journals of the 1960's that the price American society had paid for the freedom given women was the emasculation of the American male? Could it be that the men were simply reading the women wrong, interpreting women's interest in their own fulfillment as including an inevitable demand for a submissive, family-oriented male who would take over the responsibilities the women were abandoning? Or was it the same lack of communication and belief in what the other sex said about sex roles and activities that we had seen in the group discussions about women?

We decided to move in a new direction to determine which explanation made the most sense in interpreting the results of the Masculine Inventory. In doing so, we began what turned out to be the second major phase of our research. In this phase of the study, we decided to go beyond the kinds of generalized statements in the Inventories, and ask people to express opinions about specific situations and personal interactions. We felt that if we asked for opinions about specific situations, the respondents would be more realistic than they had been when asked the more general questions of the Inventory. It was one thing, we thought, for a man to agree that a woman "should have an equal role in family decision-making" when this was offered as an abstract statement, but might it be quite another thing to ask the man how much of a role his wife should have in selecting a new car? Similarly, it might be one thing for a woman to agree that she wanted an opportunity to be creative and to function in the world, but another for her to agree that she would accept the offer of a job at a better salary and higher status than her husband's job.

We developed two new questionnaires, the Family Decision-Making Survey and the Behavioral Survey, to test both male and female responses to these and similar questions. (Both surveys are included in Appendix C, together with instructions for completing and scoring them, and interpreting the scores.) The first survey was intended to move our research into the area of family decision-making; the second, into the area of sex role behavior in potential family conflict situations, and into current perceptions of sex-linked characteristics. As we did in our first studies, we combined two kinds of data collection: we gave the questionnaires to masses of people and then held small group discussions for more intensive study of the "why" of their responses. The people surveyed in this phase of the research were all American, and numbered about 1,000 men and women living throughout the United States. Most were married, and most were working at white collar or professional occupations.[5]

The questions posed fell generally into two categories: first, who did men and women think should make decisions involving family living and, second, *actually* how are they made. We listed twenty-two decisions which a family faces. Some, such as what to do and where to go on a night out, had to be made regularly. Others were made less frequently but recurred—like deciding where to go on vacations. A third group involved decisions which would occur only once in a lifetime, such as deciding upon the living arrangements for an aged parent. We asked the respondents in this study to consider each decision and tell us whether, in the United States today, they believed each decision was one which was primarily the husband's decision, primarily the wife's, or one in which decision-making power was shared equally. Then having told us what they thought was *true today*, we asked them to tell us how they thought each decision *should be* reached.

The data came back loud and clear. Both men and women said that almost all family life decisions *should be* shared equally by both husband and wife. However, with equal assurance they noted, that in the United States today, most of these decisions are made primarily by *women*. Both men and women agreed that women have a far larger share of the actual decision-making power within the family than they should have.

They agreed, also, on which of these decisions should be the prerogative of each sex. Women should decide on how to cast their own votes, what color to paint the living room (by the way, men were even more convinced this should be a female decision than women were), what the wife should do with her spare time, and whether or not she should buy a dress she did not really need. Men were allocated responsibility for their own votes, what to do with their spare time, and whether or not they should change occupations. When the latter decision involved a subsequent move to a new community, our respondents felt that this ceased to be a male prerogative and should be a shared decision.

All the other decisions, both men and women said, should be shared equally, whether or not the wife worked. These involved family life, such as determining sexual patterns, whether to have a baby, and the living arrangements for an aged parent. Shared decisions included every one of the economic factors in the survey, except for buying an unnecessary dress. These financial decisions involved both the general—such as how to spend some money which had been saved or received as a gift, and the specific—like whether to buy a color television, or an automobile, or to move to a more expensive apartment. Recreational, social, and intellectual decisions were also perceived ideally as shared. These involved such questions as where to go on an evening out or on vacation, how often to visit inlaws, what newspapers to receive, and whom to invite to a party.

But significantly, both men and women said that this ideal lies far from an everyday reality. They felt that only half the decisions which should be shared actually were equally shared. The women believed that one or two of these decisions which should be, but are not, shared, fall to the man. The men thought they had only one extra one. But, both sexes said the lion's share of the decision-making goes to women. Thus, both men and women reported that women have predominant responsibility for more decisions than they ought to have.

We wondered if family and economic status of the couples made a difference in their attitudes toward decision-making. Should decision-making power differ between married couples, depending upon whether or not the wife worked? Their answer was no; this should have no effect on decision-making power. It still ought to be shared, and it still was too thoroughly dominated by females. Next we inquired about the addition of a baby to this picture: would that have any effect on the decision-making picture? Again the answer was no.

Now, what did we have so far? The Inventory data had shown that women were not as family-oriented and submissive as they thought men wanted them to be and men had denied that they held such an ideal. Similarly, men were not as family-oriented and submissive as they thought women wanted them to be, and women disclaimed men's perception of their ideal man. But now, pinned down to specifics, both men and women were saying that women had too large a role in the family decision-making structure, that the actual decision-making power therein was not shared to the extent it should be. These findings were unexpected, and made us all the more eager to move the research into its next dimension, the study of how men and women each thought the other would act in real family situations.

The Behavioral Survey was primarily designed to explore this area of male-female relationships.[6] Each of the family situations described contains the elements of a potential sex role conflict. For example, we included a set of situations intended to test men's reactions to their wives' activities. One of these scenarios involves a husband who comes home from work expecting to find dinner ready, only to find an apologetic wife who explains that she has been delayed at work, arrived home only a few minutes before, and has just begun dinner. We asked our respondents what the husband would *say* in such a situation, but we also asked them what he would *think*. The intent was simply to see how often people would say that the husband might think one thing but say something different.

We used this same format to ask about the husband's reactions to a wife who spends a great deal of time away from home on volunteer work in the community; or to a wife who tells her husband one Sunday that she is considering returning to school to complete the studies that marriage and child-rearing interrupted, or finally a wife who tells her husband about an offer she has received of a job at a higher salary and higher status than those of his current job.

The survey permitted the respondents to describe husbands who were consistent as to thought and verbalization, or husbands who were inconsistent. Of course there were two kinds of consistent husbands possible: the husband who was always understanding and accepting in both thought and word, and the husband who was regularly hostile and rejecting. While theoretically there could also be two kinds of inconsistent husbands, we did not expect to find too many men who said hostile, rejecting things while they were thinking amicable thoughts, and so the third type we expected was the inconsistent husband whose friendly words masked hostile thoughts.

We found all three types of husband. In fact, both men and women said all three types existed, although they differed on the proportions. Men felt that of every ten husbands, seven would be consistently positive, two would be consistently negative, and one would be inconsistent, saying something positive but thinking something negative. For women the picture was quite different: they thought only five out of the typical group of ten men would be consistently positive, that three would be inconsistent, while the other two, as in the profile drawn by the men, would be consistently negative.

The responses to the Behavioral Survey indicated, at last, a core of agreement between the sexes. Both men and women felt

that at least half of the men today are understanding and accepting in both word and thought of their wife's activities. Beyond
this, however, these responses also substantiated the discrepan-
cies between the sexes suggested by the earlier Inventories.
Women were three times as likely as men to suspect that the
husband was thinking one thing and saying another.

Consider, for example, the situation in which the husband
comes home from work expecting dinner, only to find an apologetic wife. It is not ready because his wife has been delayed at her
job and gotten home only minutes before him. What does he say?
Almost all of the men and women we questioned said he would
say things like:

"Great. I can sleep for an hour."

"Let me help with dinner."

"OK, as long as it's not going to be a TV dinner."

Those who believed men to be consistent said he then would
be thinking these thoughts as well. But the 10 percent of the men
and 30 percent of the women who believed he would be inconsistent also believed that at the same time he was murmuring these
friendly words, he was thinking:

"She's got a helluva nerve getting home so late."

"Dinner should be on the table when I get home, and my wife
should be waiting at the door."

"Dammit, you should be here when I get home like my mother
always was."

It is also of interest to note that, except for this situation, only
one in ten of either the men or the women felt that the husband
would actually tell his wife that he was angry or annoyed that
dinner was not ready. The roaring husband bellowing his anger,
exemplified by Father Day in *Life with Father*, is clearly one of
America's vanishing species.

We found, too, that the sexes differed in the thoughts they
attributed to the husband. Both men and women attributed
thoughts to the husband no one believed he would actually voice;
they also attributed statements to him which no one believed to
be his true thoughts. For example, in the "late-dinner" situation,
the second most frequent thought which men attributed to the
husband was one indicating suspicion. "Where was she really?"
"That's the second time this week she's been late; what's going on
in that office?"

Yet women apparently never considered that the husband might be suspicious, for those we studied seldom wrote down this thought. Apparently, educated middle-class women today fail to recognize that the suspicious man still exists among their educated middle-class husbands. Another sex difference with interesting and poignant overtones was the fact that one woman in six believed that the husband would think, "Poor dear, she's working too hard." Actually only an occasional man ever attributed that thought or anything like it to the husband. Apparently it was not a prime male consideration that the dual responsibility of work and family care might be "working too hard." It was often uppermost in women's minds, and more intriguing, women thought men agreed when in fact they did not.

The data from the Behavioral Survey also indicated that men did take different kinds of wifely activity with different degrees of seriousness. The clearest line was drawn at the wife's accepting an offer of a job with both higher pay and status than her husband currently enjoyed. Most men liked this idea; in fact three out of every five said the husband would think this would be an excellent opportunity for his wife and their family. But there were many men who had indicated on previous questions that they thought husbands would accept dinners being late, or a wife's returning to school, or doing volunteer work, who also felt that a husband would *not* be happy to hear the news of a great job offer made to his wife. And when they drew this line, men most clearly supported women's charges that men would lie in such situations, for most of those who said the husband would not like it, also said that he would not tell his wife about his feelings but instead would say something mildly positive. The data also suggested an explanation of why the man would not say what he was thinking; most often, both men and women indicated, he would be brooding about what a threat her job offer was to his masculinity, with thoughts like:

"Why doesn't she leave well enough alone and let me wear the pants in this family?"

"My God, does she want to take over money-earning too and run everything?"

"That'll be just great for my position with the kids and our friends."

No man or woman felt a husband would really say this, even those who believed he was thinking it. Here apparently we have one of the seriously sensitive areas in the relationships between the sexes. Women know this, for in a separate question, a majority of the women said that if they were the wife faced with this situation, not only would they *not* take the job, but they would not even *tell* their husband about the offer. These women were convinced that even knowledge of the offer might damage the husband's ego, no matter what the decision finally was. Judging by the magnitude of the men's reactions, they were undoubtedly right.

Within this study, we also looked at the opposite side of the coin: the situation of the husband and the interaction of his family role and job responsibilities. We described two situations: In the first, the question was whether a young and ambitious man, with wife and children, felt "trapped by his family responsibilities." In the second, we added that this young husband and father feels that he must take work home from the office evenings and weekends, and we asked if he felt guilty over the time taken away from his family by this practice.

For the "feeling guilty" situation, the data were much like the ones we have just discussed, but for the "feeling trapped" situation they were dramatically different for men. In this situation, the proportion of men who believed the husband would feel one thing and say another soared from the usual 10 percent to 30 percent, paralleling for the first time the extent of inconsistency which women attribute to men. So here we had another line drawn by men: many would not feel free to say that they did feel trapped. Although nine out of every ten men felt the young husband would feel trapped, only six believed he would actually say so.

We are not so naive as to be surprised to find that people are not completely frank with each other. Social hypocrisy has been going on for centuries, and the "little white lie" may very well serve a useful purpose. But there is a big difference between polite deception, and the ambivalence and conflict revealed by our research that seems to typify the contemporary American marriage. We believe that what is peculiar to present-day sex relationships is the conflict for men between their immediate response in those situations involving feminine activity levels, and the social and/or personal pressures which make them hesitate to say what they really think. We think even more serious is the male-female discrepancy in perception of hypocrisy which adds up to a situation in which the male today cannot win. If in these areas involving his wife's activity level he opposes and resists her activity, then he is being old-fashioned, reactionary, and unenlightened. On the other hand, our data suggest that if the male does take the socially accepted view that women should function independently and individually, his wife will not believe him; but will be convinced that he is thinking negative, hostile thoughts. So here we have another aspect of the male dilemma—he is labeled a social reactionary if he states his opposition to his wife's independent functioning; he is seen as a hypocrite if he voices acceptance of that functioning.

We also believe that taken together, all of our data suggest a tremendous amount, not only of conflict, but of confusion among members of each sex about their individual and interacting roles. Men emerge from our data as saying, "We are not as family-concerned or socially submissive as women would like us to be: we have less decision-making authority than we should, and often cannot express what we feel about the conflicts of marriage and occupation, or about the activities we desire for the women in our lives." Women appear to have more decision-making authority than they think they should have, and feel conflict over their activities, particularly if they involve occupational status. They feel they and their husbands disagree about the activities women should properly pursue, and are convinced that women are more aggressive, self-assertive, and self-oriented than men want them to be.

We found that men's acceptance of women's activity and independent striving had limits. We saw the evidence of what the women had been telling us: "Men say things that are liberal and accepting of our outside activity but they don't mean them." The data indicated that at least when the question under discussion involved relative status at work, the women were right.

There were female counterparts to this male hypocrisy. That is, there were situations in which women too said things they did not mean, presumably from fear of the consequences of saying what they did mean. Do women resent the amount of time an ambitious husband takes from the family to devote to his job? Clearly they do. Would most women feel free to tell their husbands about it? Our data indicated they would not, but instead would murmur some encouraging and understanding phrases.

The lack of communication, the unwillingness or inability to talk things through, and the loss of sharing is dramatically expressed in the results of the last phase of our research with the Behavioral Survey. In the last section we listed eight different human characteristics and abilities ranging from the classical combination of "good looking," "ability to earn money," and "sexual competence," through "intelligence" and "good education" to the more sedate trio of "ability to be a good father or mother," "ability to help the spouse socially," and "ability to be a good companion." We asked the respondents to indicate which would be the most important characteristics for men and for women at two different points in time; the first when each was considering marriage, and the second after 15 years of marriage.

Since we had four situations—men and women before and after 15 years of marriage—and since we had both male and female respondents, there were eight different sets of data, a complex set of findings to discuss here. But the complexity was elminated by the fact that in all eight instances the same characteristic was named as most important, as the overwhelming first choice selected by at least 40 percent and as many as 60 percent of the respondents with no other characteristics picked by more than 20 percent. This overwhelming first choice? The ability to be a good companion. This attribute was chosen by thousands of male and female respondents as the most important attribute for men and for women to consider in a spouse, both when considering marriage, and after 15 years of marriage.

Perhaps equally striking was the fact that "sexual competence" was never selected by more than 10 percent of the samples, and often by as few as 2 or 3 percent as the most important attribute. Instead, at the time of marriage, physical appearance and ability to earn money were often selected as second in importance, with wage earning and ability to be a good mother or father becoming important after 15 years of marriage.

Thus despite being raised in a sex saturated age, with books, films, and advertisements all reinforcing the notion that sexual attractiveness is the critical dimension of human interaction; our respondents replied, "Now the ability to relate and provide the human interaction summed up in 'companionship' is critical in the beginning of marriage and it continues—even increases in importance as the years pass."

Throughout the 1960's and into the 1970's we have continued to collect data from the therapist co-author's clinical experience and from research data on both the Feminine and Masculine Inventories, in part to keep the research current, and in part stemming from the hypothesis, many of our fellow researchers kept advancing that the sexual revolution and feminine liberation movement had changed the basic attitudinal set of American men and women, particularly their attitudes toward sexual roles and behaviors. Yet, as we write this in mid-1973, with our most recent sets of data only a few weeks old, the essentials of the findings we have reported and discussed hold true. In fact, one of the most critical findings; the discrepancy between each sex's ideal for itself, and what it believes the opposite sex wants it to be, appears from clinical experience and from the newest statistical research data, to be more pronounced than ever. The discrepancy between how men see themselves and how they see woman's ideal man is even greater than it was, for they continue to see themselves as ambivalent, and to see woman's ideal as family oriented. Similarly, the discrepancy between woman's self-perception and her perception of man's ideal is even greater, for there has been some movement for young women toward the activist, self-oriented end of the Inventory scale, and movement, too, in their perception of man's ideal—toward the family-oriented, passive end of the scale. And so, the discrepancy between how women see themselves and how they see the women they believe men want is even greater than it was two decades ago when the research was begun.

The more we study the responses to our Inventories and Surveys, the more we see two frightening consequences of living in this age of confused sex roles. First, both men and women seem to be convinced of each other's need for continual external verification that whatever they are doing is right and sound. Thus, the working mother needed to be reassured that her children will not suffer from her absence at work, and that her husband does not mind if dinner is late or he had to help with the dishes and diapering. The young husband working late and bringing work

home on the weekend needed reassurance that his wife understands and really does not mind his homework, and that his
children, too, are proud of their father's ambition, a pride that
more than compensates for the time they are not able to spend
together. The second consequence is that, to maintain this front
of acceptance and assurance, both men and women are living a
lie. Thus, the wife does not feel free to say, "All I want to do is stay
home, keep house and care for my family." And the husband who
is stunned and dismayed to find his wife has been offered a job
exceeding his own in status and salary does not feel free to say so.
But like so many lies, these apparently are not effective, for why
then would our data indicate that in these critical family situations, men do not believe what women say, and women do not
believe what men say.

And so, what finally comes through the research data and
data from clinical experience, and perhaps the clearest single
finding, is the statement of the importance of and need for companionship. It's almost as if after two decades of living adult
lives, trying to meet a complex set of shifting behavioral standards and expectations, trying to anticipate each other's need and
reactions, and trying to achieve and bring each other to feverish
levels of sensual and sexual response, both our male and female
respondents seized the opportunity to express the feeling that
what they really wanted was someone to talk to, someone to
respect and be respected by, and someone with whom there could
be communication and a relationship characterized by warmth,
tenderness, and affection.

Looking over all of the data we see a picture of confusion,
sensitivity, vulnerability, and hypocrisy in both male and female
behavior. There is no question, of course, that these are perplexing times for both sexes. Our research has shown that the problems are no less difficult for men than for women; that men as
well as women are confused and uncertain in their relationships
to each other and in their attempts to adapt to the changing
conditions around them. We have discovered how men and
women feel about themselves and each other; the time has now
come to consider why.

·NOTES

1. The original was devised by Alexandra Botwin, Ph.D., of San Francisco, California.

2. The Inventory of Feminine Values consists of thirty-four statements, each of which expresses a particular value or value judgment related to women's activities and satisfactions. The respondent indicates the strength of her or his argreement or disagreement to each statement on a five-point scale, ranging from "completely agree" to "completely disagree," through a midpoint of "I have no opinion." The statements are sometimes stated positively, sometimes negatively to avoid a respondent being able to adopt one position by always agreeing or disagreeing.

Seventeen of the thirty-four items are considered to provide a respondent with the opportunity to delineate a family-oriented woman who sees her own satisfactions coming second after those of her husband and family, and who sees her family responsibilities as taking precedence over any potential personal occupational activity. Marriage, child-rearing, and succorant nurturing are the main avenues of this woman's achievement. The other seventeen items delineate a self-achieving woman who considers her own satisfactions equally important with those of her husband and family and wishes opportunities to realize any latent ability or talent that she might have. The score on the Inventory represents the difference in strength of agreement to the two groups of items. A respondent who took identical but opposite positions would have a score of zero; a respondent who consistently took the strongest possible passive position would have a score of -68 and a score of $+68$ if the strongest possible active position were taken. Positive scores between 0 and $+68$ represent intermediate degrees of an active self-achieving orientation, while negative scores between 0 and -68 represent intermediate degrees of a group or family orientation.

The reliability of the Inventory has been estimated through the split-half technique and, when adjusted through the Spearman-Brown procedure, is .81. The items have face validity in that they have generally accepted connotations, but they also have been submitted to validation by seven judges (psychologists and sociologists) who agreed on their categorizations as family- or self-oriented.

Three forms of the Inventory were used in the research with females. Each form used the same thirty-four items in varied order. Female subjects were asked to respond to the items in terms of self-perception (how they themselves felt); how their own ideal woman felt; and in terms of man's ideal woman, i.e., how they thought men would want women to respond.

The Inventory has been administered to 107 different cluster samples in the United States and to 56 different cluster samples in other countries. These cluster samples were selected because of availability and are not presented as random samplings of any groupings within the cultures studied.

Independent investigators using the Inventory in 37 groups involving 4,131 females came up with similar results to ours.

The American cluster samples consisted of college undergraduates, physicians, lawyers, artists, workingwomen, and nurses. Respondents were both black and white, and the noncollege respondents had all received a high school education. The age range was wide—ranging from the late teens to the seventies, although a majority were under forty. A total of 11,431 American women have completed the Self-Perception form of the Inventory of Feminine Values.

The foreign samples involved 17 different countries: England, France, Germany, Austria, Czechoslovakia, Finland, Greece, Turkey, Japan, Philippines, Israel, India, Iran, Argentina, Brazil, Peru, and Mexico. Within these samples a total of 15,886 women completed the Self-Perception form of the Inventory.

Generally the forms were administered to groups of respondents by a member of the research team. However, with some professional groups (physicians, artists, and psychologists), the Inventories were mailed to a list provided by a professional association and returned by mail after being completed by the respondents. When the mail procedure was used for data collection, the response rate was consistently close to thirty percent.

3. The six American samples totaled four hundred twenty-three men involving clusters of college undergraduates, businessmen, physicians, lawyers, and artists. Like the female samples, the male respondents were both black and white and ranged in age from late teens to the seventies, with the majority in their forties.

The six foreign samples came from cooperating researchers in England, Finland, France, Greece, Japan, and Turkey. Totaling seven hundred ten men, they included mostly businessmen and college students.

4. The Inventory of Masculine Values was the same format of thirty-four statements about values and attitudes as the Feminine Inventory and had the same response pattern ranging from "strongly agree" to "strongly disagree" through the "no opinion" midpoint. Thus it was scored the same way.

The content of the Inventory of Masculine Values was generated from that of the Inventory of Feminine Values by changing female references, pronouns, and orientations to male equivalents when there was a sexual referent to the item, and doing sufficient rewriting to keep the item sensible within current social patterns. Thus the item "a capable woman has a duty to be active outside the *home*" was rewritten to read "a capable man has a duty to be active outside the *job*."

The reliability of the Inventory of Masculine Values, through the split-half procedure, is .87.

The data on masculine values discussed here came from 52 cluster samples of American men totaling 5,324 American male respondents to the Masculine Inventory.

While covering the same age range (late teens to seventy) as male respondents to the Inventory of Feminine Values, the American male sample was more totally (eighty percent) under forty. Respondents included students, businessmen, and professionals, most often teachers.

The 2,796 female respondents to the Inventory of Masculine Values came from 47 cluster samples of college undergraduates, graduates, teachers, housewives, and professionals. They covered the same age range as the men, and like the male samples were predominantly (84 percent) under forty. In both male and female samples about half of the respondents were married.

All data for the Inventory of Masculine Values were collected from respondents meeting in groups, with the data collection supervised by a staff member of the research team.

5. The twenty-two decisions in the Decision-Making Survey can be grouped into three areas: economic types like buying an unnecessary dress, or moving to a more costly apartment, or deciding how to spend some money received as a gift. The second area involved recreational, social decisions such as what to do for an evening together, or whom to invite to a party, or what the husband or wife should do with their spare time. The third area concerned family life decisions like deciding upon the sexual pattern of marriage, whether to have a baby, or whether the husband should change occupations.

In the pilot phase of the decision-making study, we used four forms of the Decision-Making Survey: respondents were asked about the same twenty-two decisions in terms of different combinations of the wife working or not and there being children or not. Thus, we tried the survey when the wife was and was not working and when there were and were not children. The initial data indicated that only two variations produced different results: whether or not the wife worked. The presence or absence of children had no significant effect on the response pattern, either in general or in terms of specific decisions and so, in the major survey, we used only two approaches: first respondents answered in terms of a hypothetical couple in which the husband provided good financial support and the wife did not work, and then they responded to the same decision situations, in scrambled order, in terms of a couple in which the wife did work because the husband did not earn enough to enable them to do all that they would want to do.

The Decision-Making Survey was administered in the United States to eight hundred one women and one hundred fifty-six men. This total sample consisted of three major subsections. First, three hundred forty-seven women and seventy men were recruited in the New York area. This was primarily a college sample, two-thirds graduate students and one-third undergraduates. The second section of the sample consisted of three hundred eleven women and seventy-one men who were recruited through the women's participation in a series of continuing education seminars conducted by the University of California. These women were all high school educated, many with some college education, and those who were employed were engaged in a wide variety of highly skilled but not professional occupations. Finally, the third subsection was recruited from the mailing list of McCall's magazine, and represented a young college-educated population. Data from the college sample were collected by a member of the research team meeting with the students. The other two sections of the sample completed the decision-making forms by mail.

The Decision-Making Study was replicated in England by The Observer, a pictorial magazine, which printed the form in one issue, inviting readers to complete the Survey and mail in their completed form. One thousand fourteen men and two thousand nine hundred eighty-four women took advantage of this offer. A majority had been married between six and fifteen years and on the average had two children. Half were college graduates and a fifth had advanced educational preparation. The respondents included students, housewives, business people, and a wide range of professionals.

6. For the behavioral survey, respondents were asked to indicate how both the husband and wife would think and act in twenty different family situations, such as the husband's coming home to find his working wife had been delayed and so dinner was not ready. The Behavioral Survey is a free-response instrument (in contrast to the checklist format of the Decision-Making Survey), and so content analysis was used to categorize the responses to the different situations.

The Behavioral Survey also included a list of personal characteristics which respondents were asked to rank in the order they believed men and women considered important in each other in general, in terms of prospective husbands and wives and after fifteen years of marriage. It used an objective ranking procedure.

The reliability of the Behavioral Survey was evaluated through the test-retest procedure, and more than ninety percent of the respondents gave answers of the same nature after a lapse of several weeks. The validity is obviously no more than face validity in the sense that we must assume that the situations pose realistic choices for the respondents and that their consistent responses represent how they believe people would think and act in these situations.

The Behavioral Survey was always administered with the Decision-Making Survey, and so the samples in the United States and England are the same samples discussed earlier for the latter.

CHAPTER 4

The Ambivalent Man

No physiological or psychological test has yet been devised to measure masculinity with accuracy. There are too many variations in patterns of human behavior, too many variations in the definition of masculinity itself. But let us imagine, for a moment, a football field with all the different kinds of male personalities lined up from one goal line to the other. At the extreme right end of the field is the Marlboro man, rugged, more at home in the wild than in the city, living his workdays in the company of men and his nights and weekends in mixed company where the women are there for the pleasure they can provide. He is a man's man, a leader among men, an individual who works with, but not for, other people. He says what he thinks, bluntly and sharply, and does not worry about what others think or do, since he can take care of himself in any situation. He takes pride in what he does, what he creates, and what he accomplishes. If he marries, he holds his wife responsible for all domestic chores and responsibilities, for while he will cook over an open fire and wash his pan in the river, he would never dream of doing a dish in the house. His wife and children are expected to respect his wishes and needs and keep out of his way while he, in turn, protects and provides for them.

At the extreme left end of the field is Caspar Milquetoast, still masculine in terms of his physiology, and in terms of his marriage to a woman, but in behavior a meek, passive figure, easily browbeaten and the willing servant of any man, and particularly any woman, who exerts the slightest degree of psychological or social pressure on him. Thoroughly domesticated, this man exists totally within a sphere whose limits are set by his wife, who organizes and plans all his activities. He seldom speaks his mind;

he is restrained and inhibited in his relationships with people
—always a follower, never a leader. He, too, is expected to provide for his family, but his wants and needs always come last.

In the center of the field is a man within whom lie competing
drives. He is one who has some of the needs for independent
action of the outdoor man, but who is domesticated in the sense
that he also has needs for a wife and family, for relationships with
women of a more stable and permanent nature than a fleeting
encounter on a Saturday night. This man exhibits some of the
aggressive behavior of the outdoor type, but it has been tempered
by the social and psychological constraints which have over-
whelmed the Caspar Milquetoast. He has strivings for independent action, individual success and recognition, but these, too,
are qualified by his interest in, and concern for, his family and
their achievements and success.

Where does the average American male stand? When we
asked the men in our Inventory of Masculine Values how they felt
about themselves, they clustered a little to the right of center at
about the 40-yard line, on the side of the field toward the outdoor
man; more Marlboro than Milquetoast, but with components of
both. When we asked these same men what their ideal man was
like, they described a man even more on the rugged side than they
themselves were. But when we asked them what kind of man they
thought the women they knew would consider ideal, this third
man was on the other side of midfield, more Milquetoast than
Marlboro.

So we see that most of the men we studied are not the men
they would like to be; they are not as aggressive as they would
want; they are not as active and outgoing as they might wish, and
finally, they are not as free and independent and self-oriented as
their ideal. But they are a lot more active, free, independent, and
aggressive than they think women want them to be. For men are
convinced that women want a mild man, who when single is
restrained in his personal and social relationships, and who when
married will be more concerned with his family than his career,
and whose idea of the best way to spend his free time will be with
his family.

Confusion mounts when you consider what women told us.
Their ideal man? Simple—a strong, aggressive, and self-assertive
man, pretty much like the ideal that men described for us, and

not at all like the Milquetoast that men think women want. And then the final irony. We asked women, "What do you think a man would want to be like?" And they answered almost unanimously "strong and aggressive, much stronger, even more aggressive and more self-assertive than we'd like him to be."

Here, again, we have the male dilemma in a nutshell. The man who decides to hold himself in check and control his drives to self-realization, to limit his outgoing impulses in the hope that he will be more like what women want is, in fact, moving *away* from what women want. The situation is so full of ambiguity and confusing cues that it is no wonder that men as a group have little clear idea of what behavior they think is sensible and appropriate.

As we look over the specific things men said to us in our Inventory, we see that only when we dealt with the most stereotyped statements about masculine behavior, such as, "A man would like to create something recognized as valuable and important" or "A man should be energetic in the expression of his ideas," did the men take an unambiguous attitude toward traditional masculinity. They agreed wholeheartedly that they would like to create and to express ideas energetically. They agreed, too, that "one achieves one's greatest satisfactions through one's own efforts," and that "a capable man has a duty to be active in a field of endeavor outside of his job," and that his "personal development" is more important than the approval of others.

Fine. Here are men who fit anyone's concept of "man." But once we went beyond these stereotyped references and began to ask for opinions on more specific situations, the consensus among the men disappeared and their responses were far from unanimous. Should a man want to become a leader when he joins a group? The answer? About half the men said yes, about half said no. Should a man argue when people try to assert authority over him? Again, men as a group split: half said yes and half said no. This pattern went to surprising lengths. Should a man try to act in accordance with how other people feel and think when he is in a crowd? Half said yes, half no; the men as a group were clearly divided. What would a man prefer to do with a group of people: talk or listen? The same response came back: for every talker, there was a listener.

The intriguing thing is that questions like these dealt with men in general social situations, not necessarily with women only. And in every one of them, the men we questioned were divided in their opinion on how they would behave. And yet we were asking about some basic social values, values historically held at a high premium in American society, values such as leadership, fighting against the imposition of authority, saying what one feels and thinks, and talking rather than listening. Even more striking is the fact that the men in our survey were men with good jobs, with solid educations often including college, and in many samples, men who had "made it" or were well on the way to making it, by the usual standards of job, status, and income. They were physicians, attorneys, businessmen, and artists, men who by external criteria would seem to be those who could, and who would want to, function in the world with a firm sense of purpose and with drive and vigor. And yet they expressed, as a group, no clear-cut concept of their masculine role in relationships with people. No one item or piece of data is significant in and of itself, but it is also intriguing to note that, when we asked these men if American men today are too much concerned with "the impression they make" on others, they said "yes, *they* were too concerned, but their ideal man would not be." Here, then, was a simple instance of men noting their own dissatisfaction with their sensitivity to social pressures.

To clarify further the effect of the social setting on men, we asked a series of questions about marriage and child-raising which were intended to go beyond the general realm of man in society, and to be increasingly specific about the age-old conflict between career and family. At the most general level, we asked the men how important marriage was to them: would they, for example, marry a woman below their ideal, simply to get married. A clear majority answered no. How about "sacrificing some of their ideals" if this were necessary to get married? This time the men were not certain. About half said that marriage was worth some sacrifice: the others were consistent in maintaining that not only would they not compromise on the woman, they also would not give in on what they believed. We asked for more specific opinions and reactions in the following eight statements.

1. The personal ambitions of a man should be subordinated to the family as a group.

2. It is unfair that men are obliged to compromise their personal goals and ideals for the sake of a good marital relationship.

3. A man will have achieved the main goal of his life if he rears normal, well-adjusted children.

4. There is no conflict for a married man between fulfilling himself as a husband and fulfilling himself as an individual.

5. Marriage and children should take precedence over everything else in a man's life.

6. A father's place is in the home when he is not working.

7. A husband who insists on being the sole provider will be more ambitious and responsible.

8. A man would rather be famous, admired, and popular throughout the nation than have the constant affection of just one woman.

What happens when you ask men questions like these? We found that they fed back the same sense of ambivalence that they did when we asked them about their general social behavior. As a group these men were just not sure if "personal ambition" or "family" should come first for the married man, or if raising children ought to be the "main goal" of their life. Nor were they sure whether or not men are obliged to compromise their personal goals for the sake of a good marital relationship, or whether there is a conflict between "fulfilling" themselves as a husband and as a man. They were not even sure where a father should be when he is not working: there was no clear agreement on whether or not he belongs at home.

Even when we asked these men about as traditional a male role as supporting the family, for every man who believed that the ambitious husband wants to be the sole support of his family, there was another who believed that joint support by husband and wife is perfectly acceptable and casts no reflection on a man's ambitions. And most intriguing: their clearest expression of opinion came when we asked them whether a man would prefer fame, admiration, and national popularity to the love and affection of one woman. Two out of every three men preferred the love and affection of one woman.

So, finally, the men in our survey told us that yes, they want to create and be recognized, and yes, they want to be energetic in expressing their ideas; but they are not sure they would want to be leaders, or fight authority, or pursue their ambitions if it interfered with their family; and they would chuck it all for the love of one woman.

In recent years, many people have pondered the dilemma faced by modern women, the conflict between marriage and career. Whether couched in the careful language of the professional psychologist or in the freewheeling prose of the new breed of feminist, it all boils down to the same thing: how can women fulfill themselves both as women in marriage and motherhood, and as human beings in creative work in society.

Some have also pondered the problem of self-fulfillment vs. family orientation for men, but somehow it has always been assumed that there was little conflict between the two spheres of male activity. No choice was necessary: naturally a man could do both. If he were engaged in truly demanding work, however, his wife and family simply had to grin and bear it. But now, with the increasing depersonalization of work itself, the emergence of women as breadwinners as well as wives and mothers, and new pressures on the man to perform as husband and father, the priorities seem to be changing. A conflict does exist in many men's minds. Familiar in both life and literature is the woman who "gives it all up for the love of a good man." Now, it appears, she may have a male counterpart.

The last area we studied involved fatherhood. Interestingly enough, the uncertainty which characterized the items about marriage in general and about husband-wife relationships did *not* characterize the items about fathers and children. We received a strong yes to questions asking whether fatherhood "was worth the sacrifices," and whether a good father should spend his time at home. And one of the strongest yes responses in the study came in reply to our question asking whether a father could develop "just as strong and secure a relationship with his children as does a mother." The near unanimity of the yes on this question paralleled the agreement on the general personality characteristics of men; i.e., being energetic in the expression of their ideas, creating and achieving. This clarity of goal and purpose characterized the items related to fatherhood to a greater extent than any of the other areas within the questions we asked about marriage. It seems to be the one clear aspect of their familial role to all men; they understand it, want it, and accept it, and do not see it in conflict with the traditional male role.

In view of the conflict between job and home which the other conponents of the Inventory implied, the clarity of the commitment to fatherhood is interesting. The men in our survey saw no inconsistency here, possibly because they viewed "fatherhood" in the same generalized, abstract way in which they viewed personality characteristics and behavior. But we believe that the conflict between job and home occurs in the interactions between husband and wife and not in the interactions between fathers and children. Even if a specific husband is bugged by the necessity to stay home minding the children while his wife is away at work or at any personal activity, we think the data suggest that to the husband this is a conflict with his wife and not with his children; it is a problem involving his role as husband, not his role as father. Thus the men we questioned were able to see their roles as fathers without the confusion and ambiguity revealed in their responses about their roles as husbands.

It is useful, in summary, to reconsider as a whole the five categories of the Inventory: general personality characteristics, general social behavior, marriage, relationships between husband and wife, and father-children relationships. The men we questioned expressed clear ideas in response to two groups of questions, those involving their general personality characteristics, and those involving the relationships of fathers to their children. But they had no clear or consistent view of themselves or their behavior in the other three areas. Correlating their responses to these questions with the separate Decision-Making Survey and the Behavioral Survey, we can now draw a profile of the men we studied. The profile begins with clear, strong lines; these men believe that men should be creative, achieve satisfaction through their own efforts, and express ideas energetically. Then, suddenly, the sharp lines of the profile of a strong, outgoing man begin to blur. They hesitate to become leaders or to argue against authority, and would as soon listen as talk in a group. They are too concerned about the impression they make on others, much more concerned than they would like to be.

As they consider marriage and relationships with their wives and children, the area of greatest clarity is their feeling of the importance of developing a good relationship with their children and the belief that this is an implicit part of being a father, and worth whatever sacrifices it entails. But then again the profile takes on another configuration, almost Picasso-like, for the men are not certain how they and their wives should divide authority, but they do know that women have too much power at present, specifically in family decision-making. They see their own primary role as encouraging their wives in the development of their own abilities and potential, but are not certain how far they would go in making concessions to them to achieve this. Nor are they certain whose responsibility it is to "make a marriage work," or if they want to be the sole provider for the family.

Essentially, then, it is impossible to draw a clear profile, because there was very little agreement among these men about what being a man means. They were not sure what a man does at work, or how he behaves toward those with whom he works, nor were they sure what a man does in social situations, and least of all were they sure how a man behaves with women. The men we studied were leading lives built insecurely on a foundation of social and psychological uncertainty.

To understand this uncertainty and its significance, one must go back in time to the formative years of the men we are discussing. The men now in the age range of thirty-five to fifty were born roughly between 1920 and 1940, the years between World Wars I and II, and a period which, with coincidental symbolism, begins with the year in which the Nineteenth Amendment to the Constitution granted women the right to vote.

What was it like to be born and grow up as a male in this period? What were the privileges and prerogatives granted or acquired because you were you, a man-child, whether or not in the promised land? In the broadest social and psychological context possible, being male meant being the preferred child, the child through whom the family name would be preserved, the child who would receive the advantages of education if there was not enough money to go around. Every parent hoped to produce a "son and heir." Eddie Cantor got a sympathetic laugh with every reference to his five daughters, for everyone empathized with the plight of this poor "unsuccessful" father, who five times had failed to produce a son. This same sexual preference was seen vividly in Jewish families where it was the male child whose birth and attainment of manhood were celebrated, in contrast to the lack of ceremony surrounding either a girl's arrival or maturity.

Growing up and being a male meant relative freedom both physically and psychologically within a code of child-rearing which held that boys were supposed to be little men, independent, aggressive, and sometimes even rough and rambunctious. Girls were to be little women, passive, obedient, restricted, and restrained as they were being trained to be the next generation of Victorian-Puritan ladies. Toys and recreation for the little men had an orientation to the active, aggressive dimension, to the physical as opposed to the intellectual, an orientation to doing and mastering. Where boys played with soldiers and guns, girls played with dolls. Boys were given trains and erector sets; girls were given tea sets. Boys were decked out in the accouterments and costumes of vigorous roles outside the family; they were cowboys and Indians, doctors and train engineers, where girls role-played within the family, as little wives and mothers with the most vigorous out-of-the-family feminine role that of a nurse. But consistent with everything else, this role was seen as a serving role, the doctor's helper. Where physical skills were involved, only little boys were given tool sets, and only little boys were taught to run and climb, to tumble and to play ball. The worst insult one little boy could utter about another's ballplaying was "you throw like a girl." The girl who ran well, or who liked to climb, or who threw well was not a girl at all, but a "tomboy," a deviant, whose parents often worried whether or not she would ever grow out of it. But even more worrisome was the "sissy," the little boy who seemed to display "girlish" characteristics and play preferences.

In behavior, too, there were clear differences between the sexes. Boys were expected to be brave; they did not cry, and they defended themselves and fought back when attacked. They were in training to be men, and men were virile and vigorous, physical and active, self-assertive and self-reliant. Men were expected to

cope quietly with the world, to struggle with their personal and
business demons internally and privately, not share them with
their wives and certainly not with their families. Moreover, the
differences in standards of behavior were reinforced by almost
everything the children saw as they looked about them. Essentially men were the ones who left the house to go to work, while
women remained at home cooking, cleaning, and caring for the
children. It was men who went out for solo recreation and
amusement, for the night out with the boys had no female
equivalent. It was men who drove the cars; it was men who
smoked, men who drank.

The father worked and was supposed to earn enough to support the family, and with that responsibility fulfilled, he had few
others. He was not expected to take on any of the indoor domestic
responsibilities other than to serve as the ogre necessary on
occasion to coerce a child into obedience. A dish never entered his
hand except to pass it to someone else. And there was another
dimension to the question of father working and mother caring
for the house. It was not a distinction between equally dignified
kinds of labor but rather jobs of two clearly distinct levels of
responsibility, one work and one not, one meriting rest and relaxation at the end of the day and one not. It was tacitly assumed
that "woman's work was never done," but when the man got
home, his day was over and he was rewarded handsomely for it
by having his dinner cooked and served the way he liked it. After
dinner the kids were kept away by the mother's caution to "be
quiet. Daddy's resting." And on weekends the same thing happened except now the warning was "don't bother Daddy on his
day off." The clear suggestion was that father's well-being was
critical to the continued functioning of the family and his good
humor essential to maintaining a livable family climate. He sat
and read the newspaper, listened to the radio, had his weekly
night out, while mother washed the dishes and darned socks long
into the night. And by a logical extension of the same division of
labor, it was the girl who helped her mother set the table and
clean up the kitchen, while the boy had only to take out the
garbage before he was free to listen to the radio with his father.

As he grew old enough to leave the family and move into the
broadened social world of other children, the boy played with
other boys and not girls. There was no nursery school to place

him in a heterosexual social situation at the age of three or four, and even kindergarten was relatively rare in the public school systems of the 1920's and 1930's. So his earliest social contacts were almost exclusively male, and he began to learn the notion of a male sub-society, a society as privileged outside the home as it was inside. He was permitted to roam further afield, stay up later, get dirtier, and come home with fewer explanations.

The development of this sub-society continued in school, where most systems had separate secondary schools for girls and boys, many systems having begun this practice in elementary school. And while separate, the curricula were seldom equal, for when a school system had limited staff, its academic strength went into classes for boys who were going on to college. Similarly its recreational budget went into sports programs for boys, for it was boys whose physical development was important to their eventual role as men.

Throughout his school career it was clear to the boy that he was expected to go on and become something to justify all the interest and attention invested in his education and physical development. Compared to the limited destination of marriage and motherhood toward which the girl was headed, the future open to a boy was vast and varied. We were still nursing the myth that any boy could grow up to be President, but if he set his sights lower, he still had a career in his future, with marriage and fatherhood social incidentals. He was here on earth to do, to perform, to have responsibility, even to create.

If he generalized either consciously or subliminally in considering his future, the boy would note that it was clearly a "man's world." All the physically-oriented occupations, every business and professional job, were filled by men. Women worked in sedentary, less responsible and less rewarding fields such as office work or teaching. It was (and in this respect still is) a world in which men went into business with their sons and even with their brothers, but neither father nor mother went into business with their daughters, nor did mother or daughters go into business with their sisters. Moreover, the power positions in society were clearly and universally male. Whatever the town, the principal of the school was a man, as were the police, the mayor, and the judges, and the town was in a state where the governor, the senators, and the congressmen were male. At the federal level in the 1920's, only men had ever been members of the President's cabinet or been appointed to the highest levels of the federal judiciary and the diplomatic service. Whatever the boy's aspirations, whether he wanted to be a policeman or President, his only handicaps were, it seemed, the limitations of his own ability and ambition. And even if he did not make it in the outside world and ended up in some unfulfilling low-paying job, he could still be reasonably certain that he would rule the roost in his own home.

It was a man's world, too, as far as women were concerned. As his later social development began and the boy became interested in the company of girls, the social hierarchy was clear: the initial impetus to heterosexual relationships was male. A girl sat home by the telephone until a boy asked her out. Of course, she had to learn the techniques of her sex designed to elicit that call. Thus, she continued to play the Eve role, the temptress who through her various wiles got the male to do what she wanted.

But it was the male who *did* it: the boy was supposed to make the date, the first amorous advance and, finally, the offer of marriage. Furthermore, in line with his privileged position elsewhere, he was accorded considerably more sexual freedom. Experimenting with the opposite sex, within certain limits, was assumed to be part of growing up. He was expected to sow a few wild oats. A "nice" girl had no such freedom; she was expected to come to her marriage bed intact, for no matter how experienced a boy was, he had every right to demand a virgin bride.

Eventually, of course, he would settle down, and here, too, his expectations were similar to what he saw all around him. He would remain reasonably faithful to his wife, and she would remain absolutely faithful to him. And he would raise a family. In that family he would work to bring in the money needed to support it but, like his own father, that was all he would do. His wife would maintain the house, raise the children, and satisfy his sexual needs. While they had a social life together as husband and wife, he would have a second and separate social life as a man with other men at work, in the local social club, at the volunteer fire department, and at the ball game. If he had a family responsibility, it would be only to teach his sons to become men like him—active, physical, and self-reliant—and protect the innocence of his daughters.

So everywhere our man-child looked he could take comfort in

the favored position of his sex, except that it was so favored and so unchallenged that he simply took it for granted. In the home and out, in business, or sports, or school, or at play, he assumed that men could and did and women couldn't and didn't.

The men we have studied were babies or children in the 1920's and 1930's. If they had been old enough for sophisticated social analysis or gifted with powers of clairvoyance, they would have seen that the seeds of far-reaching social and psychological change had already been sown, change that would destroy or alter almost beyond recognition the world in which they expected to occupy such a favored position.

World War I was both an end and a beginning, a universal cataclysm that reduced the world of the nineteenth century to rubble and provided the impetus to rebuild. In that process of reconstruction, the 1920's are best labeled a transitional decade, and like most transitional periods, it was a time of inconsistencies, as new patterns of behavior emerged to challenge and conflict with the old patterns still strong enough to fight back. One inconsistency was the Presidency of Warren Harding, a man from a small town in the Middle West, with all the basic American virtues, whose administration, touted as a return to normalcy, ended in personal and political scandal. He was followed in office by Calvin Coolidge, a symbol of the older morality of New England, a man who even looked like a proper Victorian.

But the social dynamics of the 1920's were far from Victorian. Urbanization, stimulated by rapid growth in industry, transportation, and communication, accelerated. The days of the small, self-sufficient, rural town—and the self-sufficient family—were numbered. As the population increased and shifted, individual influence and local authority began to give way to the power of centralized government. The automobile changed the face of America, and the radio and movies its outlook. Prosperity induced complacency and reaction in some, dissatisfaction and rebellion in others, chiefly the less-privileged working classes and the young.

It is not stretching a point to compare the 1920's with our own recent transitional decade, the 1960's, particularly in the realm of human behavior. In both decades, the traditional standards of the older generation clashed with the restless demands and experiments of the young. The flapper and Joe College were no less puzzling and threatening to their parents than the hippies to theirs; alcohol, under Prohibition, no less inviting than marijuana; petting and free love no less tempting than the sex commune.

But however vast the external changes in the 1920's in society or in matters of personal behavior, the development that would most significantly alter the "man's world" of the future was the shift in the internal structure of the family, for this was the decade that saw the end of the extended family of several generations living together or near each other, and the beginning of the "nuclear family." And this new family unit was characterized by a preoccupation with child-raising unparalleled in history. The Government Printing Office found it had a best seller on its hands when it printed a booklet called *Infant Care* by the Children's Bureau. Ten editions appeared between the year 1914, when it was first published, and 1955; all told, approximately 36 million copies were distributed.

This preoccupation with children continued well beyond that date; it grew in momentum and intensity until America itself was often described as a "child-oriented culture." Advice swung erratically back and forth between strict discipline and utter permissiveness, but the consistent fact remained that, in the family, "the children came first."

The adults we have studied were infants in the early stages of this preoccupation with child-raising; they were the first children "raised by the book." Previously, child-raising had been geared to the needs of the adults. The infant or child was accommodated in adult society, cared for, and taught in some simple, instinctual system of rewards and punishment, only until he, too, became an adult—and the sooner the better.

Now the emphasis shifted to the demands of the child and the prolongation of childhood, at whatever inconvenience and sacrifice to the adult. Child-raising was no longer an instinct; it was a skill. Each child, male or female, was raised according to standards and practices that were intellectual in origin, stemming not from the needs of the "tribe" for survival, order, and continuation, but rather from a concern for the needs of the individual. However, under this new system, the male child continued in his position of favor, but the female, who after all had her own individual needs, began to assume a greater importance in the eyes of her parents, and in society. Women had won the right to vote; they had flexed their political muscle in the passage of the Prohibition Amendment; they were demanding greater social and sexual freedom; and they began to pay more attention to the upbringing and education of their daughters.

The Depression put a lid on the youthful rebellions and the superficial changes of the 1920's, but it brought into play new and powerful forces that in large measure undermined the economic, political, and social foundations that supported the life expectations of the young American male. And it further altered the social and psychological structure of the family. The Depression dispelled the notion of the male as the sole economic support of the family, destroyed the image of the independent, self-sufficient father who went off to work every day and replaced it with the fact of men unable to find work, unable to earn money, men with no place to go and nothing to do. Large numbers of women began to seek work, as the necessity to earn money forced many families to look for any available means of support. And as women moved into the work force, they were not as able, or willing, as they had previously been to take full domestic responsibility for the family. Men, women, boys, and girls—all were in the same boat together. Educational exclusivity collapsed, as coeducation became the pattern at the elementary and secondary levels and higher educational opportunities opened up for women. Politics, too, changed as recognition of the political potential of enfranchised women led to the destruction of the male monopoly on high elective and appointive offices and the 1930's saw women as mayors and governors, entering the Cabinet, the House, and the Senate.

Intellectually, he knew why these changes had occurred, and at that intellectual level most agreed that it was a sensible readjustment of sex roles, far more consonant with economic necessity and the ideals of human equality. Moreover, it was simple fairness for both husband and wife to share equally m the responsibilities as well as the rewards of marriage. Both the men and the women we have talked to and studied knew this, and have said this to us over and over again. But we have become convinced in talking to these thousands of men and women that, while in their minds they know this is only fair and just, in their hearts—at the emotional level—they still feel a deep conflict between the clearly defined sex roles they saw as children and expected to play as adults, and the very different roles they must play today.

The husband who changes diapers and washes dishes is troubled by vague dissatisfactions which he may or may not be able to relate to the difficulty of reconciling these chores with his earliest images of men and what they did and did *not* do. His father never washed dishes, his father never shopped, and his father never bathed and put the baby to bed. And at the end of a long day when his wife asks for help, it is hard for this man to say to himself, "Remember, your wife was at work all day and your mother didn't work." But even if he does say it, we doubt that it does much to alleviate the feeling that he is being put upon in ways that men never used to experience.

For most educated and sophisticated men there is little argument that the changes in the status of women are sensible and just. They would shudder at the notion of women as property, and zealously defend their wife's right to vote. But somehow these insights do not help resolve the frustration and anger about corresponding changes in the *husband's* status, and the feeling of demasculinization when some of his traditional privileges and prerogatives are stepped on. Being a liberal on civil rights for ethnic minorities is easy, particularly to the man who is all talk and no action, but being a liberal on woman's rights is quite another thing. That kind of liberalism begins at home.

And so the American male has spent the decades of the 1950's and 1960's searching for a viable means to live his life in the way that his intellectual insights tell him it should be lived and simultaneously trying to control his inner churnings and yearnings for the adult life his early childhood and family experiences led him to expect. It has not been an easy search, or a very successful one. Looking back over these last twenty years we see how men have tried everything to retain a remnant of the masculine image. For some, the conflict within themselves, or with the standards and expectations of their parents and society have been so severe that they have rejected heterosexual relationships altogether in favor of homosexuality. Others have resorted to the patterns of Don Juanism and supermasculinity, which may or may not mask homosexuality, but certainly stem from profound role confusion. These, granted, are extreme patterns of behavior with many other complex causes. However, within the bounds of the approved heterosexual relationship, there have been equally various attempts to cope with the same conflict.

At the extreme right end of the heterosexual spectrum is the conservative—even reactionary—man who has coped with the changing world by refusing to change himself and actively resisting the changes all around him. In matter of dress and personal conduct, he conforms strictly to the masculine norm of his economic or social class. He allows himself little freedom in the kind of clothes he wears, or the kind of emotion he displays, for fear of being thought in some way less a man, and he is scornful or suspicious of those who do. He cannot sustain any kind of a nonsexual friendship with a woman. They may work for him in a subordinate position, but he would never consider working for or even with them.

He considers all women, even his wife, as rather weak and witless creatures; delightful, of course, but he treats them with the exaggerated and condescending gallantry or the denigrating jocularity that presupposes his masculine superiority. Their role is to serve him and give him pleasure. Sex for him is one of those services, for the notion of a "relationship" of shared satisfaction with his wife or any other women is foreign to him.

He prides himself on his freedom, individuality, and self-reliance, his "masculinity." His ideals and goals are in the traditional American mold of independence, individual initiative, and hard work to achieve the good things in life, not only for himself, but for his family, which, he assumes, will share those goals and be willing to help him achieve them. His political and social views are usually conservative, too; he has a deep-rooted fear of change, unless it is of direct benefit to himself, and often a self-conscious distrust of intellectuals and liberals, of emancipated women, of the rebellious young, of individuals and groups who are in any way different from himself. His friends are men like himself; they play poker together, hunt, fish, drink, and go to the ball game together, while their wives are left to shift for themselves. As a boss he is apt to be high-handed and demanding; as an employee, anxious to preserve what he considers to be his rights. As a husband and father he is equally demanding and inflexible, and usually has a rather rigid view of what is appropriate masculine and feminine behavior among his children. He makes all the major decisions unilaterally; he does not share his business or professional problems with his wife, and he expects her to keep her problems to herself, too.

And so many of the elements which composed the secure, preferred world of the male child born in the 1920's were at best ambiguous and changing as he grew up through the 1930's. If he somehow managed to remain untouched by these changes, he could not ignore the war which capped the decade, the last big game of his youth, a ritualistic orgy of masculine aggression and physical activity. But even here the steady erosion of the male's exclusive privileges continued; for this was a war he shared with women. They went to work in the defense plants; they entered the Army and Navy and, blow of blows, even the Marines. While they were kept from combat, they shared the uniform, the rank, and many of the duties. About the only military privilege reserved for the men was the privilege of combat and death.

The men who survived the war returned home and, like their fathers back from France, tried to resume the life patterns they had left behind. They tried to re-create the world they had known as children, to achieve the adult experience they had expected to be theirs when they were little boys. And briefly it seemed as if they might find it. In this second "return to normalcy" which characterized the postwar years, the veteran was the center of attention. His education, his job, his home, his future were the focus of concern, just as he expected them to be. He was greeted joyously by women whose lives had been severely limited and distorted during the war, women who were only too willing, at first, to give up their educations and their jobs to make a home and create a future for their men. But the future had few similarities to the past.

The postwar years were the beginning of a prosperous maturity whose numerous possibilities were limited by as many new responsibilities. Again, war had altered both the physical as well as the psychological dimensions of the world. Few veterans returned to small towns or even small urban neighborhoods. They came back to cities. They might try to re-create that small town in the suburbs, but it was not quite the same.

Nor were the women they courted and married quite the same. They were not their mothers, the docile innocents of the past who saw the feminine role as serving the men in their life.

They were, in many cases, women who had had a taste of education and independence; women who sought an identity for themselves and who expected to be treated as individuals with desires and drives of their own; women who demanded that the heterosexual relationship be a shared experience. Some of them were women who had worked and would try to continue to work, to help make ends meet, and to meet their own needs for self-fulfillment. These were women to whom a man had to relate as thinking, feeling beings with human intelligence equal to his own. But all during his early formative years, he had neither been prepared to see women this way nor had he learned the skills needed for this kind of relationship. He reached his adult years to find that the social and sexual relationships for which he was prepared no longer existed.

The job, career, or profession was not quite what it was supposed to be either. The physical world for which his early play and sports had prepared him was gone; the jobs open to him were sedentary, repetitive ones, sufficiently demasculinized for him to see women about him performing the same tasks and even higher-level ones. The massive organizational efforts which the war had stimulated combined with mechanization and automation to further depersonalize many jobs, so that the satisfaction and personal realization he expected to find in work were not there.

And his family life was again one for which his formative years had not prepared him. The notion he brought to marriage that the husband was the hub about which the family revolved did not jibe with a working wife who expected to do her share of the domestic drudgery but also expected her husband to do his. His "favored child" position in the family could not survive the increasingly child-oriented culture of the postwar years. He was no longer a child, nor could he be the same kind of father his own father had been.

He discovered that, whereas when he was a child, it was his father who was given the first cut of the roast beef, now that he was a father, it was the children who were given the first cut. His generation, it seemed, was always at the wrong end of the age continuum. Nor could he raise his children the way he was raised, since his daughters should receive equal treatment and consideration, should be taught the same aspirations and given access to the same opportunities and expectations as his sons. Moreover he found that he had a responsibility for child-rearing that his father never had, that he was expected to provide a level of companionship he never perceived between his parents and simultaneously accept and encourage a level of out-of-the-house activity for his wife that his mother never considered. And he found that the only way he could fit all these new responsibilities into his life was to cut other things out, including the masculine joys of nights out with the boys, the weekends or vacations away from the family.

It is easy to caricature a man of this sort. See Archie Bunker. He is a figure of contemporary tragedy if he eventually brings about his own downfall, a familiar comic figure if he is humbled by a wily employee, a clever woman, particularly his wife, or the antics of his children. As the staunch racist, the stuffed shirt, the tyrannical husband and father, the man who marries the dumb secretary half his age to prove his masculinity, he is an easy target. But it is too glib to claim his excessive attitudes and behavior are due to sheer ignorance or some secret sexual insecurity. Not too many years ago, they would not have been excessive at all. There is something of the conservative, even the reactionary, in every man who longs for "the good old days." If he is married to a woman whose concept of femininity is as old-fashioned as his concept of masculinity, if he is challenged neither by the social circumstances of his own or his children's generation, he may live and die with his masculine ego intact. But that is not often the case in today's complex and rapidly changing world.

Equally familiar at the other end of the heterosexual spectrum is the man who has given in totally, the timid employee, the henpecked husband, the ineffectual and all-but-invisible father. There is nothing really tragic about him, since it is assumed he was never much of a man to begin with. Nor is he often the subject of comedy, unless through some sudden reversal he reasserts himself. His kind of docile demasculinization is not funny, either to men or women. He is usually the target of satire, which implies a standard of masculine behavior he can never hope to achieve. The reasons given for his plight, too, are familiar—a domineering mother, an overbearing and castrating wife, a world that is just too much for him to handle. But here again, there is something of him in every man. What man has not at some time said to himself, "What the hell. Why fight it?"

Most men, of course, do fight to protect a sense of their own manhood, whether on the job, in society, or at home. Their opponents, real or imagined, are as various as the circumstances that lead to the conflict. But the chief target, in many men's eyes, is women. There is little lasting satisfaction, most have found, in wrestling the women in their lives to the mat, or in being pinned themselves. And so they have learned to compromise, not always willingly or with good grace. They "draw the line," see it crossed, and then draw another one a little further back. Or they bluff and bluster in public to maintain their own self-respect and the respect of their friends, only to give in grudgingly in private.

But little by little, most men have found themselves living in a world that is dramatically different from anything they expected, much less saw, when they were children. Not only do they work with women, they now permit their own wives to work. They no longer lift their feet when their wives come by with the vacuum cleaner; they may very well be running the vacuum themselves. They have moved over in the outside world to give women a little more opportunity and responsibility, a favor repaid by women giving them more—and not always welcome—room in the home. To men like this it seems that they, and they alone, have made all the compromises, all the accommodations, all the sacrifices. In principle they may be all for "feminine fulfillment," but in practice it seems to mean masculine deprivation.

These are the men who, in responding to the statements in our Inventory of Masculine Values, fell roughly in the middle of the Marlboro-Milquetoast scale. By this measure, too, there seemed to be a divergence between principle and practice, for most of these men were in agreement on the general personality characteristics of masculinity, but there was no unanimity of opinion on just how these characteristics can and should be expressed in social behavior and male-female relationships. They were, in essence, stating a belief in standards they felt were no longer possible to uphold. The question that must be asked now, the question that many men ask themselves, is: "Are these standards wrong, or is there something wrong with me?"

All too many men avoid the question completely by harboring

a sneaking suspicion that there is something wrong with the world, and they set about, in words if not in deeds, to chastise it or try to make it into something more to their liking. At their worst and most dangerous, they react with fury to attacks on the values and standards of their youth. They may insist upon superpatriotism, for example, equating that with masculinity, and fight to defend their homes, their neighborhoods, and their schools from their black fellow Americans as ferociously as they fought the Germans and the Japanese. They may make a manly virtue of the ability to fight, and war the supreme test of that ability. Perhaps remembering the excitement and masculine camaraderie of their own wartime experiences, they may willingly sacrifice their sons to the war in Vietnam. But by some curious inversion of logic, while condoning mayhem abroad, they often demand law and order at home.

Work, whatever the level of their own employment, may also be a masculine virtue in their view. They curse the bums and loafers who do not work or who live on government handouts, at the same time denying them the education and the opportunity to find jobs much above the menial level. Their view of the opposite sex may also be highly unrealistic; they still insist upon the old double standard, and the distinction between "good" and "bad" women. Some of them may be the secret readers of hard core pornography, in the audience at the men's smoker, at the same time they decry the new moral laxity in today's books and films. And they are often infuriated by the long hair, the unisex clothes, and the sexual freedom of their children, whose dress and behavior seem totally opposed to their own values.

In describing men of this sort, the point that should be made is that the values and standards they defend so heatedly are not necessarily erroneous ones. There *is* virtue in patriotism, work, and sexual morality. The mistake they make, a mistake often shared equally by those who challenge them, is to consider these values in the abstract, as symbols or universal truths, totally divorced from the changing social and psychological conditions that both shape and are shaped by them.

Most men try to ease into a compromise. They try to close the gap between principle and practice, between what a man may believe and the ways in which he is permitted to express that belief. Denied that expression, and feeling as a result a loss of respect for himself and his own sex, a man, through anger and frustration, may very well resort to extreme demonstrations of his masculinity. However, many men resolve this conflict in rather harmless, and sometimes constructive ways. They also avoid the big question, "Are the traditional sexual standards wrong, or is there something wrong with me?" Over the past twenty years they have created a whole new world of masculine outlets in fantasy if not in actual fact. After initial resistance, they have permitted themselves a few more freedoms in their dress and have rationalized lengthening sideburns and an occasional moustache as a suitable expression of their masculinity. Again, after some initial shock and consternation, they took great pleasure in the miniskirt and other outward manifestations of female sexuality. The automobile continued to be an important symbol in their lives. They drove cars so big that their wives could scarcely see over the dashboard, let alone park or get them in the garage. Or if for economy or shortage of gas they drove a smaller car, they adopted the external equipment and internal attitudes of a Grand Prix racer.

Their life-style, too, reflected the need for masculine outlets. They lived in "ranch-style" houses and undertook ambitious "do-it-yourself" home-improvement projects. The do-it-yourself movement, which began in the 1950's, is usually explained as the necessary response to the disappearance or increasing expense of the local craftsman. But it can also be seen as a reflection among masses of men of the need for some creative act, often denied them in their jobs, a need for physical labor, to work with their hands, to build, construct, repair. It is one of the few traditional ways left of expressing their masculinity.

In books and movies, these same men became preoccupied with the "loner," the man, usually of middle age, who suddenly found himself at odds with his wife and his world and fought to regain his sense of self-importance and individuality. He participated vicariously in the independence and the rough-and-ready masculinity of the cowboy hero on television, an idol left over from his childhood and surely one of the most durable of the masculine symbols. And he manufactured a new kind of idol, the sports hero, like Joe Namath, the swinging bachelor who went fully armed into battle every Sunday afternoon, and who went out every night, it was assumed, with a different woman. They even created a new world of sexuality, the *Playboy* world that featured the bosoms and buttocks of "nice" girls pictured not in a sleazy hotel room, but in their own fluffy apartments or in a book-lined bachelor pad. While *Playboy* certainly expressed denigration of the female mind and body, it seemed a rather harmless denigration. These were girls that you could take home to mother, could marry; and they might make wives who would stay in the kitchen and the bedroom where they belonged. And this dream world was given the appearance of solidity and respectability by the accompanying articles of enlightened social comment and "quality" fiction.

In the world of sports, another traditional male outlet, professional football surpassed baseball and emerged as a major spectator pastime, both in a stadium and at home in front of the television set. The reasons were not hard to figure out. The sport had an obvious masculine appeal in the violence of physical contact, the appearance of warlike combat, the strategies and masculine camaraderie of the team. Women do not play the game; they may even cringe, or pretend to cringe, at its brutality.

Whatever the accommodations or compromises the middle-of-the-road man has been able to make, however, the conflict between the expectations of his childhood and the realities of his present situation remain, and the gap between traditional sex role definitions and contemporary demands shows little sign of diminishing. Hence his ambivalence and confusion, documented by our Inventory of Masculine Values and continually reflected by his attitude toward himself and the position he finds, often with some surprise, he occupies in today's world. Nowhere is his confusion and ambivalence more tellingly expressed than in his relationship with his wife and his role as husband and father. For sex role confusion is not the exclusive preserve of the man. Women, too, have demonstrated their ambivalence and confusion. They, too, face a conflict between their expectations and the realities of the contemporary world, between the traditional and the modern definitions of femininity. They, too, have often reacted in extreme ways in the defense of some principle, have been forced to choose between alternatives with equally unpleasant overtones and consequences, have made sometimes constructive and sometimes destructive compromises and accommodations. When men and women like these marry, live together, and share the responsibilities of child-raising, their ambivalence takes on a new dimension. It is no longer merely a male dilemma. It is a dilemma shared by women as well.

CHAPTER 5

Women in Conflict

Just as there are no physiological or psychological tests to measure masculinity in men, there is no way to determine how "feminine" a woman may be. Appearances are particularly deceptive in her case, for the most hard-bitten man-hater may adopt the provocative dress of a movie starlet, while the most passive, obedient, home-loving wife and mother may trail around in a pair of pants and a shapeless sweater. Even a woman's behavior may not be a reliable guide, so practiced has she become in the art of acting to please—or deceive—a man. And influencing that behavior is the fear that she will be thought "unfeminine," a sense of guilt whenever she displays aggression, ambition, or any other so-called masculine trait.

But for convenience's sake, just as we imagined the different kinds of male personalities lined up on a football field, let us imagine a group of women lined up on a stage in a "femininity" contest. At the extreme left of the line is the career woman, an attaché case in one hand and a copy of *The Wall Street Journal* folded under her arm. She is hell-bent on self-achievement, on dominating situations and people. She expresses her ideas and opinions strongly, cares very little what other people think of her, gives orders rather than takes them. She considers herself any man's equal; superior, in fact, to most. Married or unmarried, she comes first. She spends her workdays in the company of men; she even prefers their company on evenings and weekends, for she has little patience with women who are not as self-achieving as she is. Women may not like her, or enjoy her company, but they may identify with her. She is a symbol of female emancipation. Anything a man can do, at least careerwise, she has succeeded in doing. As for men, they may respect her on the surface, but underneath they fear and resent her. Even the Marlboro man, her masculine counterpart, knows he has to watch his step if he gets in her way. And both men and women enjoy pointing out the chinks in her armor if she has them: a henpecked husband or two, or no husband at all, neurotic or neglected children or no children at all, a haphazard homelife or no homelife at all. By most contemporary standards, if she is not overtly masculine, she is certainly unfeminine, even though she may wear a dress to the office and go to the beauty parlor three times a week.

At the extreme right end of our lineup is the submissive, passive, husband-doting, child-adoring, home-loving female. She has a laundry bag in one hand and a copy of *Woman's Day* under her arm. Her dream from earliest childhood was to find the right man, marry him, have his children and keep his house for the rest of her life. She does not use whatever education she may have had in work outside the home; she cannot take time off from her domestic chores even to collect money for the Community Fund. Whatever notions of self-achievement she may have are satisfied in the constant affection of her husband and her pride and joy in motherhood. She does what her husband tells her to do: she relies on him completely in matters outside the home and even in domestic situations. Her friends are women like herself; her range of interests not much wider than the problems of child-raising, housekeeping, and interior decoration. She feels a woman's place is in the home, not in politics, business, or the professions. That is man's work, and in her view, the man is a creature apart, the inhabitant of another world. She is "just a woman" who may glory in the unique characteristics of her sex, but who thinks all ideas of independence and equality are absurd. Her husband and children come first in her life and she expects to find fulfillment through them. Again, by most contemporary standards, this woman would be judged extremely feminine, even if a bit on the dull and dim-witted side.

Perhaps neither of these female extremes actually exists in great numbers but between them is a wide range of women who do. At the center of our imaginary lineup is the woman who has characteristics of both the career woman and the housewife. Like the housewife, she believes in the importance of marriage, husband, children, and home. But she also has some of the needs of the self-achieving career woman. She knows there is something more to being a woman than just being someone's wife and someone else's mother. She would like to create and accomplish something on her own, and she believes that a capable woman should be active outside the home. But there are just so many hours in any given day, and she has been told, or knows from her own experience, that it is next to impossible to be a part-time wife and mother or a part-time career woman. Which comes first, her own needs or the needs of her husband and children? Her conflict is aggravated by every possible shade of opinion. There are some who urge her to go out and get a job; others who tell her in no uncertain terms that her place is in the home; and still others who assure her she can do both. Is it any wonder that this woman is in conflict?

Where does the average woman stand? The women on our Inventory of Feminine Values clustered somewhat left of the middle, more *Wall Street Journal* than *Woman's Day*, but with components of both. But when we asked these same women what their *ideal* woman was like, they described a woman slightly more on the *Woman's Day*, home-oriented side of the line. The third time around, when we asked them what kind of woman they thought the men they knew would consider ideal, they described a woman who was really *Woman's Day*, husband- and home-oriented.

What we see, then, is that most of the women we studied thought of themselves as pretty well balanced between self-achievement drives and a sense of family needs. However, their ideal woman was more family-oriented than they thought themselves to be. And then a real surprise—they felt that their men wanted a full-blown home-loving wife and mother. Now, again, confusion begins to mount, for what did the men tell us? They said, "We want a well-balanced woman, one who will achieve on her own, and still be home-loving and husband-loving." Ironically, this is exactly the way the women described themselves. Why had they guessed so wrong about what a man wants in a woman? If they were wrong about the men, were they also wrong about themselves?

A closer look at their responses to the Inventory will throw some light on this discrepancy. These women, remember, were questioned as to their self-perception, their ideal self, and their concept of man's ideal. The amazing fact is that at least 40 per-

cent in each sample, and an average of 65 percent of all the
women tested, reported a self-perception balanced between
husband, hearth, and home and their own needs for self-
achievement. Most of these women, granted, had at least a high
school education, and certainly had been exposed to our culture's
increasingly insistent demands on the educated woman. Some of
them were, in fact, professional women with active careers outside the home. Still a large majority recognized the importance
of, and derived satisfaction from, both family-oriented and self-
oriented activities and goals.

Their perceptions of the ideal woman were equally well balanced with, however, a slight tilt in the direction of hearth and
home. Some expressed an ambivalence between what they
thought they were like and what their ideal woman would be like;
housewives wished they were more self-achieving, and self-
achievers wished they were more home-oriented, an indication,
surely, of the guilt they felt because they were not all that they
thought they ought to be. But in the majority of cases, real self
and ideal self were in close correspondence.

It is significant that such a large and diverse cross section of
women expressed essentially similar opinions about themselves
and their roles. But no less significant is the nature of those roles.
Self-achievement for women, the notion that they should be free
and given the opportunity to seek personal fulfillment in roles
other than those of wife, mother, and housekeeper, is a relatively
new one in our culture. Women have always worked outside the
home, and do so today in ever-increasing numbers, but until
quite recently they worked not because it was a "right," much
less a psychological necessity, but because they were forced to for
economic reasons. If a woman devoted her full time to a career, it
was assumed she did so because she could not find a man to
support her. More often, the jobs she took, usually the only jobs
that were open to her, were on a part-time basis or of a fairly
menial nature, and she took them because the man she had found
could not support her. If there was a conflict between work and
home, between her obligations to herself and her obligations to
her husband and family, and she had a choice, naturally she gave
up all but her domestic duties.

Now, suddenly, at any rate among the educated, middle-class
segment of the female population that we tested, work and home,

self-fulfillment and fulfillment as a wife and mother, are considered to be of almost equal importance in the life of a woman. That in itself may be the most startling turnabout in the sexual revolution of the 1960's. But even more startling is the fact that the men we tested seemed to agree with it, for they, too, in describing their ideal, pictured a woman who was balanced between self-achieving and family-oriented drives. In other words, both men and women seemed to hold similar views about "woman's role." It would appear that they no longer considered it "unfeminine," in the traditional definition of that word, for a woman to be something more than a wife and mother. A woman is apparently no less a woman for displaying energy, intelligence, and the will to achieve, characteristics formerly considered to be the sole province of the male, necessary to pursue interests outside the home.

Furthermore, as was pointed out in the previous chapter, both men and women seemed to be in agreement about the ideal man and his roles. He should be active, outgoing, aggressive, self-achieving; but ideally, he, too, should strike a balance between his self-oriented and his family-oriented activities and goals. The surprise here was not in their shared concepts of masculinity —traditionally, the male was and still is supposed to be active, aggressive, self-achieving—but in their mutual belief that the man should spend more time at being a husband and father. Even so, this was not a reversal of the usual male role. It has always been assumed that a man could function successfully inside and outside the home. It was merely a redefinition of his responsibilities and a reallocation of his priorities. A highly important redefinition, of course; but a man has never been thought less a man for being a considerate husband and a conscientious father. The dramatic reversal comes, according to our Inventory responses from both sexes, in their shared concepts of women's role. Both men *and* women, ideally, can and should strike a balance between self-oriented and family-oriented pursuits.

If this is, in fact, the true picture, what then is the problem? Assuming that this balance could be found, there might be some difficulty arranging the details of a life-style to accommodate two self-achievers in the same family. But our research has shown that this is only one, and usually the least, problem to be resolved in contemporary male-female relationship, for the simple reason that most women do not believe that men want a self-achieving woman, and most men do not believe that a woman wants a self-achieving man, even though in both cases that is what they say they want. It is more than a mere credibility gap between the sexes, for we have found that most men and women act in accordance with what *they believe* the other wants, rather than in accordance with what the other *says* he or she wants.

We have seen, in the previous chapter, the anger, frustration, and ambivalence expressed by a great number of men caught in the conflict between traditional and transitional definitions of their masculine roles, between past expectations and contemporary realities. It would not be illogical to assume, then, that they would express similar ambivalence when it comes to the new definitions of feminine roles. And in their responses to particular items on our Inventory of Feminine Values they certainly do. But what about the women? Are they walking confident and unafraid into this bright new world of shared domestic responsibilities and increasing opportunities and freedoms outside the home? No, they are not. Perhaps it would be better if they were, for that would at least be one less area of conflict for the men to deal with. But women, too, are expressing confusion and ambivalence about their contemporary roles; and again, their responses to the Inventory prove it. Although collectively both male and female responses may add up to a rather enlightened and understanding view of contemporary women's roles, individual questions revealed significant areas of disagreement and uncertainty.

Take, for example, the items on the Inventory dealing with women's personality and social characteristics. As a group, the women we tested seemed to be torn between the old and the new definitions of femininity. A resounding majority felt that they were always considerate of other people's feelings, that they were capable of putting themselves in the background and working hard for someone they admired, and that they could accept help from others. No one could argue that these women were "unfeminine" by any definition. But these same women, in an equally resounding majority, said that they expressed their ideas strongly, that their personal development was more important to them than what others thought of them, that they argued with people who gave them orders, and that when they were with a group of people they usually emerged as leader. Apparently they saw no conflict between the passivity and submissiveness of the traditional feminine role and the more activity and independence of its modern counterpart, although a conflict certainly exists.

The women we tested were also positive that their ideal woman shared the same characteristics that they approved of in themselves. And similarly, they were uncertain about those characteristics in their ideal woman that they were uncertain about in themselves. But in describing man's ideal woman, they made several interesting about-faces. They agreed that those passive, submissive characteristics they saw in themselves would certainly be shared by man's ideal. They were not certain whether her personal development was more important to her than what others thought of her, but they were sure she would prefer to listen rather than talk and would seldom argue with anyone who tried to give her orders. Curiously enough, the men did not always agree. They accepted the passive, submissive traits that women ascribed to themselves and to man's ideal, but they were all for a woman developing as a person, all for one who questions authority, and less enthusiastic than the women thought they would be about one who always does what others want her to do. They wanted a woman to express her ideas strongly, but, somewhat illogically, they preferred a listener rather than a talker, just as the women predicted they would.

An interesting pattern seems to be emerging here. Either these women as a group wanted it both ways—a combination of both the old and the new feminine roles—or they had not made up their minds which way they wanted it. As for the men, they seemed willing to accept both ways. But it cannot be as simple as that. Conflicts are bound to occur, and when they do, it appears that the women may be blaming their own uncertainty and ambivalence on the men. When a woman says that she considers her self-development more important than the opinions of others, and that she argues with those who try to give her orders, but then claims that man's ideal woman would do neither of these things, what exactly is she saying: that she will do what she wants *in spite of* the man in her life, or that she will not do it *because* of him? Either way, the man seems to be the loser and she is off the hook. Perhaps the man is aware of this, and he may even

be doing the same thing, for what exactly is he saying when he claims that the woman's new independence of thought and action is all right with him? Is he telling the truth? Or is he, cleverly, passing the responsibility right back to the woman, saying, in effect, when you make up your mind, dear, then I'll tell you what I *really* think?

This same pattern continues in the items on the Inventory that concern woman's need for self-realization. The women agreed overwhelmingly that "one attains satisfactions through one's own efforts," "that a woman would like to create something," and that "a woman should have interests outside the home." They also agreed that their ideal woman would feel the same way, but when it came to man's ideal woman, they were less certain. Again, they seemed to feel that a man would not be 100 percent in favor of a self-achieving woman. And again, the men denied this. In describing their ideal, a clear majority were in favor of self-achievement for women. But the interesting paradox is that in response to the item, "I would rather be famous, admired, and popular throughout the nation than have the constant affection of just one man," 81 percent of the women denied this for themselves, 82 percent denied it for their ideal woman, and 89 percent denied it for man's ideal woman. The men were less certain; only about half of them thought that their ideal woman would give up everything for the constant affection of just one man. The women were obviously willing to do just that, while in the same breath they claimed they wanted to make it on their own. If they want it both ways, is it any wonder that the men may be somewhat confused?

As a general rule throughout the responses to the Inventory, both men and women in describing their ideal adhered to the liberal, enlightened definition of femininity. It does no harm, after all, to pay lip service to such a noble ideal. Of course a woman should be equal, independent, and free to realize her full potential as a human being. But at the same time, whenever an item appears on the Inventory that tests their response to one of the more old-fashioned concepts of femininity, they agree on that, too. Of course a woman should be capable of putting herself in the background and working for the husband and children she loves. There is no harm in paying lip service to that noble idea either. But in those areas where the old and the new, the traditional and the more modern definitions of femininity come in conflict, there is considerably less agreement. For example, in response to those items that deal particularly with male-female relationships, both men and women stated positively that a woman should marry a man she could really look up to, and that the greatest help a wife can give her husband is to encourage his progress. But they also stated with equal certainty that a wife's opinions should be just as important as her husband's, and that it is not exclusively up to the woman to make a marriage work. In the abstract, they may see no conflict between these concepts, but what happens when they try to apply them to the realities of their everyday lives?

Here, predictably, both men and women as a group are not quite sure of themselves. For example, there was no agreement between the sexes as to whether a wife should give in to her husband more often than he gives in to her. They did not differ about the institution of marriage itself. Men and women alike conceded that marriage requires sacrifices of a woman, and the women agreed that they were willing to make those sacrifices. But at what point does sacrifice end and denial of self begin? On the items relating to the touchy conflict between home and career, there was no unanimity about whether or not an ambitious, successful husband would want his wife to work. And the women, while stating on one hand that they believed a woman's place was in the home, and the needs of a family came before one's personal ambitions, also stated on the other that a married woman should desire her own personal success as well as her husbands.

What about the sacrifices of motherhood? Nowhere was woman's ambivalence demonstrated more clearly than in the items on the Inventory dealing with this area. The women were sure that the joys of motherhood make up for the sacrifices, but they were not sure that marriage and children should come first in their lives, or that their main interest was in raising normal, well-behaved children. And in response to a pair of statements that said, in essence, the same thing, they answered one positively and the other negatively. They agreed that a working mother can get along as well with her children as can a mother who stays at home, but they denied that a woman who works can be as good a mother as one who stays at home.

In summary, it is, of course, difficult to make hard-and-fast generalizations from the information we obtained on the Inventory of Feminine Values. The number of men and women tested was enormous, and there were significant variations among them in age, economic class, educational level, and even race and geographical location. But if we attempt to draw a profile of the average woman, based on the Inventory statistics, she, like the man revealed on the Inventory of Masculine Values, appears to be in a state of transition. Gone are some of the certainties of the old femininity: she is not sure that a woman's place is in the home and that her sole satisfaction should come from the achievements of her husband and children. She is beginning to see herself now as an individual with needs as important, and in some cases even more important, than those of her husband and children. But as yet she is not certain just how far she should go in attempting to realize those needs, or how far her husband wants her to go. She is reluctant to give up the safety and security of the old-fashioned woman's role, her more or less comfortable position as a wife and mother. This is surely one of the reasons why she sees her ideal woman and man's ideal woman as more home- and family-oriented, more passive and submissive, than she thinks herself to be. She wants the womanly satisfactions of house and home, but she is also intrigued by the human satisfactions that greater freedom, equality, and opportunity might offer her. It is not fair to say that she does not know what she wants. There is nothing wrong with wanting both. The trick is to find some viable way of achieving both.

Just where does this leave the man? Severely limited in the ways he can express traditional masculinity in society, he might very well try to reassert himself in the family setting, but apparently he does not. He, too, has been sold on the concept of the new femininity—in principle at least. But in practice it seems to be another story, for while he can accept new female roles and responsibilities, he has not yet been able to adjust to the new male roles and responsibilities that would make them possible. In the words of an NBC commentator who interpreted our surveys, men seem to be saying, "Yes, woman should be emancipated; women should have an equal say; women should be free to think and do what they like. Only let it all start with someone else's wife, not mine."

The trouble is that it has already started, and whatever the man does or says, it is not likely to stop. It started well over a century ago when women first began to speak up for their legal rights. They have been speaking up ever since, until today their voices and organizations, their demands and demonstrations share the headlines with the most militant of the minority groups. But women are not a minority, as the new feminists often point out; they are the majority. And with that kind of power base, some of the radical fringes of the feminist movement foresee abolition of marriage, child-bearing and -raising, and the overthrow of the home and the family unit. Some even prophesy the day when, through genetic alteration or some form of artificial evolution, there will no longer be any physical differences between the sexes.

Few women of the middle-aged, middle-class group that we studied belong to these radical groups; but they do belong in increasing numbers to political parties, social action groups, and women's organizations that are working for peace, social justice, equal employment opportunities, reform of divorce and abortion laws, and other goals that they feel will benefit not only women but society as a whole. These are the same women who, secure in their positions with their husbands and with their children old enough to start taking care of themselves, are leaving home to find jobs, or are going back to school with an eye on a future career. Others, who feel trapped in their suburban split-levels or their city apartments, are seriously considering making some change in their lives—any change. Almost all of them are voicing a vague or a positive dissatisfaction with the traditional "woman's role." As the Inventory of Feminine Values has shown, they are a far cry from their mothers, bound willingly to hearth and home, who were ready to start being grandmothers as soon as they had finished being mothers and who never stopped being housewives, even if they had jobs outside the home.

What has happened in only the space of a generation to bring about this change? What is today's woman like? Why should she, all of a sudden, consider self-fulfillment as important as fulfillment as a wife and mother? Why is she, in search of one or both, giving herself and her husband such a hard time? And just how has she arrived at this transitional, semiliberated state, poised in the middle, uncertain which way she wants to go, uncertain, too, of which way her husband wants her to go or whether she should go on without him?

In trying to answer questions like these, we can speak in only the broadest terms, for in many ways—psychological, sociological, economic, and even ethnic—the personal histories of the women we studied are unique to each individual. These women did share a number of things. They were born in the twenties or thirties, and were shaped by the same cycle of war-prosperity-depression-war-prosperity that influenced the men of that period. But that history served not to limit women's opportunities and means of self-expression, but to expand them. Granted, some might claim that women had no place to go but up. For one thing, the typical girl child of the period almost invariably took a backseat to her brother. It was his birth, coming of age, education, and future that were of primary importance to his family.

But what had been a closely knit family group, sometimes consisting of grandparents and aunts and uncles, who, if they did not live in the same house, often lived nearby and shared domestic duties and the tasks of child-raising, began to close in on itself in a preoccupation with children that often amounted to indulgence. Indulgence by parents became self-indulgence as the children of that generation matured; and when they married and had children of their own, they, in turn, indulged them. In the process, in the near-obsession with giving children "all the advantages," girls benefited too.

Women began to feel their oats in the 1920's, and with the Depression we saw that they went to work to help support their stricken families. And by the late thirties, among middle-class families at least, it became as important that the daughters as well as the sons get as much education as possible, often with the rationale that just in case something should happen to the girl's husband (and provider) she would, with her education, be able to provide for herself. Parents willingly sacrificed themselves and their immediate pleasures to improve their children's chances—boys and girls alike—in the next generation. Americans have always looked to education as a means of upward social and economic mobility, and in the thirties and forties education for women assumed a new importance. Women who were doing something for themselves, with or without a man, began to appear on the scene. There were Eleanor Roosevelt and Frances Perkins in politics; both were often the object of male derision, but women could identify with them. In the movies, Katharine Hepburn, Rosalind Russell, Claudette Colbert, and others played sharp-witted, sophisticated women, obviously educated and often the equals of their men in some career. Amelia Earhart was a heroine, not a hero, and Marie Curie excited universal admiration for her pioneering scientific research. Mothers, frustrated by the drudgery of their lives in housework or menial employment, wanted more than that for their daughters. And education was the way to give it to them.

This is not to say that girls came first in any family, unless they happened to be an only child. Nor is it to say that all girls were given quality educations overnight. A mother might very well prefer and encourage her daughter to marry an education, instead of going through the painful and expensive process of acquiring her own. And many girls frankly went to college to find a man. When they did, they quickly gave up whatever plans they might have had for their own future to help support their husbands through school and the early years of their marriage. The basic definitions of femininity did not undergo any revolutionary change. A girl still looked to marriage and motherhood for her final fulfillment; she still assumed the passive, submissive role. But it did not hurt to get an education, or at least a smattering of one, along the way. In some cases, women were actually given the same educations as men and were encouraged to work toward similar goals.

For the first time in their lives, then, this maturing crop of young women began to taste the freedom, independence, and opportunity that education could give them, and which had heretofore been solely a male prerogative. They were acquiring at least the possibility of an alternative to the conventional feminine image. This new feminine image blossomed in the depression years when men and women worked together to find a way out of their troubles. And with the advent of war, the women worked alone on the home front, while their men went overseas to fight. They learned masculine skills and used them well; they made good money and kept their families in good order. For the first time in history, the government recognized their importance in the labor market. Day-care centers, canteens and special schools were set up. The women at the top made it their business to help their sisters. They badgered Congress and government officials until women received the cooperation and assistance that was their right and due.

But then the war came to an end, and women stepped down from their new and unfamiliar pinnacle and went back to *"kinder, kirche, und kuchen."* They shared the desire of the men to re-create "the good old days," or if the old days were not so good, to create the kind of life that they had been told they were fighting for. As always in America, that life was centered almost exclusively on the acquisition of material things, of tangible assets and indications of success. For the husband it meant a good salary and a wife to take care of him while he made it. For the wife it meant the best house or apartment, as many machines and appliances, and as many children as the family could afford. The postwar baby boom in this country was unequaled by any other country in the world. Industry in high gear for war production shifted gears and flooded the market with indispensable and expensive things. Families in search of jobs moved en masse to the cities, and then, if they could afford it, moved again to the suburbs.

Wives did not have to be talked into this postwar return to domesticity. The women who had not yet married were anxious to settle down, and more than willing to give up their educations and opportunities for the men they loved and the children they wanted to have. At mid-century then, women seemed to turn their backs on the gains of the previous decades. The budding new image of femininity withered and the old wife and mother image bloomed again. But it was not a very hardy flower, no matter how exuberantly it seemed to grow. Just as the postwar world was vastly different from what men had been raised to expect, so the soil and climate had changed significantly for women. And like the men, they began to discover that there was a large gap between their expectations and the realities of their everyday lives.

For one thing, a woman had been told from childhood by her parents, her teachers, various experts and authorities that she should find her fulfillment through her husband and children in marriage, and that the most important and creative work that she could do was housework. Just look, she was told, at all the unhappy and neurotic women who were trying to make it in business and the professions simply because they could not make it anywhere else. These women were not women at all; their educations and their ambitions, their attempts to compete with men, had "defeminized" them. Few women wanted that. And so they denied their educations and ambitions and devoted their full time to the career of being a housewife.

The first bubble to break was the notion of creative housework. In their move from city to city, or city to suburb, many families now lived in virtual isolation from grandparents and other relatives. The burdens of housework and child-raising fell squarely on the wife's shoulders. Hired servants had disappeared from the scene, and the husband could be counted on for only grudging assistance. Still it was not much of a problem, unless she made it one, with all the appliances and laborsaving devices available. But to claim that the endless errands, the repetitive drudgery, was "creative" soon became a joke to many women. Husbands were absent most of the day at work; as soon as the children were old enough to go to school, they took off, too. The woman found herself alone in her postwar paradise. The real business and excitement of life seemed to be someplace else.

What about finding her fulfillment through her husband? How was she supposed to do that? She could encourage his efforts, take pride in his success, and wear, use, drive, and live in the things he could afford to buy her. But it was at best a vicarious fulfillment, and where does encouragement end and nagging begin? The wife was not expected to share her husband's business or professional interests, or even his commitments to other outside activities. She did not know where he went, what he did, or, in some cases, whom he was seeing on the side. But she found she didn't enjoy being ignored. She had to have some proof of his love and her importance; and she tried to get it, sometimes by making excessive sexual demands on him, or by demanding that he share her domestic career, neither of which contributed markedly to her fulfillment or the success of the marriage.

As far as fulfilling herself through her children, a woman often found that they, too, could be a mixed blessing. For one thing, they have a habit of growing up and leaving home. Even *while* they are growing up, they spend most of their waking hours outside the home—at school or at some sport or activity that has been devised for them. Motherhood has its joys and satisfactions, but most of those joys, women discovered, are limited to a very few years. After that, what? And paradoxically, in the postwar years when most women devoted all their energies to being mothers, motherhood itself was revealed in an interesting new light.

Mom and apple pie were clichéd catchwords during World War II. They, and a few other slangy symbols of the American way of life, were supposed to be what it was all about. Perhaps they were not meant to be taken seriously, just as the politician who stands up for motherhood has become a joke. But the fact is that, in America, the words mother and motherhood have always been accorded a special sentimental significance.

But after the war, authorities and experts, armed with Freudian insights and alarmed at the statistics about the American mother's sons who had proved unfit for or incapable of military service, put forth the theory that mothers were to blame. It seemed that too much mom, just like too much apple pie, could make you sick. Mom became momism, and every variety of neurotic or psychotic pattern of behavior seen in her children was laid at the mother's doorstep.

Here was another reality, overstated and oversimplified perhaps, that women had not expected. Even if they survived the criticisms of motherhood, or took solace in its sentimental significance, they lost their positions of favor when they became mothers-in-law, the butt of endless jokes and the target of less than humorous hostility from their sons and daughters. Thus in quick succession, a woman realized that the much-touted fulfillment that she was supposed to find as a homemaker, wife, and mother could easily mean, if she did not watch her step, endless hours of unrewarding housework, a husband who wanted nothing more than to get her off his back, and children who could not wait to leave home, if they were psychologically capable of doing so. And even if she were a perfect homemaker, a perfect wife, a perfect mother, she also realized that those roles accounted for only fifteen or twenty years of a lifespan that had another twenty years to go, and only a very few hours of a long, boring, repetitive, and lonely day.

To fill those empty hours and years, many women decided to go back to work. Some of them, of course, did not have the luxury of choice. They had to work, to help pay for all the things they wanted for themselves and their children, the same things, incidentally, that so many of those children would grow up to despise and reject. But the women who could afford to shop around for an occupation or career got a rude shock. Another expectation they had been given growing up, one of the things their education had taught them, was that it was possible, even essential, for them to find another kind of fulfillment, intellectual fulfillment in useful and creative work. That's what an education was for. They had been told that they had minds as well as bodies. But when women began to explore the possibilities of work outside the home, they discovered that they were not exactly welcome in the job market. There was no depression, no war; these were the affluent fifties and sixties. Competition was keen even among the men, and every year thousands, millions of jobs open, of course; and an ever-increasing number of women filled them, but at the lower echelons of employment, and more often than not at lower levels of pay than men received for the same work. Girls just out of college snapped up the few good jobs, the ones with a possible future. How could a housewife pushing middle age, a housewife who had finished or cut short her education years ago, compete with them, let alone with men? The jobs they were qualified to fill were just as boring and repetitious as the housework they had to do when they got home.

A few women, it is true, had risen to the top, or close to it, in their careers or professions, but these were women who had been working all along, who had never married or who had somehow managed to combine family and job responsibilities. The woman who had been a full-time housewife was faced with two unpleasant alternatives. She could either take any job she could get, or she could go back to school to brush up on her skills. With husbands and families, including children of their own to educate, this latter alternative was a greater burden than many women could bear. And even if they had the time and the money, they found that few colleges at this time made any accommodation for the rusty housewife who could be only a part-time student. Here again, women had to compete with the bumper crop of children they had brought so lovingly into the world. Furthermore, the day-care centers, part-time arrangements, and the special provisions made for women during the war, provisions that might have made employment or education more feasible, had virtually vanished from the postwar scene.

Even when a woman was able to surmount these formidable roadblocks on the way to useful and profitable employment, she ran head on into the biggest block of all: the attitudes and prejudices of men. If a man wanted his wife off his back, he did not necessarily want her out of the house as well. Even if there was such a thing as too much mom, everyone seemed to agree that she should be there, if and when the children really needed her. In a world full of demasculinizing pressures, competition from women at home or on the job was just about the last straw for men. Contrary to what they had been brought up to believe by their parents, contrary to what they had been taught in school and college, contrary to what they expected for themselves and what society expected of them, many women began to feel that they were little more than unpaid servants in their own homes, and second-class citizens in society at large.

The time, obviously, was ripe for some kind of rebellion, and it came in the mid-1960's with the rebirth of the Feminist Movement. Sparked by Betty Friedan's *The Feminine Mystique*, a small but vocal minority of women began to make their voices heard. Like Gypsy Rose Lee's mother in the musical *Gypsy*, they asked, "When do I get my turn?" And as yet, no one has been able to give them a satisfactory answer. Some reply that women have never been out of the spotlight. Through their Eve-like influence over men, whether they chose to exercise it or not, they already rule the world. Equality is a step down for women, according to Bernard Shaw. According to the hard-core sexual conservatives, women are intellectually as well as physically incapable of ruling anyone, even themselves. They are written about endlessly, they are the object of both praise and blame, they talk endlessly among themselves about their "problems." If a single theme could be discerned in all this discussion, it would perhaps be the necessity for women to "be themselves," to be all that they are capable of being in their various physical, psychological, and intellectual roles. Hardly a revolutionary bit of advice. Men have been exhorted to be themselves for centuries. But still the discussions continue, because it seems no one is quite sure what it means for a woman to be herself; no one is quite sure, including women, of just who today's woman is or who she should be.

Curiously enough in all this talk, the word *feminine* has taken on a whole new set of meanings. The radical feminists use it as a term of derision; the conservative anti-feminists, male and female, use it to describe the old-fashioned, soft, pretty, passive wife and mother they hold up as their model. Those in the middle are not sure *how* to use it, again because they are still uncertain of what it means to be feminine. Can a female physicist with a better brain than many men be feminine? Is a female shot-putter feminine, even if she has bigger muscles and better coordination than many men? Is the woman who has no ambitions beyond being a wife and mother feminine? Some say yes, some say no, and the confusion seems to arise from the fact that today women are asked, and want, to fulfill functions and play roles that have only an indirect relationship to their biological sex. In other words, the old-fashioned definition of femininity, which was based on woman's physical functions and those psychological characteristics which are related to it, either in fact or through her culture's interpretation of them, is no longer adequate to explain what it means to be a woman. All of these factors—her biology, her psychology, and her culture—are in the process of change. And the definition of femininity is changing along with them.

Men long ago escaped the bondage of their bodies, in the sense at least that they expressed an interest in exercising something more than just their physical and sexual capabilities. Today, women are in the process of doing the same thing. It can be argued with validity that women are more firmly imprisoned by the menstrual cycle and the complicated apparatus that enables them to give birth. Still, with the advent of the Pill and liberalized abortion laws, they have gained greater physical control and freedom than ever before. Human psychology and cultural attitudes, however, are not so readily influenced by science and the law. Thus, men and women as individuals and collectively as society are still in the painful process of exploring what this new freedom means and where it will eventually lead.

It is perhaps the most painful for women themselves, particularly young women still in college or just out who have so many choices. The women in or near middle age in our survey perhaps have a narrower range or choice and therefore less chance for conflict. Even so, as we pointed out earlier, they displayed enormous confusion and ambivalence about their sexual roles, which may not be so surprising after all, given their circumstances. Their lives are half over. Their attitudes have been shaped by psychological and social forces that, to their children at least, seem to be part of the dim, distant past. In many cases, they are still burdened with the unrealistic expectations of that past, and they are puzzled by the realities of the present as the men in their lives. Their view of the future has a rather desperate quality to it. If they are ever going to find out what being a woman *really* means, they had better hurry up. They have not got much time left.

How do women like this behave? Promised so much at such an early age, many of them have reached the midpoint of their lives with disappointment and frustration etched permanently into their faces. With husbands, children, homes filled with expensive possessions, even in some cases interests outside the home, these women should be the envy of their less fortunate sisters all over the world. But something has gone wrong: their husbands are no longer interested, or have left them for younger women; their children have grown up and gone away from them; their possessions and their lives give them no particular satisfaction. Just where is all that feminine fulfillment they were promised? The women who put all their eggs in one basket—their bodies—are perhaps the most desperate, now that they are getting on and that basket is beginning to fall apart at the seams.

The middle-aged woman who dresses like a teen-ager, dyes her hair, paints her face, and starves herself to squeeze into a size ten is a familiar sight on the streets of even the small towns in this country. Who are they kidding? No one but themselves. But ironically, they did not think up the charade all by themselves. They are merely doing what our culture has told them to do. From childhood on they have been bombarded with the notion that youth, beauty, and sensual and coquettish behavior equal femininity. They don brassieres and lipstick at twelve or before; they are "going steady" at fourteen. Fifty percent of them are married by the age of twenty-one. "Can you tell Mrs. Smith from her daughter, Sally?" a soap commercial asks. The sad fact is that in many cases you cannot, either physically or mentally. Perfumes and deodorants, diet sodas and even cigarettes, promise youth, beauty, and success in bed, and many women are unsure enough of themselves to fall for it. We have recently learned, through the most skillful advertising techniques, that black is beautiful. How long will it be before someone comes up with the idea that middle and old age are beautiful, too? It all depends on the woman. But most have been gulled into the belief that when their necks and breasts begin to sag, they are in serious trouble. They double and redouble their efforts to prove that they are still young and desirable, in appearance, in behavior, even in their biological functions by demanding sexual reassurance from their husbands or by having an affair or one last baby before it is too late. They grow old gracefully only when it is impossible to do anything else, and sometimes not even then. It is not entirely their fault, of course, for men have been brainwashed with the same idea. If their wives no longer satisfy them when their chins and bellies begin to sag, they try a younger woman.

Motherhood, too, is part of the conventional definition of femininity, and just as women are reluctant to let go of their youth and beauty, so many of them are unwilling or unable to let go of their kids. The super-mom is an easily recognizable figure in American life, Mrs. Portnoy perhaps being one of the more recent and obvious literary examples of the breed. They nag, cajole, feed, and even seduce their children into crippling dependence or self-destructive rebellion, all for the sake of their own "feminine fulfillment." They instruct their daughters in the seductive wiles of womanhood, and then teach their sons to resist them. The secret of their power is in their dependence—again a major part of the conventional definition of femininity. They become martyrs if their husbands and children fail them, saints if they succeed. In their continual plea, "Do it for Mother, darling," they hang like millstones around their families' necks. They may think they are pushing their children up, but more often they are dragging them down. And their reward for being super-moms is husbands, sons, and daughters who cannot make it on their own or who, if they can, want nothing more to do with mom.

There are other extreme behavior patterns within the broad spectrum of the changing definitions of femininity. It is generally conceded nowadays that women have a brain as well as a body, and some women are as relentless in the pursuit of intellectual fulfillment as others are in the pursuit of youth, super-femininity, and super-momism. The career woman is often caricatured in our society; she is sometimes a caricature of herself. Liza Elliott in *Lady in the Dark* is one of that type. She has everything —brains, beauty, ability—but something is obviously wrong. Eventually, the glasses come off, the hair comes down, she consents to go to bed with a man, and she lives happily ever after. But in real life, the career woman may not be quite so fantastically glamorous, and she clutches at her brains and her job in the same way that other women clutch at their beauty and their babies. Both types, when challenged, staunchly maintain that they have everything they want in life, just as the man who only has one eye may claim he likes it better that way. No one is more contemptuous of the dull domestic routine of the housewife-mother than the career woman; and the housewife-mother scorns the loveless, childless life of the career woman. Both claim that they are what being a woman means. But do the ladies protest too much? Many of them are guilty about being "just a housewife" or "just a career woman." They are afraid that they are missing something; and their overreactions and their defensive behavior mask that fear and guilt.

A more subtle expression of that same defensive behavior, whether it comes from the housewife-mother or the career woman or even the woman who combines both, is the "specialty syndrome." While some claim and work for female equality, others maintain serenely that women, in their own way, are superior to men, that there is something unique, wonderful, and even holy about being a woman—something special. She has long been credited for her "emotional depth," her "intuitive understanding," her "commitment to culture," her "superior moral sense." These almost God-like attributes are certainly important, whichever sex possesses them. But do they belong exclusively to women who are supposed somehow to work their "civilizing influence" on their husbands and children, or are they high-sounding consolation prizes graciously awarded by the men and gratefully accepted by women as a substitute for more tangible power and influence? It is claimed, too, that if women were given, or took the power, there would be no more wars because women are not aggressive, no more poverty and social injustices because women are more sympathetic and understanding than men. If this were, in fact, true, why haven't more women, using what influence they do have, united to achieve these goals?

Other authorities have claimed that the woman is special for biological reasons. She lives longer than man, for one thing. She is less susceptible to heart attacks and ulcers. She goes mad less frequently than the man. Her body and mind are better equipped to deal with the physical and psychological stresses of everyday life. Nature, in order to ensure the continuation of the species, has endowed her with the properties necessary not only to bear and rear her offspring, but to protect her mate. Thus, she is "superior" to the man. But why superior, if superior is used to imply a value judgment, i.e., better than the man? Is the female gorilla superior to the male, or is the hen superior to the rooster? The question usually does not arise. Why then should the woman be considered superior to the man for either physical or psychological characteristics which are, in fact, merely *differences* between the sexes? The woman and her proponents who claim "superiority" for biological reasons are on no less shaky ground than the men who claim, and act upon, their "superior" size and strength.

There are other interesting paradoxes that test the speciality syndrome. Men claim, some smugly and some apprehensively, that women *do* have all the power; they control the money, they raise the kids, they can get their husbands to do anything they want them to do. Any woman in her right mind should be content with that. But if this were true, and some women like to think it so, then not only are women *not* special, they are even more responsible than the men for the messes we have made. "Behind every great man there stands a woman"—another popular speciality myth that implies that a woman is somehow responsible for men's greatness. But women stand behind the failures, too, and are not quite so eager to claim the blame as they are the credit.

The speciality syndrome is nothing more or less than a put-up job, an artful self-deception practiced by both men and women to disguise the real differences and similarities between the sexes. The man who tells his wife that women are something special usually hopes she will settle for that. The woman who tells herself that she is something special just by being female relieves herself of the responsibility to be anything else. It is as restrictive and shortsighted a version of femininity as the housewife-mother or the career woman view.

The "women's lib" version of what it means to be a woman is another form of speciality, and equally restrictive. These radical feminists advocate the same kind of superiority and separatism for women that some black militants advocate for the blacks. In their total rejection of men and motherhood, in their rage against "penis power," they also deny those characteristics and abilities that make their sex, not unequal or inferior to the male sex, but merely different. There is a difference between wanting to be exactly like a man, or better, and enjoying the same freedom, independence, responsibility, and power that a man enjoys. And it is perhaps even more difficult and unrewarding to learn to live without a man and a family than it is to learn to live with them. Most women who already have husbands and children, or who are looking forward to having them, would not even entertain the idea, however just some of the "women's lib" complaints against men and society may be. For them it is not a question of "separate and superior" but of "together and equal."

Thus today's woman has expectations for a kind of fulfillment, both physical and intellectual, that she cannot find in present reality. She is no longer content with traditional feminine roles or their special rationalizations. Ahead of her stretches a number of possible alternatives which, singly or in combination, seem to promise more complete fulfillment. And all around her voices are shouting contradictory definitions of what it means to be a woman: love men or hate them, have babies or don't have them, get a job or stay at home. Today's psychological and social pressures have narrowed the traditional road for the man; for the woman they have opened up a whole new territory. She stands at the crossroads, trying to figure out the signs, trying to figure out which way she wants to go. One thing is certain: it will be as tough to go back to the restrictions and dull routine of being "just a woman," to the conventional feminine roles however soft and secure, as it will be to go forward. Society expects more of her today; she expects more of herself. Why, then, doesn't she make up her mind?

Woman's mind has always been a fertile field for exploration and speculation by poets and writers as well as psychologists —most of them men. If she is given credit for having a mind at all, she has always been accorded the privilege of changing it. She is supposed to be fickle, flighty, ruled by her emotions rather than her intellect; she has infinite variety. No one can tell what she is thinking; no one can tell what she may do next, least of all herself. Certainly the behavior of some women would seem to confirm that view. Or is it just another speciality myth? What wonderful license it gives a woman to know that she is expected to do the unexpected, that she is not supposed to be responsible. And what a wonderful sense of superiority and protective benevolence it gives a man. In a more scientific extension of the same view, some argue that women are prisoners of their biology, of their ovarian cycles which prevent the uninterrupted concentration necessary for purposeful or creative action. Others claim that women, so long dependent on men, have lost the ability to think and act for themselves. Furthermore, as second-class citizens, they have been schooled to accept and believe in their own inferiority. The man is taught to fear failure; the woman is criticized and is self-critical if she succeeds.

There may be some truth in these arguments. Brains as well as muscles do atrophy with disuse. And those measurable differences between the intelligence of men and women are invariably ascribed to psychological and cultural, rather than physiological, causes. But after all is said and done, women *are* capable of making up their minds, and using them in independent and creative action—if they want to.

Some women, of course, do not want to. They snicker at the new feminists' demands for equality and opportunity. They are perfectly happy just the way they are. With husbands to support them and tell them what to do (or whom they can tell what to do), they have got it made. Why rock the boat? Still other women are quite willing to do a little rocking, but are less eager to jump overboard. They may very well feel inferior to men, due to a lack of education or opportunity, or indifference to these. And the fact is that women *are* dependent on their men, whether by preference, necessity, habit, or social custom. And they are bound to their husbands and children in many ways that make it difficult to take *any* unilateral action, from going to a movie to getting a full-time job. When a man makes such a decision—and many of them still do, or if they do not, they are theoretically granted that prerogative—a woman moves in to fill the gap in the line. If a woman makes it, she is also usually responsible for training, bringing in, and supervising her *own* replacements.

And so she crouches in the trenches, getting closer but not yet up to the front lines. Part of her would much rather be back home; another part wants to go over the top. But is she brave enough, strong enough, smart enough to survive? She is not sure. Is what she may win more rewarding than what she may have to leave behind? She is not sure of that, either. She is in conflict, first of all within herself, and if she is married that conflict naturally expands to include her husband. The result? At best, a series of minor skirmishes, thrusts and parries, advances and retreats; at worst, all-out and open warfare.

CHAPTER 6

Man vs. Woman in Marriage

The battle between the sexes, whether it is a minor skirmish or a full-scale war, is customarily fought within the confines of marriage. Men and women can be friends and lovers, outside the bounds of matrimony, but they often find themselves becoming the bitterest of enemies as they assume the roles of husband and wife. What happens? What goes wrong? Why does that bed of roses they expected to find turn out to be a bed of nails? Why do so many marriages end in divorce?

The causes of battle can be traced without much difficulty to conflicting expectations for marriage and conflicting views of the role that each sex should play in that marriage. Few of the men or women that we questioned in our surveys would challenge the institution of marriage itself as a worthwhile goal. The typical woman, in fact, was taught and trained from early childhood to proceed with all due speed in that very direction. And the first thing she learned was to emphasize her "femininity", to suppress anything in her character that might be considered "masculine" or that might upset the traditional distinctions between the sexes. She learned to compromise. As a little girl, she compromised her aggression, energy, and high spirits to avoid being typed a tomboy. In high school, she compromised her intelligence so she would not scare off potential dates. In college, she compromised her own creative and career ambitions for fear that they would interfere with her future as a housewife-mother. If she married in college, she even compromised her education. If she worked after college, she compromised her ambition in a job usually well below her abilities. And in courtship, she made the same compromises, which may have been, by that time, simple force of habit.

Don't be too smart, too aggressive, too independent, the woman was told or learned through bitter experience. She also learned to get what she wanted in more subtle, devious and "feminine" ways. She played the conventional courtship game. If a man were interested, or if she were interested in a man, she might very well practice a few harmless little deceptions to hold his interest. Perfectly capable of lighting her own cigarettes, hailing her own cabs, and even paying her own way in a restaurant or to a movie, she deferred shyly to the man's display of dominance and his willingness to demonstrate his ability to provide. Perfectly capable, too, of expressing ideas and opinions of her own, she again deferred to the man. She assumed the passive, submissive, conventional female role; in a phrase, she bolstered his ego at the expense of her own. If she was not swept completely off her feet by physical attraction, she made a shrewd assessment of his potential as a breadwinner and a bed partner, and then set about proving to him that she was what he wanted as a housewife, helpmate, and mother of his children. She could not be too eager in bed or elsewhere; that might give him the impression that he was being trapped. Nor could she be too docile and dependent; that might be equally frightening to him. In essence, she was biding her time, although in various ways she might be extremely active in her pursuit of the man. Marriage for her meant safety, security, status, fulfillment as a wife and mother, and last but not least, a chance, after long years of compromise, to have things her way for a change.

The man, too, played a conventional courtship game. Just as the woman pretended to be more "feminine" than she perhaps really was, so he had to be more "masculine" than he really was. He took over; he decided where they would go and what they would do on their dates, which, of course, he also paid for. He made the sexual advances which she parried or accepted, depending on which she had decided was the best way to snag him. If she was looking for someone to take care of her, so, in other ways, was he—a woman to gratify him in bed, raise his children, and make his life as comfortable and convenient as possible. And to achieve that goal, he made a few compromises himself. He could not abuse the superiority the woman so demurely conceded to him; he could not be *too* "masculine." But at the same time he could not display weakness or dependence. This woman he was courting was, after all, nearly his equal. She had been educated; she had a job. She was not all flattery and deference. They had the same interests, ideas, and enthusiasms. They did things together, and when they spoke romantically of their future life, they imagined a "shared experience." But the man was biding his time, too, waiting, like his wife-to-be, to once again have things *his* way.

Naturally enough, both the man and the woman were on their best behavior during courtship. Their little spats and quarrels were made up with a kiss. Love, in their optimistic opinion, would conquer all. So they married, and their costumes on the day they walked to the altar, the ceremony itself, were no less anachronistic and unrealistic than the personalities they had assumed to get them there. Once married, once they had given up most of their other freedoms, both felt, paradoxically, that they were at last free to be themselves. And when the honeymoon was over, literally and figuratively, both woke up to the delayed realization of just who this person was that they had married.

The marriage manuals are full of the kinds of problems a couple like this encounter from their wedding night to their retirement years, if their marriage lasts that long. And it has been rightly said that a marriage that doesn't have some problems is hardly worthy of the name. Central to all these problems, whether they are about sex, money, career vs. home, parenthood, or whatever, is the matter of the relative responsibilities of each sex, the male and female roles in marriage, individually and as a collective family unit.

The man and woman who deceive each other or themselves in courtship, or who come together insecure in their sexual identities are in trouble even before the marriage begins. And the man and woman who think that marriage alone can resolve that insecurity are in for even more trouble. Given the additional difficulties of living and working together, a husband and wife who are confused about what to expect and what is expected of them, about what is essential and what superfluous in their relationship, are in deep water indeed. Pity the man who thought he could count on the pretty, passive deferential little thing he courted for help and support in marriage only to discover that she is a very assertive and strong-willed woman. Pity the woman, too, who thought she married a man whom she could lean on only to discover that he can barely stand up, let alone support her. According to the old wives' tale, she is supposed to marry him first and then change him. But she may not be up to the job, or if she is, neither she nor her husband may be overjoyed with the result.

A recent study[1] has shown that women are often passive and submissive before marriage and dominant after. Obviously, marriage can and usually does signal dramatic changes in both husband and wife. Some of those changes are necessary and constructive in the marital relationship. But when they aggravate an already insecure sexual identity, or when they run counter to what one or both partners expected their life together to be like, they often succeed in destroying the marriage.

When a marriage goes on the rocks, everyone agrees that the parties involved probably never should have gotten together in the first place. But it cannot be denied that something was responsible for the attraction, and that something may exist well below the level of their conscious awareness. A man who has never resolved his relationship with his mother may attempt to duplicate it with his wife. A woman with a secret wish to dominate may search out a man whose secret wish is to be dominated by a woman. The list of subconscious, even neurotic, motives for marriage is endless, and the motives themselves endlessly varied. They are the stock in trade of the psychoanalysts and the marriage counselors. And they, too, speaking in the broadest terms, can be traced to a confusion or ambivalence in the roles of the sexes in marriage, or the participants' interpretation of those roles. When they are added to the confusions that exist on the conscious level, and the small everyday conflicts that are endemic to any marriage, it is perhaps a wonder that an even greater number of marriages do not end up in divorce.

Every marriage is a unique relationship, just as the men and the women who enter into them are unique individuals. But the problem common to all marriages is one of personal identity, and the question that is most often asked, or felt and acted upon if it is not actually spoken, is "Who comes first, the husband, the wife, the marriage?" When children appear, they are added to the list, as if each family member were anxious to win some kind of race, or throw it in favor of someone else. Indulged in their own childhood and adolescence, accustomed to being the center of attention whether they are male or female, preoccupied with their own fulfillment and happiness, critical and analytical of themselves, each other, and their relationships, both husband and wife find it extremely difficult even in love and marriage to think of someone else first. Thus in the sexual relationship, whose convenience, pleasure, or simple release should be paramount, the man or the woman's? Who should take responsibility for the major decisions that affect the welfare of the entire family, the man or the woman? Who should perform which of the domestic duties of the marriage? How are the responsibilities of parenthood to be divided between the man and the woman?

And so it goes, straight through the long list of marital situations, each one of which is a potential source of conflict between the sexes. It is very easy for the man or the woman to say that "the marriage comes first," and they may very well believe it. But that motto is most often invoked when one of the partners is asking or demanding that the other give up something that he or she considers to be an individual right or privilege, an essential to his or her sense of personal identity. A relationship that is built on nothing but self-denial and sacrifice, from one partner or the other, or both, is not much of a marriage. Nor is it much more than a contractual arrangement if it is based on the principle of "taking turns": the wife has her way one day and the husband the next. If they are not able to be or achieve something more together than they could be or achieve separately, or by taking turns, why bother with marriage at all?

Some have claimed that the battle between the sexes, whether it occurs inside or outside the home, in bed or in an office, is a simple struggle for dominance and for power. This often seems to be the case, and when it is, sex, money, work, domestic duties, children, and the other component parts of the marriage become weapons in a cold- or hot-war conflict between man and wife. And as with the other pseudo-wars and conflicts we have engaged in in the mid-twentieth century, there is little resemblance between the way they used to be fought and the way they are fought today. The man, long accustomed to superiority and dominance by virtue of his sex, took his power for granted and used or abused it at his whim. He engaged in sexual intercourse in or outside of marriage for his pleasure and at his leisure. Even intercourse outside of marriage was tacitly condoned, if he could get away with it; but it was taken for granted that his woman, whether wife or mistress, was eternally available and absolutely faithful.

Today, the balance of power has almost reversed, at least

within marriage. Even with greater social mobility and sexual freedom, the woman who "fools around" is still an object of criticism and contempt, while the man who does the same thing may be excused with a shrug. Women are apparently more willing to forgive such an action by their husbands than the husbands are by their wives, vestigial indications perhaps of male possessiveness and female dependence. But within marriage, the sexual picture is quite different. With our increased sophistication in the physiology and the psychology of sex, it is the woman who has achieved the upper hand.

Sex, for most married women, is no longer a dirty word, an onerous duty, or merely a means of procreation. Rather it has become the primary frame of reference for male-female interaction. Such has been the concern with the forms of sexual interaction, the techniques for sexual gratification, and the levels of satisfaction by which a couple can measure their sexual success, it can and has been argued that many American couples have an exaggerated concern with sex and sexual gratification. In part this is explained by the culture's obsession with sexuality and sexual symbolism, but in part we believe it also reflects the absence of wider concerns, the lack of individual identity, and the inability to communicate and provide the companionship each needs and desires. Given these lacks, and the consequent feelings of isolation and loneliness both men and women have turned to, and become preoccupied with proving and gratifying themselves in the sex act.

It is possible to have a workable marriage without sex; and conversely a marriage in which the sex is terrific may be a terrific failure in every other way. But, obviously sex is here to stay, and far from being a mindless and repetitive animal act, it is a unique and essential means of self-expression and communication between the sexes.

But it is a mistake however to endow sex with a greater importance than it deserves, to be controlled by rather than control the sexual urge. And, of course, it is an equally serious error to ignore or deny it. Men are most often guilty of the former mistake. The penis is their chief means of sexual stimulation, expression, and release, the easily visible barometer of the intensity of their feelings and the urgency of their need. In the past, it did not seem to matter how, when, or with whom that release was achieved.

Dominant everywhere else, the man was no less dominant in the sexual act. He was the aggressor, the penetrator, the one on top, and his sexual gratification was of paramount importance, no matter how bizarrely it was achieved. Far from being a medieval or Victorian interpretation of the male role, this is still a prevalent view, not only among men but among women as well. Freedom to use his penis how and where he will is considered a measure of the man, and many men feel the necessity to prove their "masculinity" in the sexual act. If they cannot prove it with their wives—and curiously, many husbands are at their most inhibited with their wives—they look for an opportunity to do it elsewhere with a stranger, if not in actual fact then in sexual fantasy.

This man dreams of "ravaging" a beautiful, young woman, of taking her and possessing her, of being free to express himself sexually every chance he gets; and he may spend much of his life in that elusive pursuit with disastrous consequences. The man who relies solely on his penis as a means of achieving identity is, of course, in serious trouble; and most men are sensible enough to realize that having a penis and using it is not all there is to life, or to being a man. Sex for sex's sake, the urge to aggressive sexual pursuit, promiscuity, and selfish gratification may very well be part of the male makeup, but it is not the whole.

Some women, too, pursue sex for sex's sake, and for the same sort of reason—as proof of their "femininity." To be desired by many men, not only their husbands, is a mark of status, of self-importance, of identity. And it is ironic that our culture, which puts such exaggerated emphasis on all the outward signs of female sexuality—youth, beauty, breasts, legs—so severely chastises women who do something more than merely display their sexual assets. That may be the reason why many women are guilty, not of making more of sex than it should be, but of making it much less. Many have been schooled from a very early age in the necessity of purity and virginity if they are to attract a man. Taught, too, that men are "selfish beasts" and warned about the discomfort, inconvenience, and even possible boredom of the sex act, as well as the dangers of pregnancy and childbirth that can result from it, they grow to fear and avoid sex whenever possible. A woman, they also learn, must repress her own sexuality because a man might not like her to express it. Perhaps because they were denied the freedom to express themselves sexually, perhaps because they were denied or circumscribed in other means of self-expression, women swallowed, and even had a hand in cooking up, a purer version of sexual fulfillment which, for lack of a better phrase, might be called the myth of romance.

It is the fantasy of a woman who buys this particular myth to *be* possessed by a man who is so completely under her spell that he is willing to sacrifice everything for her, to protect and love and take care of her for the rest of her life. That is her identity. Thus the woman's power, the proof of her femininity, results from her passivity, not from loving but from being loved, and from being able to command while her lover obeys. The sex act has little or no importance in the romantic myth. During the forties and fifties, the formative years of the adults we have studied, the romantic book or movie always ended before the hero and heroine climbed into bed. But sex is impossible to avoid in a real-life marriage, and the woman who subscribes to the romantic myth is in for a rude awakening. She learns, however, to retain her power by bargaining with her body, and to deny her husband access to her bed for one flimsy reason or another while she dreams of a romance unsullied by sex.

Somewhere between the two extremes of sex for sex's sake and the myth of romance lies the vast but infinitely more realistic and difficult area that might be called love. Here, by today's definition men and women are on a more equal footing. With the insights of sexual psychology, the Kinsey research, and the Masters and Johnson studies, not to mention the countless volumes that have been devoted to various aspects of sex, human sexuality has become an accepted reality. But in this area, again, greater equality has been achieved at the expense of male superiority, and in some cases, the balance has tipped in favor of the female. If pursuit has become easier for the man in this era of increased sexual freedom, he is no longer allowed to get away with merely satisfying himself. He must satisfy the woman as well, and if that woman happens to be his wife, her demands for satisfaction are even more urgent, because as yet she is not permitted as much freedom. Thus the man finds himself in a double bind. He is not a "man" in his own eyes if he does not assume the dominant sexual role and gratify his own desires, but in his wife's eyes he is not a man if he cannot satisfy her as well.

Women have always had the power to accept or reject male

advances, and to gratify the egos of their husbands or lovers by real or pretended sexual excitement. Their femininity once depended on just how desirable they were to men, how often and how avidly they were pursued and propositioned. But today women consider themselves as something more than sexual objects, and rightly so. They have learned that their bodies are more sensitive to a variety of erogenous stimulation than a man's, and that they are capable of profound and prolonged orgasms the same and even different from man's. Thus the meaning of femininity has taken on a new dimension, and a woman feels she is less than a woman if she is unable or is denied the opportunity to experience her total sexuality.

Women are certainly more aggressive in the sexual pursuit than they used to be, but few would willingly give up their favored positions as objects of the chase. They make themselves available in various subtle or obvious ways; they still resort to the Eve-like role of the temptress, but now they say to the man, in essence, you must not only chase me, you must satisfy me completely if and when I allow you to catch me. She has acquired, in other words, a new and potent weapon in the battle of the sexes, even more powerful, in many ways, than the superiority that was once accorded to the male. For the man requires a woman for his gratification, too, and the burdens of chasing, catching, and satisfying her as well as the responsibilities that follow in marriage and child-raising, are sometimes more than he can handle.

It is assumed that in love and marriage, ideally, the man and the woman are seeking a completion of identity and purpose that they cannot achieve alone. But in such a union, man and woman do not, suddenly and magically, become one. Individual identity remains of vital importance, for, as the old saying goes, you only get out of marriage what you put into it. The attempt to establish and maintain that identity is often translated in marriage into a simple struggle for power or dominance. We have discussed that struggle in terms of the sexual relationship, but it also occurs in other areas of the union, particularly in money matters and in the area of decision-making.

Money, according to the Freudians, is intimately related to the psychology of the individual. It represents, in the broadest sense, control, and the way it is put to use reflects basic traits of character. Money is most often cited as a cause for divorce. If a husband and wife spend more than they earn, or if a husband is a miser and the wife a spendthrift, or vice versa, or if neither can agree about how or how much of the money they do have should be spent, there are bound to be problems. But beneath the bickering about unbalanced checkbooks, household budgets, a new car, a new fur coat, or new shoes for the baby, a much more basic struggle is taking place. It is, simply a struggle for control. In the old days when the man made most of the money and most of the important decisions, the woman could find only a vicarious identity in how much her husband earned, and how liberally and conspicuously she was permitted to spend it. But today, when women often bring in a share, they have also come to demand a greater part in deciding how it should be spent. Even if they do not earn some of the family income, they have been given, or have usurped many financial decisions, perhaps as a compensation for their dependence in other spheres, perhaps as a proof of their importance. For many men take pride in how much money they can give their wives to spend as they like. It is a roundabout way of proving their importance. Some even take pride in how much alimony they have to pay to get rid of their wives.

A daughter can also be the victim of her parents' ambivalence and lack of a secure sexual identity. While the mother may in essence seduce her son to reaffirm her femininity, so the father may seduce his daughter to demonstrate his masculinity. But more often, particularly among those men who adhere to the traditional definitions of femininity, and to the double standard that goes along with it, the father insists upon purity, passivity, and obedience in his daughter—the characteristics of a "good woman." If he is convinced of the inferiority of women, it will show up in his preference for his son and the indifference or lack of encouragement he displays in connection with his daughter's achievements. Mistrustful of his own sexual orientation and male sexuality in general, he will try to protect his daughter from it; and if he is mistrustful of and hostile to female sexuality, he will try to thwart or punish indications of it in her. The mother, of course, will encourage the behavior and values in her daughter that she considers to be properly feminine. If she has gotten everything she ever wanted by manipulating a man, that is what she will teach her daughter to do. If she is hostile to men and male sexuality, that will be passed on. And just as the father may hope to live vicariously through his son's achievements, even his sexual exploits, so the mother pushes her daughter toward the goals she has not been able to realize. For a woman this may mean a better marriage than she has, or education, career, and independence—whichever, or a combination of both, the mother feels is lacking in her own life.

The nuclear family is potentially explosive, then, particularly when the parents compel acceptance of their own narrow values and standards of sexual behavior, or when their conflicts and ambivalence result in confusion and anxiety in their children. Or when father and mother transpose their insecurity into permissiveness, their children go out into the world without any values and standards at all. No less dangerous is the family that is organized and held together by the kind of sacrifice best described in the phrase, "We are doing it for the children." Marriage may have originally evolved, in part, as an orderly and discriminate means of perpetuating the species. But if having babies and bringing them up is all there is to marriage, why bother? There are a lot of easier ways to do that, and some of today's young people, so badly stung by their experience with marriage, are experimenting with those ways.

Children are often used, however, by husband and wife to justify both the means and the ends of marriage. One wonders what happens to marriages like these when the children grow up and leave home. Many, of course, end in divorce; others continue from force of habit or because it is too late to change. But while the children are still part of the family unit, no sacrifice is too great for parents like these if it is made for the kids. The husband works long hours at a job he hates to support them. The wife spends her day cooking and cleaning and picking up after them until she thinks she will lose her mind. Their whole lives revolve around the wants and needs of their children, or what they imagine those wants and needs to be. They rarely have time for themselves, or to be themselves. If they have problems as man and woman, husband and wife, they are subordinated to their problems as parents. They try to conceal the true nature of their relationship for fear of harming the children; separations and divorces are postponed "for the children's sake." Self-denial is the keynote of such a marriage, and the first pillar to go is the identity of the parents as individuals. Neither the husband nor the wife comes first; even the quality of the marriage takes second place to its offspring.

These parents see their children as the only justification for their own existence, not as individuals in their own right; and the children, even if they are not deceived by the elaborate games played for their benefit, see their parents as little more than the means to their own gratification. Thus a child may be given power in the family setting completely out of proportion to his ability to handle it. He may play one parent off against the other, while, in turn, one or both of them may attempt to annex him as their own personal property as proof of their importance and superiority in the marriage. Or the child may be denied any power at all, so anxious are his parents to justify their sacrifices by compelling him to be and do all that they were not able to be and do themselves. The result: the identities of both parents and the child are completely submerged and all are handicapped rather than enhanced by the parasitic nature of their relationship.

The younger generation's reactions to these various parental ploys will be discussed in the following chapter. It is obvious, however, that their rebelliousness, ambivalence, their seeming sexual and social restlessness, and their fierce and single-minded pursuit of utopian ideals and values can be attributed at least in part to their own parents, just as their parents' problems can be traced to *their* parents in the generational chain reaction that promises to accelerate, continue and even intensify unless it can somehow be interrupted. Remember, the middle-class, middle-aged Americans we studied were the offspring of the generation that was the first to experience the upheaval in traditional standards of sexual behavior. They were also the first, or among the first, to experience the advantages, and disadvantages, of being the most important thing in their parents' lives. Perhaps it is not so surprising, then, that they have made their children the center of *their* lives, that they try to reinforce their identities vicariously through them, and that in their ambivalence they fall back, at least to the extent that they are able, on the definitions of sex roles that were passed on to them or that seem to promise their children the greatest freedom and fulfillment, whether or not they have realized those goals for themselves. But what have their children got to fall back on? Definitions, traditions, and sex role behavior they have seen not working for their parents, and have even less relevance, two generations later, to present-day reality?

Parents of the present generation have certainly been confronted with this lack of relevance, but in all too many cases they have attempted to maintain the illusion of adherence to traditional sex role behavior. In fact, the truth of their everyday lives is something else again. The father who refuses to wear an apron in the presence of his son, but then knuckles down to his wife in other ways, is fooling no one, least of all his son. Nor is the woman who overwhelms her children with motherly love to make up for the times that she cannot stand the sight of them, or is out of their sight working at something other than being a mother. The couple who cheat on their income tax, or on each other, and then expect their children's behavior to be above reproach, are in for a rude surprise. Similarly the couple who deaden their sense of reality with alcohol, and can find no explanation why their children do the same with drugs.

Individuals or couples are not solely guilty of perpetuating irrelevant masculine and feminine standards, for society itself has been ponderously slow to recognize the realities of contemporary sex role behavior. Are not women constantly regaled through the mass media with products and gimmicks to make them more "feminine" or somehow make them better lovers, wives, and mothers? Aren't men promised "masculinity" if they smoke a certain cigar, drive a certain car, or use a certain cologne? Are not their fantasies fed by the proliferation of pornographic novels and X-rated films? But in the most powerful and influential medium of all, television, the cracks in the mirror it pretends to hold up to "real life" are beginning to show. The daytime soap opera is, of course, aimed at the bored and lonely housewife. In it she sees herself as a brave little woman, still beautiful and desired by men even though she is pushing middle age. Her husband is a drunk or on trial for murder, her relatives and friends are out to get her, and her children are ungrateful hippies; still her magical femininity sees her through.

Soap operas have recently made pretensions to "relevance." Drug addiction, promiscuity, and abortion are now grist for their mills, but the situations they present and the solutions they offer are almost invariably slanted toward the traditional standards of "proper" sex role behavior. The subject of homosexuality, for example, has rarely, if ever, been considered.

Men identify with cowboy heroes, hard-hitting doctors, detectives, lawyers, and newspaper reporters who abound on the late evening shows, men who again reflect traditional masculine sex role behavior, even to the extent of using exaggerated violence. Most of these men have no wives, but they enjoy the undying and unquestioning devotion of dance-hall hostesses, nurses, and secretaries. If they do have wives, they are almost invariably passive, obedient, and understanding, or as an alternative "kooky" and endearingly "feminine."

It is in the early evening domestic situation comedies, designed for "family viewing," however, that male and female roles emerge as nothing short of parody. The families on most of these shows are strangely truncated; bachelor or wifeless fathers and widowed or divorced mothers abound, along with a variety of cute and precocious kids. Granted that broken homes allow for more flexible plot situations, but they do little to present realistic models of the man, woman, and child of the 1970's. Seldom are men and women pictured together in what might be considered a normal marital relationship. If they are, it is usually the man who is bested by his clever and long-suffering wife in a comedic situation, a bow perhaps to the female audience which has its fingers on the dial. At a time when real men and women are trying desperately to understand themselves and each other in a new world, television, the most powerful mass communication medium, presents almost nothing but distortion of their roles.

The social structure of many middle-class suburban neighborhoods also feeds parental unrealities. Here the emphasis is on organized play for children of various ages, certainly a commendable goal, even if it is partially designed to get the kids out from underfoot. But many parents look to Little League sports, Boy and Girl Scouts and extracurricular school activities as a welcome relief from their own responsibilities, and in the hope that their children will thereby acquire virtues and values that their elders are too busy to instill or incapable of portraying themselves at home. The parents who actually participate in these activities, instead of merely driving their children to and fro, may be trying to re-create a simple, straightforward childhood situation as much for themselves as for their children, while others may be acting out their parental fantasies, like the volunteer coach who is a father to nine or more active, able, vigorously competitive substitute sons.

The American school system itself, in many ways, is also the instrument of promoting an avoidance of parental responsibility as well as a means of perpetuating social and sexual prejudices and conflicts. Witness the battles in the North and the South, over desegregation. More to the point in our discussion here is the discrimination practiced against girls in the public and parochial schools. Statistics show that the percentage of girls who go on to higher education is greatly disproportionate to their number as well as to their academic abilities, which during adolescence may often rate higher than those of their male classmates. Obviously, they are not encouraged to go on, and the attitude of the teachers and guidance counselors who discourage them reflects parental attitudes or they would not be employed for long in the system.

Few parents would be able or willing to educate their own children even if the law permitted it. Most, in fact, are more than willing to hand them over to the school systems without a qualm. It is only when the systems, on their own initiative or at the instigation of more actively involved parents or community leaders, come up with a program that ruffles parental prejudice that they begin to speak out. The current conflict over sex education in the schools is a pertinent case in point. No one can deny that sex education is the primary responsibility of the parents; and if they were doing their proper job, it would hardly be necessary to teach it in the schools. But the fact is that most parents are as incapable of instructing their children in this sensitive subject as they are of teaching them the new math or the rudiments of grammar. They are not necessarily ignorant of the physiology of sex, although a surprising number are. It is the psychology of sex, so intimately connected with their own ambivalences and prejudices, that is the problem.

During the late 1960's with student riots in the hallways and pushers on the playgrounds, the school systems began to encounter a barrage of abuse. Some, particularly the big city monoliths, seem to be in the process of long-needed and long-delayed reform. But the parents who blame the schools for their children's misbehavior and, in fact, for all of society's ills are, again, avoiding their own share of the responsibility. Schools do not exist in a social vacuum, as the campus demonstrations of the ninteen sixties so dramatically proved. Neither does the family unit, as isolated and fragmented as it may seem to be. It is from the home that children come; it is their original environment, their point of reference in the larger social context that they must eventually reflect.

This, naturally enough, puts an enormous burden upon parents to create and maintain the sort of home environment that will enable the child, boy or girl, to emerge from it secure in the sense of his own identity and worth, both essential for survival in the larger social environment, and both equally essential for the re-creation, when the time comes, of his or her own family unit. Parents at odds with themselves and each other, insecure or ambivalent as to their sexual identity and roles, cannot hope to achieve such a goal for their children. Even under ideal circumstances child-raising is an enormously demanding task for parents of either sex, although children are perhaps more resilient and adaptable than they are generally given credit for being. They often survive in spite of, rather than because of, their parents. As they grow older, they may be fortunate enough to latch onto other more effective and relevant sexual models. But it would seem, at least from the youthful rebellions of the late 1960's, that the one thing they will not sit still for is hypocrisy, whether it comes from their parents, their teachers, or from society itself.

Hypocrisy is, in essence, an attempt to deceive oneself and others by saying one thing and thinking something else, or by pretending to feel and believe something and then acting so as to contradict it. Gloomy as it sounds, we have found that hypocrisy is a very prevalent characteristic of the many marriages we studied. The most revealing indication of this hypocrisy emerged in the personal interviews that were used to complement our written Masculine and Feminine Inventories. When the discussions turned to an evaluation of their responses to the Inventories, or when the subject of traditional vs. a more modern interpretation of relative sex role behavior in marriage came up, husbands and wives quite frankly stated that they thought their opposite members were lying. Remember, the men had stated that they were all for a woman who was both self-achieving and family-oriented; and the women had stated that they wanted a man who was primarily self-achieving but who was also family-oriented. On the Inventories and in person, however, both men and women clearly did not believe each other. And clearly their opinions were based on their own experience in marriage where actions usually speak louder than words, and where it matters little what is felt or thought if those feelings and thoughts are contradicted in word or deed.

One man explained it to us this way:

Sure she says she wants an aggressive, strong husband. She's said that to me a lot of times; she even beats the hell out of me to be more aggressive. But she never seems to realize that all the words don't mean much when she pushes in on every decision, when no sooner do I decide we should do something, and the words are hardly out of my mouth before she's questioning it, challenging it and usually we wind up reversing it. She's in on every conversation we have with everybody. I don't mean I want her building me up, although that wouldn't be so bad once in a while either, but I don't like her pushing in with her opinion every time I say something, and if she does, it would be nice if she agreed with me now and then. It makes a man feel like an ass if his wife never shows the slightest respect for his opinion; it almost seems as if my taking a side guarantees that she'll be on the other side. How does that tie in with her wanting me to be agressive, or strong, or firm? The only time she wants me firm is in bed, and even then it's only when she's ready.

A woman who decided to try going back to work told us this story:

He said, sure why not, if you can find something to keep you busy. I had no trouble doing that, for my old office was glad to take me back on a part-time basis. For a while it worked out fine, and now I realize why—for him, nothing had changed except a few more dollars were available. I was there when he left in the morning and I was there when he came home at night. The first battle came when we hit a hectic period at the office and he came home one night before I did. I ran in with a barbecued chicken and some potato salad and he grouched and grumped all through dinner. It had been an exhilarating day and I started to tell him about it, but first the paper and then the ball game were just too terribly important to be interrupted. That night we went to bed, I started playing around a little because I was still exhilarated and bubbly, but he just rolled over and conked out. Maybe I just got sore, or maybe we really got busier in the office, but we started having nights like that more and more, until we had a big blowup over it. That's when he said he thought he had a *wife*; if he just wanted a room-mate, he didn't have to get married. So I quit the job, and now he tells you he wants a woman who can express herself, and create, and be active ... maybe he does, but not on his time.

If these stories are typical—and we have discovered that they are—then obviously there is not only a generation gap in this country between parents and children, but there also exists a credibility and communication gap between husbands and wives. And the reason in both cases might be an inability of men and women to communicate real thoughts and feelings, to express them in words and resolve whatever conflicts arise at that point, instead of acting first and creating an even greater conflict whose resolution may be well beyond the power of mere words. Men and women who cannot communicate with each other and their children, or who are caught at hypocrisy, whether of words and actions, make a humpty-dumpty of their relationship. Once it cracks and breaks, it may take more than all the king's horses and all the king's men to put it back together again.

And we believe that the importance our respondents attached to "companionship" is the direct reflection of this absence of communication among the adults we have studied. The wife who complains that "he never talks to me" is asking for companionship not sex and not sex role satisfaction. Similarly, the husband and wife who spend their time together separated by a newspaper at breakfast and whose closest moments come when they wordlessly watch the same television program both feel an emptiness in their marriage which they don't recognize as a reflection of the lack of human interaction, the lack of companionship.

Mutually effective and gratifying patterns of communication are, we believe, the most important aspect of marriage. These may begin in bed, but they are inextricably related to every other activity of marriage as well; their importance ends only when the marriage dissolves. But because they are so vital, and so intimately connected with both the man's and the woman's concept of themselves—their identity—such patterns are difficult to develop. And when a conflict arises in sex role behavior in a marriage with poor communication, it is the most difficult to resolve. This is not to say that men and women do not argue. They do, with a vengeance, and marital arguments, within certain limits, may well be a good thing. At least they prove that the marriage is still alive. Marriage dies when no mutually gratifying resolution of sex role conflicts can be found. How much more difficult it is, then, to find that resolution when both the man and woman are insecure or ambivalent in their own sexual identities, quite apart from their sex-related roles in a marriage.

Their children pay a price for that ambivalence, and they themselves, in addition to the agonies of an unworkable relationship, pay the price of divorce. Divorce laws are becoming more liberal in many states, and the "no fault" concept is often part and parcel of this new legislation. To state it most simply, if a man and wife want a divorce, it is no longer necessary to prove that one or the other of them is at fault either for adultery, severe mental cruelty, or any of the other "causes" cited in previous legislation. It is enough merely to express the desire to separate. Under such circumstances, it is logical to suppose that the divorce rate will rise even higher in this country, if only because those who once could not afford the long and expensive procedures involved, or who did not bother with them unless they wanted to remarry, will now submit to the legal formalities. The new laws certainly have merit and have long been needed. The problem, however, is not one of ease of divorce, but the hasty assumption made by many couples that divorce will solve all their conflicts. They will no longer have to live together, it is true, but when there are children involved, or where the husband is required to support his wife whether or not he lives with her, the divorce may result in a whole new set of problems and conflicts, not the least of which are the profound psychological effects of such a move on both sexes.

But when marriage can too easily be terminated, the sexual and psychological problems that lead to divorce in the first place can never fully be understood or resolved. Husbands and wives are seldom forced to face up squarely to those shortcomings and failures in themselves or in their relationship that were the root causes of their trouble, even if the divorce was ostensibly the result of seemingly unrelated incidents. Under these circumstances, they may very well go on and make the same mistakes in a second or even a third marriage and continue the damage already done to their children.

Perhaps in discussing contemporary male-female ambivalence and sex role conflicts in marriage, we too should adopt a "no fault" point of view. It is without question difficult to fix the blame on one person or the other when such a complex relationship as a marriage blows up. But one trend has clearly emerged from our research: the long-suffering female is largely a thing of the past. Statistics show that it is often she, and at some stages in the marriage, *more* often she, who institutes proceedings for divorce. She is no longer content to ride in the backseat of the marriage or anywhere else. She is behind the wheel in an active and aggressive pursuit of her own happiness and fulfillment; that combined with her ambivalence about just how and where that fulfillment can be found is leading to a dizzy and dangerous ride for the whole family. This transformed female at his side is a threat to the male, already beset by a host of other threats and challenges to his once unchallenged control. He may be as whimsical and selfish a driver as she is when he has the wheel. But two bad drivers, instead of merely one, are even less guarantee of a safe and mutually satisfying trip. Thus the male dilemma appears as a male-female dilemma, for in our surveys and interviews, both men and women have demonstrated their inability to comprehend, cope with, or even communicate their sex role conflicts within themselves and in their marriage.

It is this realization that has led the radicals in the sexual revolution to advocate the overthrow of the conventional marriage. They see it as a deterrent to sexual equality and self-expression, an unnecessary concession to social respectability, even a superfluous adjunct to parenthood. But, in general, most of the critics of marriage view only one side of this multifaceted human institution, and that side usually in its worst light. Is marriage simply a means of assuring free and readily available sex, or a check on the essentially promiscuous nature of the human animal? Yes, it is both these things, but it can also encompass one of the most rewarding and fulfilling forms of human self-expression. Is it merely a means of securing the orderly disposition of property and the legitimacy of offspring? Yes, but it also serves a much wider and more important purpose; it is the cell of the social organism whose healthy function in large measure determines the health of society itself. Further, it is by no means the static human state that it is often made out to be. One has only to look around at one's contemporaries to see that any marriage is as variable as its partners; one has only to look backward to the marriages of one's parents and grandparents to realize that marriage reflects not only the personalities of its partners but also the temper of the times; one has only to look forward to the "arrangements" of the younger generation to understand that even without legal sanctions and religious rituals a marriage can still exist. If, in fact, there were a single word that could describe this particular condition in its multiplicity of functions and forms, that word would be *flexible*.

For this reason alone, there is little cause to fear that marriage is a dying institution. Changing yes, as it has always changed, to encompass the changing physical and psychological needs of its participants and the changing demands of the society in which they live; and with that kind of change, its continuing good health would seem to be assured. It is pointless to argue whether marriage is mankind's "natural" state or whether it has been imposed upon us by social considerations: the point is that it can work and that, in some form, it seems to be necessary.

There have always been alternatives, among them free love and communal or even homosexual relationships, all of which have been with us in various guises for many centuries. But in general, each of them exploits only one or two of the many aspects of conventional marriage to the exclusion of its widest potential; and while they may offer satisfactory solutions to some, only the monogamous heterosexual marriage contains within its flexible boundaries the means to achieve the fullest range of human expression and communication on the physical, social and psychological levels.

The literature on marriage, from anthropological investigations to how-to manuals, is voluminous; marriage—and divorce —are big business; for some it is a full-time career, for others a part-time hobby; it can begin in clouds of love on a park bench, and end in clouds of hate in front of a judge's bench. But wherever it begins and ends, whatever happens in between, marriage is, first and foremost, a commitment. Probably because that commitment is so often made impetuously, or for the wrong reasons, because it is so difficult to keep even if it is made for the right reasons, a vast body of do's and don'ts, musts and must nots, have grown up around marriage; and these along with the social attitudes and legal sanctions that penalize those who fail in their commitment have made marriage either a romantic dream impossible for anyone to achieve, or a frustrating and costly nightmare. Fortunately, the present-day trend is toward a simplification of this age-old commitment. The rituals and restrictions surrounding marriage are in the process of loosening up. And that is all to the good; perhaps we can at least begin to see just what the nature and extent of that commitment should be, and how it can be kept.

It is important, first of all, to view marriage in its widest functional context. Whatever form a relationship between two people may take, it must offer both the freedom and the opportunity to seek constructive and fulfilling avenues of self-expression on all three levels of being. Marriage, then, is an extension of the individual human personality, for it offers means of self-expression, sexually, socially and psychologically, that would be impossible any other way. Yet, at the same time, it is an individual restriction, for the needs of both partners must be considered of equal importance, and neither can behave in ways that are detrimental to the full function of the other, or to the full function of their shared relationship. The commitment resides in the willingness to explore these avenues of self-expression together with another person, sharing those that cannot be achieved separately, and supporting each other in those that can. If that commitment is genuine, if it is deeply felt and actively expressed, then the marriage will work. It will be not a denial of self, but a sharing and strengthening of self.

Stating it this way may seem a vast oversimplification of a very complex relationship, but if a marriage is not built around this essential core, it will surely crumble or become an unsatisfactory compromise. Few marriages, in fact, begin with this kind of commitment, for it requires a maturity and a knowledge of one's self and one's partner that take time to achieve; but if the marriage does not permit its partners to grow toward maturity and achieve the security that comes from that kind of knowledge, a full commitment to it can never be made. Even a genuine commitment will be severely tested during the changing course of a relationship, although the willingness to make it, and to try to keep it, mark a significant milestone in personal growth. But it is only a milestone, not the end of the race, and if the relationship inhibits further growth, or if it is not flexible enough to withstand the inevitable tests, a continuing commitment to it will be virtually impossible.

It is a cliché to say that every marriage is unique, yet it is surprising how many couples approach it with fixed expectations of what it will be like, and how their partner will behave——expectations that can only be based on the assumption that marriage is an end, not a beginning, and the person who says "I do" will be exactly the same person ten, five or even one year later. Marriage is not just the conventional way of growing old together, it is one more step in the complex process of growing up. With growth, change is inevitable, not only in the physical or economic circumstances of the marriage, but also in the personalities of its partners. This does not mean, however, that there can be no certainties in marriage, and that a couple has "to play it by ear" day by day in their relationship. A commitment to marriage is a commitment to the future, a means of giving some order and purpose to the chaos of everyday experience, a relationship in which both partners can depend upon each other and find something more than monetary security in the shared rewards of working toward a common goal.

Marriage, then, seems to be a collection of opposites. It is both an extension and a restriction; it must allow for individual growth and change, but within a framework of shared and mutually gratifying experience. It is a paradoxical combination of freedom and dependence, each made possible only because the other also exists. How could anyone hope to make a lasting commitment to such an arrangement? The marriage manuals usually claim that love is the magic ingredient that somehow makes it all work, but realistically, the love that precedes marriage is a pale shadow of the love that grows and matures as a marriage and its partners grow and mature. A psychologist might claim that a secure sense of self, a strong individual identity, is necessary for that kind of commitment, but again realistically, very few men and women, particularly those who marry young, have achieved that desirable goal. In fact, it is more often marriage itself that can, and should, enable them to achieve it. All of the other motivations so often cited for making a marital commitment—sex, security, social acceptance, the desire to have and raise children—are also only a part of the picture. Marriage cannot guarantee satisfaction of any of these needs. It can only offer the opportunity to fulfill them.

However it happened, women are generally accorded the lion's share of buying power in this country. Advertising and commercials are geared to them in the belief that they can persuade their husbands, one way or another, to come up with the necessary cash. If this is in fact true, then today's women have another important weapon to add to their arsenal; they can call not only the sex shots, they call the money shots as well. And this power can also be abused. The woman who requires the newest, the biggest, and the most expensive "whatever" for her security "as a woman" is no less misguided than the man who thinks the size of his bankroll is proof of his manliness. It works the other way, too, when a woman equates a man's earning power with his masculinity, and a man equates a woman's femininity with her ability, usually not to waste his money, but to spend it wisely. What happens, then, in a marriage where both husband and wife are preoccupied with money and all its sexual, psychological, and social implications?

The battle of the buck in the contemporary marriage is a difficult and complex one. Ideally, the decisions about how money is spent should be mutual, particularly when there is not very much of it, regardless of who made it in the first place. But because money is power, and power is necessary to reinforce an insecure sense of identity, the battle rages on. Do women really have a disproportionate share of that spending power? Perhaps in the field of consumer buying they do, but paradoxically, the products that are manufactured, advertised, and sold to them pay the salaries of men. The ad man who handles a home appliance account has no right to complain if his wife wants a new washing machine every year or so.

When it comes to the management of money in the overall economy, however, women have scarcely any power at all. The boardrooms and executive suites of American industries, banks, insurance companies, and brokerage houses are almost exclusively filled with men. And in the government, the biggest spender of them all, women are equally underrepresented. Much is made of the personal fortunes, usually inherited, of a small number of women in this country; but while they may own a considerable sum and spend some of it, they seldom manage it. Traditionally, women are supposed to be scatterbrained about money, but one wonders if that, too, is not another "speciality" syndrome, perpetrated by men and adopted by women to rationalize their economic dependence. Perhaps women would be less scatterbrained about money, less avid buyers and spenders, if and when they no longer felt it necessary to reinforce their identities in that way. Both sexes, however, are guilty of using money, just as they use sex, to gain the upper hand in marriage.

The corollary to spending power is, of course, earning power. And here again women are at a disadvantage, as a quick survey of income statistics shows. In our materialistic culture, where both husband and wife often feel compelled to demonstrate and display their affluence, earning power has become a mark not only of the value of work but also of the worth of the individual. And presto, the lid opens on a Pandora's box of new potential conflicts between husband and wife. To keep up with the Joneses, the wife finds that she must also work. And if she does work, why should not her efforts be rewarded on a scale comparable to the man's? Add to this the fact that work in this country has always been considered a human virtue, and more recently, in the view of the psychologists, a human essential. Thus the problems that result when both the husband and the wife work become tangled up not only with money and the control of it, but also with the whole question of individual identity and who comes first in the marriage. The husband has for years demanded special consideration at home because he is the one who goes out and wrestles with the world. Now that so many women are also doing it, they want equal treatment in the working world and some special considerations at home, too.

The distinctions that once divided the occupational world into "man's work" and "woman's work" are in the process of disappearing. Want ads in newspapers no longer specify which sex is wanted, although the nature of the job and the salary offered are telling clues. In theory, there is no reason why any job should automatically bolster a sexual identity. Again in theory, it is human identity that both men and women seek in useful and creative work. But in fact, it is far easier for a woman to aspire to "man's work" than it is for a man to settle for "woman's work." Nowhere is this better illustrated than in the area of housework, which was, and still often is, considered solely the province of women. For decades, housewives have been told that their work is useful, essential, creative, fulfilling; they are nothing short of "domestic engineers." But if this were indeed the case, why then, as the new feminists have pointed out, are men so dead set against doing it?

The time has already come in many marriages when the husband has to help around the house whether he likes it or not, even to washing dishes, cooking, and doing the laundry, in addition to those "masculine" jobs like mowing the lawn and putting up the screens. Because housework is so laden with feminine connotations, many men feel emasculated doing it; and for the same reason many women feel degraded when it is automatically assumed that they *must* do it, simply because they are women. Someone must do it, however, and if both husband and wife have demanding jobs outside the home, it would seem logical that they share in household responsibilities.

It seldom turns out to be as logical, or as easy, as that, once again because both men and women find themselves in a situation which has no counterpart in their early experience and expectations, and because work outside and inside the home is still tied to traditional definitions of masculinity and femininity. Hence the conflicts that arise are yet another example of the struggle within marriage for dominance and control. Who should cook the supper if the husband gets home from work before his wife? Who should do the dishes if the wife has to study for an exam? How should weekend chores be divided when both husband and wife are free? These and a thousand other variations on the same theme crop up daily in many contemporary marriages. And their resolution does not depend solely on who is making the most money. If the wife happens to be the principal breadwinner, should the husband do all the domestic chores? He may very well expect her to do them if he brings home more money. And if it is either economically or psychologically essential for the wife to work, why should she be burdened with a double load? In the end it all boils down, again, to the question of who comes first in the marriage, the husband or the wife. Formerly it was always the husband. But today?

It is in the nature of marriage that few husbands and wives, however selfish, can think only of themselves without regard to the wants and needs of their partners. A wife may defer to her husband if both of them feel that it is necessary to his sense of identity which, in turn, is essential to the health of the marriage. It works the other way, too, of course. But most marital conflicts are not D-Day confrontations where the battle can be won or lost in a single show of superior strength or by a single strategic decision. They are smaller power plays and involve continual small decisions and compromises that can, nevertheless, add up to a satisfying victory or a disastrous defeat. And nothing complicates such conflicts more than the presence of children, for the husband and wife who become a father and a mother no longer have the luxury of thinking only of themselves or even of what they may have as a couple. They must also think of the children and what they all have together, not only as individuals, but as a family.

Fatherhood and motherhood are roles heavily laden with sexual connotations. And in a culture as preoccupied with children and youth as ours, it is no surprise that hundreds, perhaps even thousands, of books have been written on the subject. Most of them, even today, present a rather hard-line and traditional view of the roles of each sex in parenthood. To state it in its simplest terms, it is the woman who conceives, carries, gives birth to, and nurses the child, just as surely as it is the hen who lays and hatches the egg. That is a physical and immutable fact of life, although the hand of the new biology may one day change or modify it. But in the traditional view, it is also a psychological necessity. A woman who has not given birth is somehow incomplete as a woman, and she is uniquely equipped in mind as well as in body to do it. However, once this miraculous feat has been accomplished, and motherhood moves beyond mere biology, the woman's role becomes the subject of more varied interpretations. The traditionalists claim that she must always be there, offering love, security, physical and mental stimulation —functions she is supposedly uniquely able to perform again simply because she is a woman—and they cite human and animal research to prove it. The man, meanwhile, is presumably standing by to offer whatever help he can. But infant care is primarily "woman's work."

The more liberal interpreters of infant care say that someone should be there, but not necessarily the mother. It can be the father or even a parent substitute, a nurse or a relative. As the child grows and his desires and needs become more complex, so do parental roles and responsibilities; but again, in the traditionalist's view these responsibilities fall largely on the woman's shoulders, not only because she is better equipped to handle them, but because she is usually the only one who is available. It is her job, quite apart from feeding, teaching, disciplining, and loving the child, to present an "appropriate feminine image." The man, of course, must also present an appropriate masculine image, along with whatever child-care charges he is willing to assume when he is available. The liberals, naturally enough, do not make such a rigid distinction between the sexes when it comes to the chores, but they too put great emphasis on the presentation of appropriate male and female images and, concomitantly, a model of an effective heterosexual relationship.

Here, without going any further into the complicated and often contradictory theories of child-raising, is an area of enormous potential conflict and confusion. The well-known perils of the ever-present mom and the never-present dad are part of it, but even more to the point is the question of just what are appropriate male and female images. Sexual imprintation is, of course, essential in child development, and the primary and most important means by which it is accomplished is through the parents of the child. But how can a father, insecure or ambivalent about his own sexual identity, hope to be, consciously or unconsciously, an effective male model for a child of either sex? And how can a mother similarly insecure and ambivalent convey the appropriate female image? And finally, how can a marriage floundering over sex role conflicts offer an effective model for any child?

The term "nuclear family" as it is used by sociologists and psychologists today carries with it almost the same explosive connotation as the term nuclear weapon. The typical American family in city or suburb lives as a small, isolated, though far from self-sufficient, unit. The child, during the crucial formative years before he goes to school, can look only to his mother and father as adult models, and it seems from all appearances that they have nothing more on their minds than his comfort and convenience. For the moment at least, *he* comes first. He quickly learns to use, and often abuse, his power as the main attraction; and because he is so important in the family hierarchy, he may become, willingly or unwillingly, a weapon in his parents' struggle for the upper hand in the marriage. Hence the husband who predicts a dire future for his offspring if he is displeased with the way his wife performs her domestic duties. And the wife who makes equally dire predictions if she resents the time her husband spends away from home. The child, even under the happiest of circumstances, becomes an extension of his parents' egos, and under unhappy circumstances, whatever unresolved conflicts the parents may have within themselves or together are acted out on or through the child.

With such conflicts, a man often falls back on the traditional definitions of masculinity, for himself and his son, that pertained in his own family situation. Or he may want his children, particularly his son, to have all the things that he did not have as a child, thus trying to re-create and relive the ideal of his own childhood situation. And it goes without saying that every father wants his child to do him credit, even though there may come a time when he keenly resents the child's accomplishments and readiness and ability to be on his own. But most of all he wants his son to be a "man," and his standards of masculinity may be very old-fashioned and rigid indeed, particularly if he feels his own manhood has somehow been compromised. Thus the standards of masculine behavior and all the values that go with it may be completely unrealistic and unattainable for the child from the very beginning. The methods by which these standards are transmitted from father to son are, of course, as various as the fathers and sons themselves. The father who encourages, even drives his son in sports and gives or withholds his love as a reward or a punishment is perhaps the most familiar. His attitudes toward work, money, ambition, intellectual achievement, and women, to name only a few, are also transmitted in various direct or indirect ways, and the effects upon the child are permanent, whether he ultimately accepts or rebels against them.

Society itself, the men and women who compose it, are the cause and effect of man's feeling about himself as male and about his masculine behavior. What a man feels about his job, the satisfactions and dissatisfactions he is obtaining from it, spill over into his feelings and attitude toward his wife and family. If the man feels dehumanized at his job, not only do his negative reactions invade his private emotional feelings but they do so on a wide scale. "They are the costs of such job related pathologies as political alienation, violent aggression against others, alcoholism and drug abuse, mental depression, and an assortment of physical illnesses, inadequate performance in school and a larger number of welfare families than there used to be."[2]

A mother is often no less responsible than a father in molding her son into what she thinks a man should be, and her view of masculinity may be even more unrealistic than the father's. It is shaped by her relationship with her husband, her own father, and the other adult males in her life, and of course by her view of her own femininity. Uncertain of that, she may demand an excessive degree of love and duty from her son to reaffirm it. Or if she has suffered, in fact or in her imagination, at the hands of the men in her life, she may do her utmost to prevent her son from growing up and becoming one. If she happens to share her husband's standards of masculine behavior, or defers to them, she, too, may encourage him to be a "little man" even to dressing him as a diminutive carbon copy of his daddy. Again the variations are infinite and the effects upon the child permanent.

NOTES

1. A. Rappaport, D. Payne, and A. Steinmann, "Perceptual Differences Between Married and Single College Women for the Concepts of Self, Ideal Woman, and Man's Ideal Woman, *Journal of Marriage and the Family*. Vol. XXXII, No. 3 (Aug., 1970).

2. "Conflicting Theories on Efficient Work: Repetition vs. Satisfaction" and "HEW Study Finds Job Discontent Is Hurting Nation," *The New York Times*, Friday, Dec. 22, 1972, pages 1 and 14.

CHAPTER 7

The Children of Ambivalence

What happened to the children who grew up in families where the mother found herself in conflict between her image of herself as a person in her own right and the traditional roles as wife and mother? What was the impact of having a father who was torn between his traditional male roles, with their freedom, power and status, and the increasing restrictions of his job and family responsibilities? How were the children affected by parents whose ambivalence and sex role conflicts resulted in a struggle for dominance and control in the marriage? And how were these conflicts aggravated in parents and children alike by dehumanizing social pressures and the gradual disintegration of the once-rigid distinctions between the sexes, as well as many other traditional standards and beliefs? These conflicts within and between their parents, and between their parents and the changing social structure, have made the generation between sixteen and twenty-five the children of ambivalence. Whatever else they have been given, today's young people have been left a legacy of these same conflicts which, perhaps predictably, they express in their own personalities and behavior.

No previous generation has been more visible or more vocal, more studied and written about, more publicized and promoted, more praised or blamed. As a result of this, the younger generation, and the attitudes and behavior that seem to characterize it, are very much a part of the American scene. Youth no longer exists in enforced or privileged isolation from the rest of society. In the 1960's they burst the bonds of parental, educational, and social authority that once held their natural exuberance in check—or those authorities gradually surrendered to them—and that exuberance had widespread and profound repercussions. On perhaps the most superficial level, adolescent styles of hair and dress were adopted even by middle-aged adults, and many of the phenomena of our so-called pop culture—its music, dance, writing and films—originated with youth, or with adults who either found it a refreshing change or an opportunity to capitalize on the profitable youth market.

On a deeper and more significant level, it was young people who led the way in the social and ideological upheavals of the 1960's, starting with the civil rights and peace movements, and more recently the ecology crusade. True, they may have derived their ideas from the intellectual writers, teachers, and political leaders among the liberal adult population, but it was their marches and demonstrations, their insistent calling of attention to themselves and their causes, that convinced an increasingly larger segment of the adult population that they might have a point there after all. In short, we saw in the 1960's a curious reversal of the usual generational progression. The young began to lead the old.[1] In fact as the nineteen sixties moved along, it would have been easy for an observer of the American scene to conclude that the young were coming to early power. They dominated the campaign of Eugene McCarthy for the Democratic nomination for President in 1968, achieved the vote for 18 year olds in 1971, and again played a pivotal political role as George McGovern gained the Democratic nomination for President in 1972.

But shortly thereafter the observer would have been puzzled, for the votes of 18 year olds had little consistent impact in either local or national elections in 1972, and the wave of youthful activism subsided so suddenly and dramatically that in the spring of 1973, the New York Times[2] ran a front page story on how ". . . political activism is moribund at colleges and Universities in New York, New Jersey and Connecticut, and students have taken on the superficial appearance of their self-centered, socially indifferent, All-American campus counterparts of the nineteen fifties."

And so, as a generation, their overall activism too had this ambivalent dimension of intense activity and sudden quiet. How did they become so loud and so active, and why did they quiet down so fast?

One can find, of course, every pattern and shade of behavior among the younger generation, from the conservative to the radical to the indifferent, but clearly the young generation who reached adolescence during the 1960's, was unique in several important respects. First, the world they live in and will one day inherit is quite different from that of the previous generation; their world is one that suddenly seems rife with political, economic, and social evils—war, poverty, pollution, injustice, hypocrisy, dehumanization, alienation, and the ever-present threat of nuclear annihilation. And second, young people have reacted, and may continue to react, to that world, with its evils and its virtues, in a way that would have been impossible for their parents, simply because they have been shaped by a vastly different spectrum of family and social forces. Young people today have, for better or worse, an awareness of self and a concern for life and the quality of life that are quite new in recent decades. Such awareness and concern are, of course, hardly new in philosophy, ethics, religion, or even psychology. They did not suddenly spring full-blown into the consciousness of today's youth. By an irony that is yet to be understood by the older generation, it was the freedom they gave their offspring, the education they provided, and the example of their own lives that were responsible for the awareness, concern, as well as the confusion of their young.

Another aspect of this generation which is unique, is that they are in the curious position of having some influence—more influence now than ever before—but no real power. Perhaps because of this, and perhaps because of their youth, they have reacted in the extreme, and not always a consistent extreme. They rallied around the charismatic political figures who courted their favor, but displayed a surprising indifference to the legislation that enabled eighteen-year-olds to vote. While decrying conformity and the mass mind, they flocked to rock festivals by the thousands, all looking and behaving pretty much alike. They also flocked to colleges in unprecedented numbers, and fought to open the doors of these colleges to the underprivileged and disadvantaged. But at the same time they seized, even invented, opportunities to disrupt these institutions and threaten their viability as educational bodies. The young chose peace as their most important objective; yet among them were groups who resorted to violent destruction of a kind and on a scale not seen since the

anarchistic bomb throwing of the 1920's. They responded enthusiastically to calls from the Peace Corps to help underde-
veloped nations, but they ignored service occupations at home
such as teaching, social work, nursing, and medicine. As one
educator noted, "I can recruit teachers for East Africa but not for
East Harlem."

In response to this youthful inconsistency and extremism, the
older generation was troubled by the symbolic behavior of the
young, their attempts to tease or shock adult society. In attacking
gargantuan social institutions without, in most cases, realistic
alternatives to offer, or the power to effect them even if they had,
they behaved like underdogs everywhere; they nipped and ran.
To mock the law and the government, they heckled elected officials and the police, symbols of those institutions. They taunted
the military by defiling the flag and burning their draft cards,
more symbols. They dressed symbolically and chose as their
cultural heroes young men and women who flaunted convention
and, somehow, made it pay. Their life-style itself could be said to
be symbolic, at least among those who went all the way in their
defiance of convention and authority. They mocked the clean-cut
American ideal with long hair, unkempt beards, and outrageous
costumes. They reversed the usual standards of cleanliness and
order; their concern was for the environment, not always for
themselves. They rejected the Protestant work ethic, economic
materialism, and even capitalism itself. Their answer to the suburban dream house was the hippie pad.

And studying those who chose such life-styles reveals another
important difference within this generation; the fact, often
pointed out, that the majority of these young individualists were
the offspring of the white middle class, with parents of more than
moderate intelligence, ability, and means, men and women, in
fact, who correspond in almost every respect with the bulk of our
survey subjects. It has also been pointed out that among the
well-heeled, white, middle-class rebels, as well as among the
youthful troublemakers from less advantaged social and ethnic
groups, it was the "bright ones," young men and women of above
average intelligence, who were the organizers and ringleaders.
We had then a very curious paradox, a shift in values which made
this generation unique.

Formerly, it was the smart ones from good families, good

neighborhoods, and good schools who were the most eagerly sought and the most readily absorbed by the system. They went into business, law, the professions, and sometimes even politics, without a murmur of complaint. Their sole concern about the system was how it could be made to work for them. The complaints came from those who may have been no less smart, but who were certainly less privileged. Their complaints, however, were chiefly concerned with those aspects of the system that made it difficult for them to fit in. In any case, their criticisms were usually temperate and their rebellion dwindled when, with some luck and a lot of hard work, they finally found their niche. But now, ambivalent about the system and its values, both privileged and less privileged rejected and rebeled.

However, the most significant aspect in which this generation was and *is* unique, lies in the willingness of the nondeviant majority to hospitably accept, empathize with, and defend the deviant subgroups. There is a generational empathy that leads young people to identify with *any* member of their own age group against any representative of the authority of their elders. And those who fail to identify, decline to oppose, for there has been no activist opposition *within* the adolescent generation to counter any of the deviant subgroups. In fact, in the late 1960's, one basic aspect of the problem of maintaining order in both secondary school and college was the inability to mobilize the nonviolent, nondemonstrating student majority to exert any counterbalance in support of order. They may not have supported a strike, and most certainly did not support bombing a laboratory, but their generational empathy was too strong for them to take action, or even to speak out against those who were striking and bombing.

Similarly, those who do not use drugs can "understand" those who do. And those still living at home within behavioral standards the staunchest Victorian would consider "proper" can defend their male and female friends living together in homosexual or heterosexual groups. Those who are politically disinterested or even traditionally patriotic can often accept the fact that their peers demonstrate, parade, and deride the patriotic symbols and practices that they themselves engage in.

And this mass acceptance of deviation of even the most extreme or flagrant sort we believe expresses this generation's basic ambivalence. While individuals have values and belief systems, the majority of adolescents seem to be so unsure of the true significance of any value or system of values, or so unclear as to the possibility of generalizing any one social system or social behavior, that they can understand and accept even those who most completely reject those values and behaviors. Nothing at the value and practice level seems, to the normal majority, to be so right, so worth defending, that they will actively organize to develop a counterforce against their peers who attack the given values and practices. And this we maintain, makes them a unique generation, uniquely ambivalent as a group.

Much has been written in recent years of the "crisis of identity" of the American adolescent, from Erik Erikson's very specific psychosexual theories to the blanket explanations offered by some commentators for all our social and psychological ailments. If identity is what it is all about, then here again today's younger generation is unique, for the adolescent quest for identity is, at one and the same time, much easier and much more difficult than it has ever been before. Easier because today there are many more acceptable alternatives to choose from in every sphere of personal and social expression. Many of the old distinctions of class, color, and even sex, no longer restrict the opportunity for choice. Even within those distinctions that still exist to some degree, there are greater opportunities and freedoms. But apart from the physical and psychological facts of life that contribute to personal identity, there are the social values, standards and judgments that determine its dimension. And these, too, at least those moral concepts once reinforced by the authority of the family, the church, government and the law, and the subtle pressures of society itself have begun to lose some of their former certainty. Hence the increasing difficulty for a young person, boy or girl, to discover just who he is and where he would like to go. The greater the choice, the greater the possibility of making the wrong one. The fewer the "givens," the greater the temptation merely to take.

In their search for identity, many young people today, in our opinion, simply do not know where to look. Putting together symbolic bits and pieces of several identities, like assembling a hippie costume, does not necessarily mean you have found an identity of your own. "Doing your own thing," whatever that thing may be, can just as easily be a cop-out as a legitimate and

creative means of self-expression. Defying conventional authority in favor of peer group acceptance can be a dangerous business,
especially if your peers are as uncertain of their identity as you
are. Substituting a pastiche of bizarre or occult beliefs from other
religious, political, or social systems in place of traditional values
of your own can be just another cop-out. Nor can identity be
found by dropping out. In their search, many young people today
find themselves in a dilemma no less perplexing than the dilemmas faced by their elders. That they may have new freedom, and
new self and social awareness, merely compounds the problem,
for they have inherited a staggering load of the old hang-ups.
They, too, are torn between fantasy and fact, expectation and
reality. They, too, exhibit the characteristics of confusion and
conflict in their sexual and social behavior. They are the unlucky
heirs of their parents', and of society's, ambivalence.

If this generation was in any sense "created," it was not only
by the mass media and the entrepreneurs of the mass youth
market, but also by the peculiar mass psychology that pervaded
the postwar years. It was a time of plenty and leisure, a time when
the child-oriented nuclear family, which had begun to emerge
before the war, came into full flower. Consider the situation of a
typical family of the urban or suburban middle class. The man
and the woman, in many cases barely out of their teens, met and
married; their first concern was usually to start building a nest
all their own, preferably at some distance from other members of
their families. When that nest began to fill up and when their
income permitted it, they moved and, if necessary, moved again.
Mobility was a hallmark of the postwar decades, characterized
by a willingness to pull up stakes and plant them again wherever
social or financial necessity decreed. The usual progression was
from an urban to a suburban environment, but whatever the
progression, the result was a kind of rootless isolation. Apartments and houses changed along with their contents; neighbors
and neighborhoods were in a continual state of flux. The only still
point in that turning world was the family itself, wherever it
happened to be. And it was on the family that parental concern
was almost exclusively centered.

For the father this meant earning the money necessary to
support the family, and because he usually chose to live at some
distance from his work, another consequence of mobility, he was

often absent from home most of the working hours and sometimes for days at a time. It was on the mother's shoulders, then,
that the bulk of the family-centered preoccupations fell; and in
many cases, she had to serve as both mother and father.

The young mother of the nineteen fifties, furthermore, found
herself in a rather peculiar position. First of all, there was her
isolation from the rest of the world. It was an era when women
were encouraged to give up their education and all but the most
innocuous interests outside the home, and devote themselves
fulltime to the essential job of keeping the house clean and bringing up the kids. It was a difficult job, surely, but with affluence,
leisure, few other interests, and the social nod of approval that
meant status, she took it on diligently and enthusiastically. In
fact, motherhood became her "career," the only one that was
considered appropriate for a woman, and she looked to it to
provide the ultimate in "feminine" fulfillment. And just as engineering technology gave her a hand with the washers, dryers,
and vacuum cleaners to help with the housework, so did child
psychologists and educational theorists stand ready to help with
the children.

Child-rearing changed in this era from the rather casual
"learn by-doing" approach of previous generations to a rigid
step-by-step procedure. The old maxim that "a child should be
seen and not heard" was transformed into the belief that he
should be both seen and heard, and continually watched. Growth
gave way to "development," discipline to "self-expression." It
was perhaps a predictable change, for many adults had become
preoccupied with personal, sexual, and social psychology in their
own lives. Why not in their children's lives as well? If, as the
psychologists maintained, the first years of infancy and childhood are absolutely crucial in later development, what intelligent parent could ignore them without the fear of causing some
permanent damage, or the feeling of guilt for somehow having
failed the child.

The business of child-watching was both propagated and
given an undeniable air of authority by the widespread publication of the books of Gesell *et al.* and Spock. Not only did such
books set forth the "principles" of child development, but they
also introduced the notion of normative behavior, that is, that
children should develop at a specific pace in stages predictable

enough for the mother to note when the "normal" child "should" stand and take his first steps, when he "should" first babble, how and with what he "should" by playing, and when he "should" be toilet-trained. Naturally enough, along with all these "shoulds" came a rather intense desire on the parents' part that the child "had better, or else," and, of course, a full load of anxiety if for some reason he did not.

Adding to the anxiety was the fact that, while the experts were happy to give the tables and the norms, they consistently neglected to tell the parents what to do, if indeed there was anything to be done, if development was not proceeding according to "schedule." And so, the anxious parents with the "slow" child had to ad lib. A frequent sight in these years was the slow walker going through his days swinging ahead of his mother as she clutched him under the shoulders and forced him erect, or staggering along at 45 degree angles to his mother, looking like a miniature leaning tower of Pisa held erect by one hand as he sought to return to the comfort of the ground. And the slow talker was bombarded with speech, with records, and his every gurgle was overinterpreted into sophisticated language which only his parents seemed able to understand.

Thus, children were raised by the book, and if childhood was a critical period for the child, it became if anything more critical for the parents. The mother usually had the last word. She was the one who had read the book and the one who told the father what the child "should" and "should not" be doing. The mother invested almost all of her time, energy, emotion, and intelligence in her offspring, and, while the father could not match that, she demanded more help than he was sometimes willing or able to give. The mark of the success of their combined efforts was, of course, the child. They congratulated themselves when he did well, and blamed themselves when he did poorly—perhaps rightly so. But they also competed with each other for his love, which could increase their already considerable parental power, and used him in the struggle for dominance in their marriage. In short, the child assumed an importance unique in the history of child-raising. He was the fragile receptacle of all his parents' fondest hopes and dreams.

Curiously enough, the psychological theories that pervaded both child-raising and education in this era were essentially

sound. It was in their misinterpretation or overzealous application that the trouble began. For example, Freudian theory, the
fountainhead of almost all child psychology, stated that frustration and sexual repression are most often at the root of emotional
illness. Parents bought that; they could certainly see evidence of
it in their own lives. Their children must be spared the terrible
consequences of both. And so they were not permitted to suffer
any frustration at all. Self-expression, whatever form it took, was
actively encouraged, and parents compared notes with the book
or with each other, vying to turn out the perfect product. If it was
not so perfect after all, there were a host of other authorities to
consult, ranging from the "how-to" columns of the ladies'
magazines to the hospitals and clinics that employed increasing
numbers of child-care specialists.

The unhappy result, in all too many cases, was that the parents, in attempting to become experts, and fully aware of the
dangers of failure, ceased to be authorities. Again the pendulum
had swung too far in the opposite direction, from the au-
thoritarian and often autocratic roles parents had assumed in
previous generations to the permissive and frankly fallible roles
that they now assumed. Authority in the family was all too often
represented by the child itself. It was his growth and development that were paramount, his wishes that had to be instantly
gratified, his conflicts eased and resolved. Autocracy gave way to
a kind of democracy in which both parents and child had a voice
in family decisions. Even if the child was outnumbered, he usually got his way, since one or the other of his parents gave in.

The principle may have been admirable—to give the child a
sense of his individual worth and a feeling that he was a member
of a social unit, with rights as well as responsibilities, liable for
privileges as well as punishments. But in practice, rights and
privileges far outweighed responsibilities and punishments. The
child learned how to use and manipulate his parents, and the
parents discovered that a childish tyrant is no better than an
adult one. Few were sure enough of themselves and their own
identities to risk thwarting the incipient identity of their offspring. And as that offspring began to grow up, and more was
expected of him in the way of application, obedience, and self-
discipline, what could have been more logical in his mind than to

revert to the childish behavior that had served him so well in the recent past?

Other social and psychological factors also contributed to the decline in parental authority. The authority of the church and the morality of religion had all but disappeared in the homes of the educated white middle class. If parents insisted upon some kind of church attendance for their children, they were usually socially rather than religiously inspired, and they drove their children to and from Sunday school as if it were Little League practice or a ballet lesson. Few, if any, children saw in their parents an earthly incarnation of a divine will, righteous, impartial, unchanging, and just. Nor was parental authority reinforced by community standards. The community was too large, too disparate, and constantly in a state of flux. Not many parents took an active part in community affairs. Power and responsibility were left to the faceless school boards or the politicians with some special ax to grind. Even if a parent did become involved, he soon discovered that there was little that he as an individual could do. Socially, the community, even if disparate, was rigidly structured; politically, it was at the bottom of an endless spiral of buck passing and red tape. In the long run, it was easier to live and let live, and rather than to do unto your neighbor as you would have him do unto you, to simply do as he did. Morality, in short, depended largely on who you were and how much you could get away with—standards of behavior, of course, that were not lost on children.

Finally, parental authority was also diminished by the anonymous nature of the father's job. Few children knew what their fathers did, or where or even why. It is difficult for any child to identify with a media buyer or an assistant general manager of the products division, let alone decide that is what he wants to be when he grows up. Perhaps even more difficult was deciding, based on his own immediate experience, just who his mommy and daddy were, what they did, and what the nature of their relationship might be. He was told often enough, if his parents were anxious to pass on the traditional male-female role distinctions, but he could see that they did not always apply in his household, just as he could see that many of the standards of behavior they tried to enforce seemed to be pulled out of thin air for the occasion, and were meant to apply to him and no one else.

Perhaps because of the isolation of the nuclear family, perhaps because parents felt the need to shore up their own ebbing authority, the children of the nineteen fifties were pushed at an earlier and earlier age into "socializing experiences"—peer group play when they were barely out of their baby buggies, preschool activities, nursery school and finally kindergarten, all before they even got to first grade. The nineteen fifties saw a proliferation of preschools, sometimes with the mothers themselves participating; but often the child was simply taken to the school and handed over to a paid professional. Its effects on the child were various. He was, first of all, removed from his parents, and the parental substitute was another adult who existed only to care for him, play with him, feed him, and amuse him without any other competitive responsibilities. And the standards of behavior most often enforced by this indulgent adult were based on whether or not he could get along with the other children. If he could obtain peer group approval, adult approval would follow.

The psychology behind the preschool education that flourished in the 1950's was again child-centered. The emphasis was on his progress, his participation, his wants, his needs. By contriving situations involving individual decisions and choice, or the illusion of them, the teacher led him to believe that he controlled what he did and how he did it, or even whether he did it. Disobedience and recalcitrance were not punished physically, or even by the old-fashioned techniques of isolation, deprivation, or ridicule. An effort was made to understand why. Positive behavior was rewarded; negative behavior was tolerated. Often the only standards were those established by the children themselves. Here again, they were the authorities.

All of these experiences made the child who began his formal schooling in the nineteen fifties quite different from earlier generations. At home and at nursery school, he was treated as a miniature adult, an interesting throwback to nineteenth century child-raising. He was often dressed as a pint-sized version of mommy or daddy; his social schedule was as organized and busy as their own; his birthday parties were no less carefully planned than an adult party; he "graduated" from nursery school in some instances complete with cap and gown. But for all the grown-up trappings, he was still a child, a "mature" child perhaps, due to the sophisticating effects of his social experiences, but destined to remain not much more than that due to the cumulative effects of his psychological experiences. He emerged, in all too many cases, with a sense of power and self-importance that would prove to be largely irrelevant, if not completely illusory, in later psychological and social contexts.

We wonder if this "mature" child did not pay a high price for all the attention paid to him, in the loss of joy. His parents' anxiety that he develop on schedule could easily result in making his achievements a relief from stress, rather than a joyous accomplishment. And his failures, when they occurred, were all the more anxiety-ridden to both child and parent. The emphasis on self-expression meant, in too many cases, that he was supposed to express what his parents wanted him to express. Toys had to be "creative" and "educational," but what parent could resist telling his child how to play with them, or offering his own interpretation of the results? Early socialization left much less time for the aimless, nondirected but truly creative and self-expressive activities that children have traditionally enjoyed. Whatever happened to doing nothing?

But surely the most detrimental trend was the absence of adult authority. There was no lack of parental pressures on the child to perform. Approval and love were thought to be the rewards, but the child quickly discovered they would not be withheld for long. To the parent who said, "Do it because I want you to," the child could always reply that he did not want to and usually get away with it. Few parents had the self-assurance to insist that the child do something because it was right, or simply because they told him to do it, and back it up with the necessary discipline. The lack of consistent and just standards of behavior, even if he cannot always understand the reason for them, is a joyless burden for even a "mature" child to bear.

Discussion of the forces that have shaped the younger generation's personal and social awareness would, of course, be incomplete without mention of the influence of television. If it is unique in no other way, this generation was the first to be brought up in the flickering white light of this new and pervasive medium. It began, with many, even before they were able to discern shapes and distinguish sounds. And it continued through childhood and into early adolescence. The figures compiled on the number of hours per day children of various ages watch television are truly astonishing.[3] One wonders how they have had time to do anything else. Television is a passive medium; you can watch without seeing, listen without hearing. But if you do pay attention, it prevents you from doing or thinking about anything else. Thus the time spent by this generation in front of television sets has had an undeniable effect on their development. On the plus side, it exposed them to experiences, albeit vicarious, that would have been impossible otherwise, with an immediate impact on their sensibilities that cannot be duplicated with any other form of communication. It gave the isolated nuclear family, adult and child alike, a window on the world, a kind of instant awareness.

But for the child, particularly, that awareness was largely self-centered. The commercials that were directed specifically to him as a potential consumer, or as an influence on family consumption, were part of it. But perhaps more telling was the impression that it was a diversion designed specifically for him. In spite of the millions of people looking at the same thing at the same time, television is essentially an individual experience. It does not, like the theater or the movies, require audience participation; audience reaction is provided along with the entertainment on the sound track.

For the child, this meant that he was doubtless satiated with emotional impressions long before he had the mental equipment necessary to handle them. Again he was invited to participate in an adult world before he was an adult, and the "reality" of television, which relies so heavily on extreme and dramatically heightened situations, could easily be mistaken in his mind for "real life." A reverse reaction might also be possible whereby those situations that are in fact real, like news broadcasts of some grim natural or man-made disaster, could be considered just another form of entertainment. In either case, television would have blurred the line that separates reality from fantasy, particularly for the child with no experiences of his own against which to measure the version of reality presented by the medium. At a very early age, then, he might have seen it all—and not had to think about any of it. He did not even have to bother making up his own fantasies, nor was he required to deal with them in his own behavior. Like his parents, the "electronic baby sitter" kept him continually gratified and amused on the infantile level, trying to spare him at all costs the frustration and pain of growing up.

The same can be said of the freedom he was allowed in the expressions of childhood sexuality. With some sophisticated awareness of their own sexual hang-ups, many parents knew that sexual repression was one of the most dangerous forms of frustration. Many were even knowledgeable about the special hazards of the pregenital and genital phases of child development. Oral and anal behavior, aggression, sibling rivalry, and oedipal conflict were frequent topics of conversation on playground benches and at suburban cocktail parties. The instinctual drives of childhood, it was assumed, were legitimate forms of self-expression; to thwart them was to ask for trouble later on. And hence many parents adopted overly permissive attitudes toward their children's sexual behavior. The more liberated ones permitted their children bathroom and bedroom privileges that would have been unthinkable to most parents a generation ago. They became anxious and alarmed only when the child's behavior was inappropriate to his sex. Often the line was severely drawn when it came to a little boy playing with dolls or a little girl fighting. Liberated they might be when it came to an understanding of how both "masculine" and "feminine" drives can exist side by side in children of both sexes, but few parents were happy about the prospect of raising a sissy or a tomboy.

Thus the confusion and conflict in their own sex role behavior, both as individuals and as husband and wife, were inevitably passed on to their children. To the father who saw his masculinity threatened by social and family pressures, it was important that his son grow into a "real" man. To the mother whose search for feminine fulfillment in child-raising had turned her into little more than a domestic drudge, it was important that her daughter be spared a similar fate. To those parents who viewed their marriages as a restriction rather than the realization of their hopes and dreams, even if they put on a brave show for the benefit of their children, it was important that the latter be spared the pains of that kind of frustration, too.

The subtleties of these contradictory patterns of sex role behavior must have been extremely difficult for the child to grasp. If he was being told, in essence, *not* to be like his parents, whom was he to be like? If he was permitted complete freedom in expressing his own sexuality, he was confronted with a welter of emotional experiences that, without appropriate models, he was in no way equipped to handle. If, on the other hand, patterns of sex role behavior were rigidly enforced, he was confined to standards that he could see from his own experience did not always pertain in the adult world.

The word *permissiveness* has recently come into considerable disrepute in our society. It is held responsible by some factions for every social problem from rebellious youth to pornography and crime in the streets. It has become a catchall term that can be bent to many interpretations but, unfortunately, there is not a much better one to describe the social and familial atmosphere of the 1950's and 1960's and its impact on the present younger generation.

Brought up in a climate of self and parental indulgence, but without appropriate parental models to guide their behavior, it was easy for children to think that their wants and needs were all that mattered. Their early school experiences reinforced these notions. The teacher was in most cases a woman and they would continue to be taught by women until they got to high school. Like their mothers, these teachers might lose their tempers and threaten, but they were seldom capable of carrying out their threats. In the 1950's many school systems even deprived the teacher of her ability to fail children or to suggest children should repeat a grade because of poor achievement.

This same pattern prevailed through grade school up to high school. The authority represented by the adult hierarchy of the school system became more and more impersonal, and students had no alternative but to reinforce their notions of their own importance in peer group approval, or through the continuing indulgence of their parents. In addition to humoring them at home, parents often went to bat for their children against the authority of the school in a way they seldom did a generation before. If the quality of education or the justice of treatment were the points of the argument, fine. But all too often, parents complained that the work was too hard, or felt their child should get special treatment. Schools, too, faced with that kind of pressure, as well as the pressures of large enrollments and a system that was not designed to accommodate any exception, began to relax their standards. In the child's mind, the contrast between what he was supposed to do and what he could get away with doing was clearly apparent. If he was permitted to cut corners at home, why not at school?

But with adolescence came some shocks. The first was the discovery that educational and social institutions beyond family control demanded much more of them in the way of consistent and conformist patterns of thought and behavior. Gone were tolerant teachers and the formless learn-while-you-play structure; in classes many times the size of the early grades, their harassed teachers told them what to do, when and how fast. What is more, they were graded for their efforts and were expected to compete with each other for the teacher's approval. However, in many cases the peer pattern had already been set. The students, often banded together to oppose the authority of the teacher, and to seek the preferred favor of their friends.

A second shock came with puberty and dating. Preadolescence had been traditionally considered a time of latency, where the child's sexual energies are sublimated and directed toward the process of learning and acquiring skills. But with the gradual slackening of parental authority to enforce that process, and with the new emphasis on the social activities of childhood, the period of preadolescence was considerably foreshortened. Children had been encouraged, remember, to express themselves both sexually and socially since infancy; but suddenly, as they approached or entered adolescence, and had both the inclination and the equipment to do just that, they were told to "wait," to "take it easy." Many parents were, in fact, seriously alarmed at the speed with which their children were growing up. Did the youths fail to realize what a wonderful, carefree time childhood was? One is only young once, why not enjoy it? So adults belatedly tried to enforce the rules and standards of behavior that would prolong adolescence. The girl who had worn lipstick at ten and a bra at twelve, had dated at thirteen and been allowed to go steady at fourteen, met with considerable resistance when the possibility of intercourse occurred. If it was too late to prevent it, she was instructed in the use of contraceptives, or even underwent an abortion to avoid a forced and undesirable marriage.

As in previous generations, the boy was permitted wider latitude in his modes of sexual expression. But he, too, met resistance when he got "serious" about a girl. Forced into early maturity, boys and girls alike, now that they were in fact maturing, were treated as children. There seemed to be no clear distinction, no discernible *rite de passage* between adolescence and adulthood for either sex. Their physical readiness far outstripped their psychological readiness. Few boys and girls held jobs outside the home, except an occasional baby-sitting or lawn-mowing assignment to supplement their liberal allowances. Few even had jobs or responsibilities at home. They were provided with both money and mobility and were expected to use them wisely. If they did not, and many did not, for they had never been taught that kind of wisdom, there was always more where that came from. Parents may have thought they were giving their children freedom and the means to enjoy their carefree teens, but they were merely encouraging dependence in the hope that the young ones would not grow up quite so fast. It was a surprise to many of them when their children, far from being grateful and obedient, used that money and freedom to defy them; it was also a surprise when, after their money was used up, children came back for more.

Prolonging adolescent irresponsibility, and paying the price for it, can have, naturally enough, disastrous consequences. One of them is the very real danger that the adolescent will never grow up; another, the adolescent's temptation to test the limits of parental indulgence in increasingly extreme ways. Belatedly enforcing rigid standards of discipline and behavior can have equally disastrous results, usually in the form of outright rebellion. In either case, the adolescent is deprived of the necessity of assuming responsibility for himself. But ironically, those adolescents of the 1960's who were willing and able to do just that, found themselves in an unusual situation, both in high school and later in college. They were, they discovered, effectively sealed off from the adult world by systems and institutions that, like their parents, insisted on treating them like children.

Moreover, the way they were expected to behave in high school and college had little pertinence to the way grown-ups really behaved. They were told to study, work hard, and get ahead, but they could see the dull, superficial, and futile lives of the middle class adults who had done just that. They could also see that society sometimes pays its highest rewards to the wheelers and dealers, those who are not too particular as to how they get ahead. And they could see that there were a great number of people who, no matter how hard they worked, or how they tried to wheel and deal, would never get ahead because they could not bend the system to their will.

To many young people the subject matter of the courses they took must also have seemed irrelevant. The high ideals of justice, equality, and opportunity, and nobility of patriotism and war which were the bread-and-butter fare of high school history and social studies courses, were belied daily by television reports of the battles against integration, racial strife in the ghettos and the horrors of the Vietnamese war, if not by their parents' fearful and hypocritical behavior when their own social or economic exclusivity was threatened. The ideas they were taught in college existed, like the college itself, in a vacuum. Further, many of those who taught them seemed to prefer it that way. There were, as always, incompetent faculty who sought the safety and protection of the institution, as well as those of undoubted ability who could not, or did not care to make the connection in their own subjects between past significance and present reality. Faculty who did express their opinions to the outside world, or who sought to lend their intelligence and skills to the concerns of society or government, were often greeted with derision and distrust, if not actually threatened for holding opinions that were unpopular in the frankly anti-intellectual climate of the fifties and sixties. Like the students, they too were treated as children, to be seen but not heard, indulged and tolerated as long as they kept their place and did not make waves in the "real" world.

Students, then were consigned to years of marking time and playing with ideas and principles that they were not allowed to put into practice. Add to this the impersonality of the college structure and the anonymous authority, the out-dated rules, of the "administration," and it must have seemed, not illogically, that the educational system was concerned exclusively with pleasing and perpetuating itself, with little concern for the individuals within it, and even less for those outside. Students who were looking for models, standards and values to guide their own behavior, for ideas and beliefs to shape their opinions and direct their actions, who were looking, in short, for a personal and social identity, looked in vain. Under the circumstances they had only three alternatives. They could drop out, as many did, convinced either of their own worthlessness or the worthlessness of the system; they could play along with the system, as many did, enjoying its privileges and avoiding responsibilities; or they could fight the system, as many did, carrying that fight from the campuses to confront the self-serving indifference, hypocrisy, and irresponsibility of their parents, of business, the professions, government, and society itself.

And for a while those who protested enjoyed some spectacular successes, closing down several colleges and universities for varied periods of time, including such major institutions as Columbia University, City College of New York and Sacramento State. In part, these successes can be attributed to the fact that many of the adult public officials and college administrators the young people encountered were the product of the same social influences as the parents we have discussed, and so they reacted with the same indulgence, with the same effort to understand, to communicate, to explain away socially inappropriate behavior. And they sought ways to satisfy the "non-negotiable demands" just as the parents had sought to satisfy and alleviate the temper tantrum.

We can speculate that one of the major social influences which led to the dying down of the demonstrations was the emergence of a new breed of administrator, typified by S. I. Hayakawa at Sacramento State, who headed an administration which would listen and talk, but which drew firm lines and set clear standards it was willing to enforce with all the measures necessary. A further contribution was a President of the United States who refused to listen, who watched football games while thousands demonstrated, and who bombed as he wished while millions protested. And a third was the discovery that social change did not occur easily, that ringing thousands of doorbells helped Eugene McCarthy gain fame but not the nomination for President, and that even when George McGovern did gain the nomination, it was a brief victory, for he soon suffered wide rejection at the polls. And perhaps more disillusioning, Eugene McCarthy proved not to be the mobilizing force around which a youth-centered new political movement could jell and mature, and with the nomination in hand, George McGovern began modifying and backing away from those very positions which had attracted the young people to him initially.

And so by 1972 the activists among American youth had a large dose of disillusionment to absorb. They had invested heavily of their time and commitments but the colleges and universities were not dramatically different. Some had given students opportunities for participation, but many more had only created structures which gave the illusion of participation, and almost all now made it clear that their willingness to tolerate disruptive activism was over. There was even less to show for their participation in the larger social setting. The war in Vietnam was over in a way, but the "peace" was a strange peace, initially seeming to be best defined by noting that only Vietnamese were now being killed, and for many months after the "peace" American bombers continued to bomb Laos and Cambodia, with little public reaction. Even the Watergate affair, which in many respects was tangible evidence to support the youthful attacks on the system and the establishment as evil and corrupt, did little to restore the fervor of the young.

We suggest that this is because as children and adolescents they had no experience with frustration, no need to fight and work for a goal over a period of time, and so they had no experience with the process of working, losing, working again and losing again only to start all over. Things came easy to children in the indulgent decades of the 50's and 60's and so when they were confronted with hard line administrators, a disinterested President, and an adult public who did not immediately accept their selection of idols, they, as a generation, had no behavior patterns or previous experiences to turn to, and they just gave up.

It is of course, much easier for the young than for their elders to challenge authority of whatever form, to wave the flags, mount the demonstrations, and ask the embarrassing questions of these institutions. They are still young enough to choose, while their elders, having made their choice years ago, have too much to lose and are stuck with the establishment. It is to the credit of the younger generation that their impatient and insistent cries of outrage, their demand that something be done about the many injustices "now," did succeed in opening many adult eyes. But now that the enthusiasm is lessened and the problems remain to be fought, the question must be asked how intelligently these young people will choose their own lifelong values? What will they be like ten to fifteen years from now? How will they live?

What kind of mothers and fathers will they make, and what will their children be like? Do they know who they are, where they belong, and where they are going?

Charles A. Reich, in his book *The Greening of America*, presented an optimistic, if somewhat romantic, view of the future of the "revolution of the new generation, a transformation that seems both necessary and inevitable, and in time may turn out to include not only youth, but the entire American people."[4] His descriptions of the almost accidental evils of technology and corporate power that have brought about our present social and psychological predicament are apt and succinct, frightening realizations of the earlier predictions of Thorstein Veblen. But in describing the heart and compelling force of that revolution, "a change of consciousness," he largely overlooks the equally powerful force of the unconscious. Ironically, the reawakened self and social awareness that are part of the new consciousness are also products of technology and corporate power which have provided the means and the leisure to cultivate such awareness. But to counteract its less attractive by-products, much more than simple awareness is necessary. As one teenager was quoted as saying, "just noticing that things are wrong doesn't give kids any moral advantage." The effective force of Reich's new consciousness depends on how it is used, and that depends upon the strength, both conscious and unconscious, of the individuals who may possess it. As Reich himself says, "The key lies in the concept of full personal responsibility."

Psychologists, of course, call it ego strength, that delicate balance between complete liberation and excessive repression of instinctual human drives, a balance upon which, according to Freud, the continuance of civilization depends. It would seem that young people today have been victims of the former in their early upbringing and education, and victims of the latter in their present encounters with the systems and institutions of society. The question may be, then, not whether civilization will continue, but whether its youth will survive. The alternatives are dropping out in a self-destructive regression to patterns of infantile behavior, or selling out in passive and equally self-destructive submission to any authority. Active, instant rebellion is a third choice, with Reich's gradual revolution yet a fourth. A bewildering selection for anyone, young or old, at a time when the best choice may very well be some workable integration of all four: exploring the new freedoms of personal, sexual, and social expression while, at the same time, submitting to and upholding those rules and standards that are both just and necessary in any social community—being actively committed to changing those standards that are neither just nor necessary, while at the same time perpetuating self-awareness and a sense of social responsibility in the next generation.

Today's adult generation had few, if any, of these choices, and it is not surprising that they watch their children vacillate with both alarm and anguish. In too many cases, they cannot even admit that the possibility of choice exists. They gave their children everything, and now expect them to be content with what they themselves had. They cannot understand why a boy who was excused from doing his homework, does not have the self-discipline necessary to stay in college, or why the girl who was encouraged to excel in college does not want to marry a nice boy, settle down, and start raising a family. They are shocked to discover that their own sexual ambivalence, and the excessive repression or the excessive permissiveness that resulted from it, has given rise to the sometimes bizarre expressions of sexuality among the young. The nuclear family has exploded, its offspring have shot off in a hundred different directions, and many parents sit unhappily amid the debris of their ruined hopes.

It is, naturally enough, a severe blow to a mother and father to have their children reject them. Parenthood was the one role in their lives, according to our survey subjects, where there was little confusion and ambivalence, particularly among the fathers. As a result, many have succumbed to an immense feeling of guilt. The whole thing is their fault: "Where did we go wrong?" The father may feel that somehow "he was not man enough," and the mother that either she spent too much time with her children, or too little. But the question that they might better ask is why did they expect, or even hope, that their children would turn out to be exact carbon copies of themselves. And if they did, would that be such a good thing after all? Young people today may well be expressing their own ideas of masculinity and femininity in their behavior, either in disillusion or rebellion against the artificial and hypocritical standards of their parents and the society of which they are a part, or in response to the new and changing standards of their own generation. After all, they were not raised as their parents were; they were not born into, and have not grown up in, the same kind of world. Their past, present, and future differ in a million ways from their parents'. Why should they not be different?

The thing that troubles most parents, however, is both the quantity and quality of those differences. They themselves went to considerable lengths to conform, at least on the surface, to the prevailing standards of dress and social conduct, to the work ethic and the norms of sexual, marital, and parental behavior. Their kids are testing, and sometimes rejecting, them all. And what are the parents to do, confronted with this kind of rebellion? Reject their kids completely and either lock them up or throw them out? Wring their hands in guilt and self-reproach? Grin and bear it, and continue to pay the bills? Or is there some other alternative?

The most frequent gratuitous advice is that parents must try to "understand" their children. But what exactly is this younger generation trying to do? Are they not, like young people of every generation before them, trying to find their own identity and a means of expressing it sexually and socially? Of course their enthusiasm, youth and inexperience often lead them into strange extremes and dead ends. But the young have always insisted on finding their own way, and making their own mistakes in the process. Perhaps the best parents can ever do is provide their children with a sense of direction and the strength to survive their mistakes. The younger generation is still, admittedly, "feeling its way," and some have made some progress—not the ones who have dropped out with drugs and promiscuous sex, nor those who express their disillusion in pointless violence. Young people like these, who represent one of the most delayed infantile temper tantrums in social history, have had their sense of self and social awareness so distorted by their upbringing that they will perhaps never be able to function at all. But there are others who are exploring new patterns of behavior and life styles in sex and parenthood without marriage, or in communal marriage and child-raising. The essential ingredient for them, as it has always been and should always be, is love, and many of them represent a long step forward toward the goal of honest, guilt-free, mutually pleasurable and nonexploitative sexual relationships. The traditional notions of male superiority and dominance, and female inferiority and dependence, no longer seem to apply. They are attempting to find expression not only for their "masculinity" and "femininity" but for their potential as complete human beings.

NOTES

1. Margaret Mead. *Culture and Commitment*. New York: Doubleday & Company, 1970.

2. "Campus Activism Fades, Style of 1950's Prevails," *New York Times*, April 23, 1973.

3. Various studies over the past decade have been consistent in finding that beginning as young as age 3 children spend 3 to 4 hours a day watching television and this average is equaled or maintained as the child grows older until he or she reaches high school where the average drops to about 2 hours a day. based on,

Sarson, Evelyn, "How T.V. Threatens Your Child," *Parents Magazine*, 47, August 1972, p. 39

Schramm, Wilbur, *et al.*, *Television in the Lives of Our Children*, Stanford, Cal., Stanford University Press, 1961

4. Charles A. Reich, *The Greening of America*, New York: Random House, 1970.

CHAPTER 8

"Why Can't a Woman Be More Like a Man?"

As *My Fair Lady* draws to a close, Henry Higgins, confused and angered by Eliza Doolittle's unpredictable behavior, asks his friend Colonel Pickering, "Why can't a woman be more like a man?" Why can't she think logically, act sensibly; why must she be so emotional? The audience knows, of course, that Eliza is in love with the professor; they sympathize with her charmingly irrational "feminine" reactions, their sympathy increased by the knowledge that Professor Higgins is far from the "masculine" paragon that he thinks himself to be. Still, both are meant to represent opposite ends of the social as well as the sexual spectrum, and this musical adaptation of George Bernard Shaw's original work, *Pygmalion*, holds out the possibility that the twain may eventually meet and live happily ever after. Shaw, a man not unlike Professor Higgins, furnished no such romantic resolution.[1] Taught everything she knows by the professor, Eliza has become too wise and strong-willed to marry the likes of him. Ironically, then, at least in the play, professor and pupil are much more alike than either of them suspects, and it is their similarities, not their differences, that will keep them apart.

Higgins' complaint in the musical version, however, is a more familiar and stereotypical statement of the differences between the sexes. He may wish wistfully for a friend and companion rather than a woman and a wife, but who, then, would fetch his slippers and find his spectacles? Colonel Pickering certainly does not perform those functions, nor does he offer the unquestioning respect and obedience that Higgins seems to require. His real feelings are more accurately revealed in another song, "Let a Woman in Your Life." In short, Higgins might be described, at least in women's liberation parlance, as a perfect example of a "male chauvinist pig." He may pay lip service to greater equality between the sexes, but what he really wants is a continuation of the old inequalities.

There are, however, an increasing number of today's men and women who are asking in complete sincerity, "Why *can't* a woman be more like a man?" Or to rephrase it, in fairness to those who do not think that being a man is such a desirable thing, "Why can't men and women be more like each other?" The fact is that in recent years men and women, like the professor and Eliza, *have* become more like each other, and this may explain why the battle of the sexes has reached a new intensity. The blurring or disappearance of many of the traditional differences have brought men and women closer together than ever before, and as they begin to rub elbows as equals in the same living space, greater friction is created between them. The few differences that still remain, once ignored or taken for granted, have assumed new significance. They are now vehemently attacked or vehemently defended depending on the side of the argument being heard. And in the ensuing smoke screen of catchwords and slogans, in the fog of emotional overreactions and misinterpretations, the real issues at stake in the battle have been largely obscured.

Clearly, men and women are different, perhaps less so than formerly; but short of some genetic anomaly or outright impersonation, the differences that remain should be as apparent to twentieth-century men and women as they were to their ancestors. These differences are, of course, the physical ones. If they were to be gradually eliminated through some means of genetic engineering, then men and women would indeed be like each other, equal and undifferentiated units in a unisex society, the utopian solution to our sexual dilemma proposed by one fringe of the women's liberation movement. It is unlikely, however, that many women or men would opt for such a "final solution," even if it were possible. The phrase *vive la différence* is certainly closer to their feelings on the matter. The trouble is that no one really is sure anymore of what *la différence* consists.

If there is an answer to Professor Higgins' hypocritical question, it lies in an understanding of the *real* differences between men and women. Our current dilemma is the unhappy price that both men and women pay in their attempts to adhere to obsolete and unrealistic standards of sexual behavior, to the old-fashioned and untenable definitions of "masculinity" and "femininity." But what are the new standards and definitions that should replace them? They too, can only be found through an understanding of the real differences between the sexes.

It is not difficult to distinguish between the male and female of the human species; it is simply a matter of physiology. But are there *psychological* differences as well? And if there are, are they a direct and inevitable result of the physical differences, or are they somehow learned or acquired in the process of growing up? These are not new questions. The relationship between physiology and psychology, between biology and behavior, has puzzled man ever since he began to inquire into the human condition. It is, in essence, the familiar nature vs. nurture, or heredity vs. environment, debate in sexual disguise. But beneath all the rhetorical trappings, it remains the single most significant issue in the battle of the sexes. Granted, men and women have far more in common than was once supposed. We are all human beings, after all, with similar human characteristics; but we are also either male or female with quite different sexual characteristics. The question is, then, can behavioral differences between men and women be explained simply on the basis of their biology? The nature adherents say yes, particularly in the case of women. Anatomy *is* destiny. The nurture adherents disagree. They do not deny that physical differences exist, but they do deny their psychological importance. Behavior is not inherited, it is acquired, and the psychological differences are the result of environmental influences.

Of the two sides in this debate, nurture has always been more popular, for it leaves room for optimism and idealism, and paves the way for the possibility of change, even progress. Environment is generally held to be the culprit when it comes to the primary motive force behind human behavior, chiefly because we cherish the notion of the equality of all men and the double vision of the essential goodness and innocence of the infant along with the essential perfectability of the adult. Heredity is a constant, environment a variable; and if perfection is, in fact, possible, it must be achieved through the manipulation of the environment, which is man-made and therefore capable of being altered by man. Even if this is a rather old-fashioned view, an artful combination of both the romanticism and rationalism of previous centuries, no one can deny its enormous importance, particularly in this country, which was founded on such beliefs, and has labored ever since to realize their fullest implications.

The most recent upsurge in this way of thinking has come with the arguments of the new feminists. They, too, bear down heavily on nurture or environment as the primary formative factor, although it may be presented in a variety of disguises—as cultural determinants, social expectations, role requirements, and the like. The gist of their arguments is that there are no natural differences between the sexes other than the obvious physical ones. All the other differences are simply the result of environmental influences. Kate Millet, one of the new feminism's most outspoken proponents, puts it this way:

> Whatever the "real" differences between the sexes may be, we are not likely to know them until the sexes are treated differently, that is, alike. Important new research not only suggests that the possibilities of innate temperamental differences seem more remote than ever, but even raises questions as to the validity and permanence of psychosexual identity. In doing so, it gives fairly concrete positive evidence of the overwhelming *cultural* character of gender . . . . [2]

The implications of this line of thought are clear: what man has done, in this case males rather than mankind, man can undo—a very comforting thought for feminists, as well as for anyone else who agitates for social reform. But even assuming this were true, carried to its logical extreme this particular recommendation might prove difficult to achieve. What if boys and girls, from the moment of birth to the moment of death, were "treated" exactly alike? In such an eventuality, just *how* would they be treated? Would they be treated like boys or like girls, or could some middle ground combining characteristics common to both be devised and adhered to? If so, what then. Would the sexes be exactly alike or equal; and if they were, would that be such a good thing? Or would they merely be *more* alike or equal with a few differences remaining? If the latter turned out to be the case, and these remaining differences proved to be to some extent psychological, rather than simply physical, what exactly are they?

Obviously such an experiment could not be carried out on human beings. And even if it were performed on several generations of chimpanzees, the results would not necessarily have human applicability. It should be said in defense of the feminists that few if any of them would insist that such an experiment is either possible or desirable. They are calling for a reevaluation and reemergence of those human characteristics that the sexes already have in common, or might have, given the proper social conditioning. Still the question must be asked: are those human traits completely independent of sexual characteristics? If the answer is no, or even a qualified yes, nurture cannot be the omnipotent motive force that it is sometimes made out to be.

Still, it is in many ways just as difficult to make an airtight case for the nature side of the nature-nurture debate. The notion that human behavior is largely determined by biology has never been a particularly popular one, and physical determinism can all too easily become little more than psychological fatalism. Yet its adherents usually consider themselves to be on safer scientific ground, because at least a few facts about the human organism can be isolated, studied, tested, and some conclusions drawn. They are not always welcome conclusions, no matter how scientifically verifiable, and there is always the possibility that later investigations will prove them wrong. We have long flattered ourselves that we are much more than mere animals, that over the centuries our human nature has gradually triumphed over our animal nature. The scientific study of man is still in its infancy, and who knows what we may yet discover about both our animal and our human qualities? Recent discoveries have, in fact, given the romanticists and the reformers more room to operate even in the physiological field. With the application of genetic engineering, it may soon be possible to improve and perfect heredity as readily as it is supposed we can alter environment.

Until the studies of both psychology, sociology, and anthropology have progressed well beyond their present limits, however, it would be unwise to come down too heavily on either nature or nurture. Perhaps the argument can be laid to rest, for the moment, in the resolution proposed by another comparatively new body of scientific investigation, the appropriately named study of humanistic biology. The work of Konrad Lorenz best illustrates this emerging discipline, with spin-offs in the books of such men as Robert Ardrey, Desmond Morris, and Lionel Tiger. They have undertaken the study of animal behavior, and from there have made sometimes cautious, and sometimes incautious, generalizations about human behavior. René Dubos sums up the implications:

> While it is obvious that man is the product of his social and cultural history, it is equally certain, on the other hand, that everything he does is conditioned by his biological attributes. The performance of each human being of each human group reflects biological necessities and propensities inherited from the evolutionary and experiential past. Human decisions create social and cultural history, but the raw materials of this edifice are derived from man's biological history.[3]

Thus, in this view, nature-nurture is not an either/or proposition, but rather a circular process. Environment is a major factor in shaping man's behavior, but his genetic endowments determine the individual responses to that environment. And to round out the circle, "In the very process of responding to environmental stimuli, each individual human being creates his physical and mental personality from the biological attributes that are shared by all men. Human societies and cultures emerged from the progressive integration of these responses."

Biology, long concerned with specific physical and evolutionary aspects of animal organisms, has now turned its attention to the whole organism and, in particular, the organism that is man. And studies of the past and present lead almost inevitably to speculations about the future. Dubos notes:

> As is well known, man has now the technical means to transform his life and himself by manipulating his environment, as well as his physiological and mental processes; soon he may even be able to alter somewhat his genetic makeup. The powers of action generated by scientific advances are so great that the classical discussion on the ideals of the good life now take on a very practical meaning.

But he warns:

> The glory of the coming age must be conceived within the framework of man's nature—of his biological limitations as well as potentialities.

There seems to be greater accord these days about the potentialities of both men and women than about their limitations, biological or otherwise. Thinking and feeling persons are in general agreement that men and women have similar human needs to grow, create, achieve, and find means of self-expression and fulfillment, and to establishing their identities in personal behavior, in work, and social and sexual relationships, and in procreation and parenthood, whatever forms they may take. But what about their limitations? Surely all of these forms of self-expression and fulfillment depend, to some degree at least, upon one's sex. How can human identity be considered apart from sexual identity? Anatomy need not necessarily be destiny, but biology is certainly a very important fact of life for both men and women.

How important is a matter that is yet to be settled. Those who argue for complete sexual equality would ignore it; those who defend the sexual status quo overemphasize it. Formerly, women were largely restricted by our culture to functional sex roles; today they are asked—and in some cases are eager—to take on roles and responsibilities that are less intimately related to their biology. As for men, they are being asked to share roles that can be performed equally well by both sexes, and to assume responsibilities in areas that were once considered strictly "feminine." In both cases, biology has not changed, merely our culture's interpretation of its relative importance. But if we adhere to the view that heredity and environment, nature and nurture, work in concert to shape the individual personality, then whatever culture may eventually decree in the matter of roles will still in some way be influenced by biology. This has always been true, and will undoubtedly be true in the distant future.

Perhaps it is a mistake to consider sex a "limitation." As our culture gradually adopts a more equitable distribution of roles between the sexes, the fact of being either a woman or a man will not automatically carry connotations of superiority or inferiority, advantage or disadvantage. Even so, men and women are not exactly alike, just as no two women or no two men are exactly alike. They may share equal human potentialities and may aspire toward the same human goals, but the means by which those potentialities are realized and those goals achieved will vary with the physiology and psychology of one's sex, just as it will vary among individuals whatever their sex.

The task at hand, then, is to discover the real differences between the sexes, and thereby arrive at new and more realistic definitions of masculinity and femininity. The task is not to blame either biology or culture for our current sexual dilemma, but to study the complex interaction between the two. To make such a vast undertaking feasible, we can follow the lead of Dr. Robert J. Stoller, who, in his book *Sex and Gender*, makes a very useful distinction between the terms in his title. He restricts the term "sex" to its biological connotations, while "gender" is taken to have psychological and cultural, rather than biological, connotations. Further, the terms "male" and "female" are used to relate specifically to sex, and the terms "masculine" and "feminine" specifically to gender. Such distinctions may facilitate discussion, but, as Stoller admits, they are not quite so easy to make in actual case histories.

> One problem that arises to complicate our work is that gender behavior, which is for the greatest part learned from birth on, plays an essential part in sexual behavior, which is markedly biological, and at times it is very difficult to separate aspects of gender and sex from a particular piece of behavior.[4]

Nevertheless, at the most rudimentary level, sex is determined, gender is learned; sex is what your body says you are, gender is what society says you should be. And these two forces combine to shape identity, or what the individual perceives himself to be.

The balance of Stoller's book is concerned with the many extraordinary variations and conflicts possible in such a situation. If there is a lesson to be learned from it, it is the folly of absolute certainty when it comes to either sex or gender. To say, even as Stoller does, "that the normal male has a preponderance of masculinity and the normal female has a preponderance of femininity"[5] is not saying much. Any number of combinations are possible, for any number of reasons, and normality, like beauty, appears to be in the eye of the beholder.

Society—or culture or nurture or whatever else it may be called—is usually no respecter of these varying combinations in the formulation and evolution of its general rules. As a beholder of sex and gender, it has postulated these rules on any number of conceptions, and often misconceptions, about men and women that may seem perfectly valid in principle, but simply do not work in practice. And once rules have been formulated and practiced for any length of time, society is often ponderously slow to change them, or even actively resists change, so that standards of sex and gender behavior that may once have had validity and purpose have become anachronisms. It is in society's favor, however, that, like the psychologists and psychiatrists who have studied the individuals within it, it is coming to recognize that there are exceptions and individual differences, that changing social circumstances demand more flexible rules, and that much broader spectrums of behavior can be included under the labels "masculine" and "feminine" and still fall within the range of normal. Differences between the genders will perhaps always remain, as will the sexual differences, but they may not be the differences upon which society has, at least up to now, based its view of appropriate masculine and feminine behavior.

Predictably, it is women who are in the vanguard in demanding revisions in these standards of behavior, not only for themselves but for men as well. And it is the men, also predictably, who resist these revisions. Perhaps that is why women so often insist upon the similarities between the sexes, while men claim it is the differences that are important. Women, after all, are attempting to escape specific sex role assignments and standards of gender behavior that are intimately related to sexual function, while men, who so far have had much greater freedom and variety in both sex and gender roles, would like to keep things as they have always been—if not for women, at least for themselves.

It may be reassuring to women, then, and somewhat alarming to men to realize that the sexes do start out as equals, at least in physiological function. If anything, women enjoy a slight edge.

> The boy and the girl up to about the age of seven are essentially the same in their endocrinologic and physiologic functioning. They produce and excrete the same amounts of estrogens and androgens, the so-called sex hormones; and their metabolic functioning is the same in relation to thyroid hormones, adrenal hormones and insulin. The functioning of the pituitary hormone is the same with perhaps one exception. Here there is a subtle endocrinologic and metabolic difference between boys and girls before birth, right on to adulthood. The girl develops faster, both physically and mentally than the boy.[6]

But even if male and female infants start out as essentially equal, any parent will testify that they quickly begin to display the characteristics of their own sex. What then determines that the male infant will become "masculine" and the female infant "feminine"? Is it the sex hormones? Apparently not. The steroid hormones, androgen, the "masculinizing" hormone, and estrogen, the "feminizing" hormone, are present to some degree in both sexes. Their secretion is determined by genetic factors, but it is largely a quantitative rather than a qualitative difference between the sexes, and as endocrinologists long ago realized, predominance of androgen does not necessarily guarantee that a man will be "masculine," any more than a predominance of estrogen guarantees that a woman will be "feminine." They may well influence the course of physiological development and function, but their influence on psychosexual development and gender behavior still remains a mystery.

That leaves the obvious physical differences between the sexes. These differences are legion—shape and size, muscular and skeletal construction, rates of respiration, and many others, all well documented in any physiology text. But the most important difference is, of course, the fact that the male child possesses a penis and the female child a vagina. Much has been written on the subject of organ awareness and its influence on psychosexual development. Freud, in fact, constructed his psychological theories largely upon this single physical difference between the sexes. Later investigators, however, have been more cautious in both their assumptions and conclusions. Working backward from effect to cause, even as Freud did, it would seem obvious even to the nonspecialist that the mere possession of a penis, or of a vagina, is no hard-and-fast guarantee that a male child will be "masculine" or a female child "feminine." Clearly, then, along with both internal physical factors, the sex hormones, and the external physical apparatus, the genitals, there must be some other influence at work.

That influence is, of course, the environment, or, to begin at the beginning, the sex role into which the infant or child is cast, usually by virtue of the physical evidence at hand, although, as Stoller points out, that evidence is not always infallible. One is forced to conclude, then that there is no primary genetic or other innate mechanism to preordain the masculinity or femininity of psychosexual differentiation. Factors of innate origin may exert influence as secondary determinants, however. The obvious example is the anatomy of the external genitalia which, in the normal course of embryonic events, is determined by bio-chemical organizer substances which, in turn, are regulated by chromosomal sex. Postnatally, the anatomy of the genitals determines the sex of assignment, the gender-specific reactions of other people to the growing child, and the proof to the child through his own body image that other people are correct.[7]

Thus if the male or female child comes into the world normally endowed, he is greeted according to the customs of that world and, eventually, responds himself to that greeting. That sex-gender-identity cycle begins at the moment of birth, and while the road ahead will present a multitude of detours and other dangers, the male child will become "masculine" and the female child "feminine." But however or whenever they reach their destinations, the experiences of the male and female child along that road are not, and could not ever be, quite the same. Even if from the moment of birth they were greeted and treated as absolutely equal, or at least alike, it would not be long before they discovered that they were not alike. Under those circumstances, if they were possible to achieve, it would be the "secondary determinants," the obvious differences in genitalia, that would prove their dissimilarity. And that is only the beginning. Other physical differences would soon become apparent as well, in shape and size, for example, and rates of growth and development. Of course, these would vary tremendously between individuals whatever their sex, as well as between the sexes themselves. The point is, however, that the male and the female child, no matter what their culture expects or demands of them, from the very first undergo quite different experiences in confirming or countering those expectations.

The body is the infant's first postnatal environment, and its exploration is one of his first concerns. The boy soon discovers that he has an appendage, the girl that she is invaginated. It may be months before they discover that stimulating their genitals can be a source of pleasure; years before they discover their excretory function and learn to control it; and perhaps even longer before they realize that everyone is not equipped as they are. By that time, naturally enough, many other environmental and cultural forces have come into play. And if, as Freud postulates, the male child comes to prize his penis and fear its loss, that is at least partially a learned response, just as is the female child's envy of the penis. This is not to say that castration fear and penis envy are not real and potent factors in sex and gender behavior. They are, and will still continue to be, as long as our culture and its spokesmen, either overtly or covertly, place such a high value on that particular organ. Nevertheless, whatever relative importance is placed on the penis and vagina, they exist first as a physical fact of life and, many psychologists feel, as an important psychological fact as well. "insofar as the body is the greatest part of its own first environment, it seems justified to stress the influence of the reactions within and to it of the developing ego."[8]

It would appear, for example, that the male has a heightened sense of organ awareness because his penis is external and visible.

The male organs are exposed and external, whereas the female organs are almost completely invaginated. This is of considerable significance, in that in the male throughout life, the genitalia may be seen and palpated . . . and this sensory appreciation through vision and palpation tends to an intensification of awareness of the organ, combining with any endrogenously aroused sensation in the organs themselves.[9]

Thus for the male child, the penis assumes considerable importance both physically and psychologically. Its physical importance is reinforced at puberty by the development of sensory receptors in that single area, while its psychological importance is continually reinforced, from childhood to maturity, by society's attitudes and expectations. The combination of these forces results in a characteristic which might be described as "external concentration," a characteristic which seems to typify male behavior in both sex and gender roles.

By contrast, the female's organ awareness appears to be much less localized and concentrated in infancy and childhood, because her genitals are internal and for the most part invisible.

> In the female infant . . . the hidden invaginated position of the major proportion of the sex organs means that the female never sees her own organs, in any way comparable to the male's, nor can she touch them to the same extent.[10] With the clitoris and even more in the case of the vagina, it is evident that the awareness of the organ on the part of the child herself lacks the degree of firmness and consolidation of the combined senses.[11]

This lack of firmness and consolidation is reinforced physically at puberty by the development of several body areas capable of erogenous stimulation, and again by society's attitudes and expectations. Paralleling the male, the combination of these forces effects a characteristic which might be described as "internal diffusion," one which seems to typify female behavior in both sex and gender roles.

Is it possible to postulate innate and immutable psychological differences between the sexes based on the simple fact of the physical differences between their genital equipment and their reactions to it? By process of elimination, that is virtually the only difference, at least in infancy, that cannot be ruled out as a cultural influence, even if its importance is only as a "secondary determinant." How important it is may be extremely difficult to pinpoint, for culture can by no means be overlooked as a factor in shaping organ awareness. But even given the high incidence of individual variation, and the complex interaction of other physical and psychological influences, the characteristics of external concentration in the male and internal diffusion in the female occur and reoccur in various guises throughout the human life cycle.

It is extremely important, of course, for both the male and female child to establish a secure sexual identity. We have become accustomed, in this post-Freudian age, to thinking of children and even infants as highly sexual beings. Even if we resist that notion, no one can deny that they are very sensual creatures. The first few months of life are devoted exclusively to the achievement of pleasure and the avoidance of pain. There is no give and take; as far as the infant is concerned it is all take, and at first even the sources of pleasure and pain are undifferentiated. But that quickly gives way to a recognition of those sources—his parents and particularly his mother—and eventually the realization that it is not a one-way proposition; he is expected to give something in return. If he is "good," the child learns, he will be rewarded, and if he is "bad" he will be punished. But more than that, the male child learns that he must be a "good boy," and the female child that she must be a "good girl." Thus patterns of appropriate gender behavior are implanted at a very early age.

Neither the boy nor the girl usually has to look very far for physical proof of their sex, but they must look to family members, chiefly the mother and father, for psychological proof and examples of the behavior appropriate to their sex. This process is quite different for the boy and the girl, and it is particularly difficult for the boy, in the typical American family at least, because the first years of his life almost completely revolve around the figure of the mother. He must, in essence, reject the mother in favor of an identification with the father who, in all too many cases, is either absent or disinterested. The problem is further compounded by the fact that most of his teachers, even up to the high school level, are women. He is most often forced to look, then, for appropriate models among his peers outside the inner family circle. The measure of his masculinity, in his own eyes and the eyes of others, frequently depends upon what he does, quite apart from what he is, and verification comes from outside himself in a psychological process that parallels the external concentration of male organ awareness. This process may very well be the origin of behavioral patterns that persist through childhood and into maturity: the importance to the male of peer group approval; the tendency to "run in packs"; and, of course, the emphasis on activity, independence, and achievement outside the family group.

The girl child has as her gender model her mother, and there is no necessity to reject the warmth and intimacy of that original relationship. If there is a danger in this kind of continuity, it is that much too little is expected of the girl in the way of independence and activity. She is, in fact, expected to renounce them in favor of patterns of behavior that do not require much more than passive and obedient imitation inside the family circle. Femininity, then, is in most cases equated with simply being or becoming, rather than doing, which parallels the internal diffusion of female organ awareness. Further, in her peer group relationships, she often searches for the same intimacy and intensity that characterize the relationship with her mother, at first among a few girl friends and then later with boys.

Psychologists have noted this same external-internal difference in studying the learning and play patterns of childhood. First of all, the boy is generally more active and energetic than the girl. Is it the result of nature or nurture? His bones and muscles are better suited to the strenuous games of childhood; some authorities believe, in fact, that the male body demands a higher level of activity. This combined with social expectations and parental encouragement results in the usual picture of the brave, rambunctious boy and the comparatively timid, docile girl, although both may be exactly the same size. However, the boy pays a price for his greater activity level. In addition to lagging behind in the rate of development, he also lags behind in the rate of intellectual growth. He does not possess, it would appear, the same degree of patience and passivity that enables the girl to master the rudimentary mental and physical skills at an earlier age. Boys talk later than girls, have smaller vocabularies, and use much shorter sentences. Learning and discipline problems occur much more frequently among boys than girls, and girls display a much higher degree of sociability at an earlier age.

Children at play also seem to conform to the same external-internal pattern. Dr. Helen Thompson, studying five-year-old children at the Yale Clinic of Child Development, noted the following:

> The question has often been raised with respect to early sex differences in play, whether the tendency of girls to play with dolls and of boys with mechanical objects is not entirely the result of conditioning. I do not believe it is. Consistent with what we have noted about the tendency of girls to move around less, to sit longer in one place and to use their hands more, it would follow logically that they would take more naturally to playing with dolls, which involves more detailed hand motions, as in dressing, rocking, and so on. Little boys, on the other hand, having been found to be more given to active movements, and to be less adept in the use of their hands (as illustrated by their greater difficulty in buttoning

and dressing) would be less inclined to play with dolls and more likely to use toys affording more opportunity for moving around and exerting physical energy . . . It is not unreasonable to suppose that society's ideas of what differences should exist between the sexes are based, in part at least, on differences which inherently exist.[12]

Erik Erikson has also written revealingly on the play differences among somewhat older children.[13] In a clinical study done several years ago, a group of preadolescent boys and girls were asked to make play constructions, and Erikson noted "the fact that girls and boys used space differently, and that certain configurations occurred strikingly often in the constructions of one sex and rarely in those of the other . . . the girls emphasized inner and the boys outer space." The girls' constructions typically were interior scenes or simple enclosures, with the figures of animals and people in static and usually peaceful positions. There were occasionally elaborate doorways, and intrusion into the scene seemed to be almost invited. Boys, on the other hand, built exterior scenes with elaborate walls and towers. People and animals were outside, usually in action. Accidents and the dangers of collapse and ruin were depicted, but a figure of authority, a policeman, was on the scene to keep order.

> The male and female spaces, then, were dominated, respectively, by height and downfall and by strong motion and its channelization or arrest; and by static interiors which were open or simply enclosed and peaceful or intruded upon.
> It may come as a surprise to some, and seem a matter of course to others, that here sexual differences in the organization of a play space seem to parallel the morphology of genital differentiation itself: in the male, an *external* organ, *erectile* and *intrusive* in character, serving the channelization of *mobile* sperm cells; *internal* organs in the female, with vestibular *access*, leading to a *statically expectant* ova. [Erikson's italics]

"The question is," Erikson himself asks, "what does this tell us about the two sexes?" He takes into account, as he must, the influence of environment; but that, to him, does not offer a completely satisfactory explanation. He goes further and suggests

an altogether more inclusive interpretation, according to which a profound difference exists between the sexes in the experience of the ground plan of the human body. The spatial phenomenon observed here would then express two principles of arranging space which correspond to the male and female principles in body construction. These may receive special emphasis in pre-puberty, and maybe in some other stages of life as well, but they are relevant throughout life to the elaboration of sex-roles in cultural space-times.[14]

Yet for every authority who claims that sexual physiology is an important determinant of gender psychology, there is another, with equally good evidence, who will deny it. Naturally enough, not all boys display the characteristics of external concentration that could be related either directly or indirectly to organ awareness; similarly not all girls demonstrate in their behavior the characteristics of internal diffusion. Thus if biology does influence this kind of behavior, it is not the only influence. Society clearly plays an important part as well. But because such behavior is prevalent enough to be considered "typical," many psychologists have concluded that there are at least some biological factors at work. Certainly it would be difficult to believe that society, ours as well as others', make up standards of gender behavior completely out of the blue. It would seem much more likely that they evolved from those inherent sexual patterns that both characterized the individual and served the group.

The influence of biology on the individual in our society accelerates during the time of adolescence, even if, as most psychologists believe, personality patterns are already firmly established. With adolescence comes an abrupt physical change for both the boy and the girl, and equally abrupt changes in the way they behave, and are expected to behave, socially. These changes effect what amounts to a crisis of identity, as Erik Erikson's work in this area has so well amplified. There is, of course, much more to this crisis than merely coming to terms with one's physical identity, but surely that is an important part of the problem. And here again it is a quite different problem for the boy than for the girl. The circumstances that surrounded original organ awareness in infancy and childhood are, in a sense, re-created, although in much greater complexity and on both the conscious and unconscious levels.

The boy, for example, confronting a whole new set of physical facts about himself, feels compelled to explore and test environ-

mental responses to them. They, in turn, influence his own behavior in the sex-gender-identity cycle described in infancy and
childhood. The same is true for the girl, although her environment permits less active exploration and testing. In both cases,
however, they are seeking outside confirmation for what they feel
inside, and if that confirmation is found, the crisis of identity, at
least for the moment, is resolved. The dissimilarity between the
sexes in adolescence lies, naturally enough, in the differences in
their physiology and their psychological reactions to those differences in their particular environmental setting.

The girl, to some degree at least, has an easier time of it. The
solid proof of her "femaleness" comes from her own body. Her
breasts begin to grow, she begins to menstruate; her *rite de passage* is provided by nature. She *becomes* a woman, although
society demands that the final physical proof in pregnancy and
childbirth be delayed. The boy must *prove* that he is a man, and
the ways in which he may attempt to prove it are vaguely defined
and subject to more or less stringent limitations. The growth and
new potency of his genitals may provide some physical evidence
of his manhood, but it is from his behavior that final confirmation must come. True, he can ejaculate, but that in no way corresponds to female menstruation, which is a continual and regular
internal reminder of femaleness, while erection and ejaculation
are more often a matter of external erotic stimulation. It can
hardly be a coincidence that primitive societies, and even our
own, have devised elaborate social rituals to accompany male
puberty, while the female is largely ignored until the ceremonies
that herald marriage and motherhood.

It would appear, then, that adolescence is a repetition of
external concentration for the male and internal diffusion for the
female, reinforced by their body images and behavioral expectations. There are other more scientifically verifiable differences,
however. Adolescence is, in general, a developmental rather than
a chronological phenomenon. Girls enter adolescence on an average of six months earlier than boys and their progress toward
sexual maturity is relatively smooth. Boys enter adolescence
later and not only take longer to reach sexual maturity, but
proceed by fits and starts, growing unevenly and erratically.
Their psychological growth appears also to be more erratic, as
the parents of any teen-age boy will testify. Girls seem, at least, to

arrive at a stage of self- and social contentment without as much conflict, while boys often express, and are permitted to express, more active discontent and rebellion.[15]

The psychological differences between the sexes during adolescence cannot, of course, be wholly ascribed to their physiological differences, for their environment and culture, at this stage, play an important, perhaps even the predominant, part in shaping their behavior. Psychologists have studied this behavior in detail—from the apersonal and somewhat abstract sexual statistics of the Kinsey group to the many researchers in developmental psychology itself. Their findings are well enough known. Boys continue to be more active and aggressive, girls more passive and dependent. "Boys are dominated by needs for achievement and independence; girls' concerns center on developing interpersonal skills and on the need for love."[16] Boys think and approach problems more analytically, while girls on the average are "less analytic, more global, and more preservative."[17] Conclusions such as these, no matter how impeccable the source, have provided ample grist for the women's liberation mill, for they maintain, and rightly so, that girls would not be passive and dependent, nor would their intelligence and powers of analytic thought be stunted, if society did not decree it. And most psychologists would agree; they are even more wary of individual variations and the dangers of generalization. There are, in any case, particularly among members of the present younger generation, a great many more exceptions to these general observations.

Still, it is interesting to note that the same internal-external pattern prevails, whatever the complex of causes. Originally, the physical differences and their psychological ramifications served essential sexual and social functions. It was the female role to conceive, carry, bear, and tend the offspring, while the male role was to impregnate, provide, and protect. Of course, we have come a long way since then. The social roles of both sexes have been altered by changing environmental circumstances: psychological attitudes and patterns of behavior have changed in relation to both social and sexual roles, and yet the sex roles themselves remain fundamentally unchanged. It is *only* the woman who can conceive and bear the child; *only* the man who can impregnate and fertilize. Thus somewhere in the maze of human potentialities and limitations shared by men and women alike, there remain quite unique and dissimilar sexual characteristics.

We have become much more knowledgeable in recent years about the nature and intensity of the sexual urge in both men and women. Freud and his followers have amply illustrated the potentially disastrous consequences of its denial, repression, or perversion. Society itself offers numerous examples of the other extreme, its unchecked expression. Clearly some viable compromise must be effected, and most psychologists agree that late adolescence and early maturity is the time that this compromise is made. Teen-agers can perhaps be forgiven for their sexual preoccupations, but the adult who is similarly preoccupied, who behaves sexually like a teen-ager, is in more serious trouble. Achieving a secure sexual identity is an essential step on the road to maturity and the quest for a secure human identity, and the young adult, male or female, who is hung up on sex is unlikely to proceed much further. Sexual drives and urges are probably comparable between men and women, but again the means of expressing those urges and the consequences of both success and failure are quite different.

For the male, teen-ager or young adult, it is usually merely a question, after finding a willing partner, of erection, penetration, and ejaculation, all active and, at least to some degree, aggressive acts. The male response is external, and his ability to "perform," the measure of his masculinity, particularly if the relationship is purely a physical one. Since his penis is easily visible proof of his response, again there is an external concentration of activity and concern. This simple physical response is, however, influenced by any number of psychological factors and is by no means infallible. A failure to perform, either because of premature ejaculation or impotence, is also clearly visible, and if it occurs either in initial sexual encounters or in later sexual relationships, it can have a profound effect upon the man. Again, his masculinity, in his own eyes and in the eyes of others, would seem to depend not on who he is but what he can do.

The woman, on the other hand, generally attracts rather than pursues, and the source of her attraction, again in a purely physical relationship, is usually not a specific part or organ, but her whole body. She receives, essentially a passive act, and the measure of her femininity is in her power to attract and, if she is genuinely aroused, the totality of her response. That response is considered to be much more complicated and difficult to achieve than the man's; it, too, is influenced by a complex of psychological factors, but there are no external signs of success or failure. If it is successful, it is internal and diffuse.

Masters and Johnson have investigated the differences in male and female orgasm.[18] In general, they have found that the male is capable of a single, intense physical "climax," and the muscular spasms that accompany orgasm are specific to ejaculation. The female, of course, does not ejaculate, although she may have an increase of normal secretion. Her orgasm is better seen as a release of physical and emotional tensions, and if she is sufficiently aroused, there may be several such releases. Do these physiological differences account for the different psychological attitudes toward intercourse itself and the satisfactions derived from it? Stereotypically the male is active, aggressive, sometimes abrupt and impatient. Orgasm is important, and once it is reached, his physical and emotional energies are spent, and it may take some time before he can be rearoused. The female on the other hand is often more interested in the sex play that contributes to her arousal. Thus how she is aroused, and by whom, may assume an importance equal to or even greater than the importance of orgasm. Further, the orgasm itself is nonspecific, even given the role of the clitoris, and, under certain circumstances, capable of early or even continual repetition.

There may, therefore, be no difference between male and female in the urgency of their basic sexual needs, but the needs themselves would appear to be somewhat different. There is a difference, too, in how these needs are met, and the traditional "masculine" and "feminine" stereotypes seem to have counterparts in real life. A recent survey of 20,000 responses to 101 questions about sexual attitudes and practices reveals that women prefer sex in the context of an intimate relationship.[19] Men are more active sexually, and more indiscriminate; they have more premarital and extramarital affairs than women, and are more interested in mate-swapping, group sex, and communal marriages. Of course, society allows the man greater sexual freedom, but the fact remains that the male penis is an external organ, comparatively easily aroused, and capable of achieving satisfaction with little more than physical stimulation. His external concentration is surely reflected in the higher incidence of voyeurism and fetishism among males than among females, and the all too frequent tendency, justifiably decried by the women's liberation movement, to treat women as "sexual objects," or simply as a place to put his penis. The male interest in pornography is another reflection of this attitude. It is the male who most often reads, and writes, this kind of material, which apparently offers both a source of erotic arousal and the privacy to conceal an inadequate performance. There is far less proclivity among women for anonymous, impersonal, or promiscuous intercourse. Of course, she too may be guilty of object love and preoccupied with her own gratification, but apparently that gratification is more readily achieved with a partner who knows and understands her body and its reactions.

There is not a "mating season" for the human species. Once past puberty, both male and female are "fertile," and intercourse is possible, whatever the season. Conception, however, is not, for that is limited by the female menstrual cycle. Only for a period of about 48 hours during the approximately 28-day menstrual cycle, when ovulation has occurred, is conception possible. Most authorities agree that the hormonal cycle that regulates ovulation and, later, menstruation, has no direct physiological effect upon desire. A woman does not necessarily feel "sexier" during ovulation, or less sexy during the rest of the cycle. Similarly in the man, the compulsion to seek sexual release is primarily psychological; there is no internal physiological mechanism that automatically triggers desire. Alone among the animal species, men and women are capable of exercising a degree of conscious control over their mating instincts as well as participating in the act of intercourse not merely for the purpose of propagating the species but also, even principally, for the physical and psychological gratification it affords.

It would be very tempting, and many writers have succumbed to the temptation, to ascribe the essential differences between the sexes to the act of intercourse itself. Some, in fact, go even further back and equate male aggression and activity to the frantically wiggling sperm, and female passivity and receptivity to the egg patiently waiting to be fertilized. But such analogies, as convenient or symbolic as they may be, are far too simplistic if sex is considered as something more than a compulsion to reproduce, or merely a means to achieve physical pleasure. The mechanisms of intercourse are ingenious and highly complementary on the physical level, but on the psychological level they can pose, both for an individual and for a relationship, a number of problems that are quite unique to each sex. The woman is, of course, concerned and even anxious about her powers of attraction and response, but her initial and even later sexual experiences may be accompanied by a degree of pain that can decrease her pleasure in the act. Perhaps more important is her fear of pregnancy, for if she conceives and the baby is brought to term, it means not only the discomforts of carrying and bearing the child, but additional years and even decades of responsibility for its upbringing. If the child is expected and wanted, there may be no problem; in fact, for many this is what being a woman is all about. But since conception is not the goal in every act of intercourse, it usually falls to the woman to take the precautions necessary to prevent it.

With the advent of the Pill and, more recently, liberalization of the laws governing abortion, "mistakes" are less likely to be made, and if they are, there is a medical out. Still, many couples are woefully ignorant of the fundamentals of sex, and it is probably safe to say that a significant number of children are still unexpected, even if they are wanted. If they are neither, it is generally the woman who bears the brunt of the termination of the pregnancy, and even a legal abortion can have serious physical, social, and psychological consequences. It is her biology, then, that can have a profound influence on a woman's attitude toward intercourse, however patiently the egg is waiting, or however passive and receptive she may be during the act itself. If her usual preference is for sex within the context of an intimate relationship, it may very well be due to the fact that mastering the internal diffusion that characterizes female sexuality requires a degree of experience in both partners. And, naturally enough, the woman needs some reassurance that if a "mistake" does occur, she will not be left holding the baby.

The man, of course, does not become pregnant, but that does not mean the physical act of intercourse is without its psychological perils. Like the woman, he is concerned about his power to attract and respond; he may also be concerned about the loss of freedom and the burdensome responsibilities that seem to accompany a sexual involvement, whether it is a marriage or just an affair. But these concerns pale beside the chief worry: the fear of impotence. Medical and psychological authorities concur in the belief that in the vast majority of cases impotence stems from emotional rather than physical causes. Just as there are any number of usual, or even unusual, things that can "turn a man on," so are there as many that can turn him off. But whatever the cause—and the man is by no means always the one at fault—the result is pretty much the same: he feels himself to be less a man, less "masculine," and he imagines that others think the same. In fact, it is often the fear of appearing unmanly, or not man enough, that operates as a prior restraint and makes sexual performance impossible. In other words, many men have nothing to fear but fear itself.

Surprisingly enough, very little detailed writing and research have been devoted to the question of male impotence. It would seem that there is almost a conspiracy of silence, particularly among men themselves. These days everyone writes and even jokes amiably about women's psychosexual hang-ups, but discussion, let alone humor, about impotence is rare. Certainly one of the reasons for this is our culture's male orientation; another is our cultural reverence for the power of the penis. Yet psychiatrists will testify that impotence, or fear of impotence, is at the core of many of our society's most serious problems. It is a contributing factor in the higher rates of mental illness, suicide, alcoholism, and drug addiction among men than among women. Male homosexuality, in many cases, also revolves around this concern. And a man's inability to perform with his wife, combined with his desire to test his potency on someone else, is at least in part responsible for the staggering instability of American marriages. Further, the resistance that many men raise to prophylaxis during intercourse, and their even greater resistance to simple and safe modern sterilization procedures,[20] insisting instead that it should be the woman who wears the necessary equipment, or undergoes the necessary operation, is surely additional proof of their fear of impotence, or their excessive concern with the appearance of "masculinity."

Impotence is, of course, merely a symptom, not the disease, but symptoms can often be as destructive and irreversible as the disease that causes them. The disease is, speaking only in the most general terms, a sense or feeling of inadequacy which may be caused, in adolescence, by something as simple as the lack of experience, or in middle and old age, by the lack of opportunity. But, again, the problem is primarily psychological and has less to do with the ability to fertilize a waiting egg than the ability to achieve erection, penetration, and orgasm—all external. If he cannot "get it up," none of these is possible.

Frigidity may be a roughly similar psychological phenomenon in women; even so, she has an advantage over the man. There is no external sign to stigmatize the frigid woman; she can go through the motions, the man can be satisfied, and even conception is possible with little or no effort on her part. The fear of pregnancy may be a factor in frigidity, or it may stem from a variety of other complex psychological causes, and the frigid woman may suffer no less anxiety and self-doubt than the impotent man. Yet since femininity is still generally related to her ability to induce the man to perform, rather than the quality of her own performance, she does not necessarily feel herself "less a woman" if she is unable to achieve satisfaction. In fact, it is generally the man who is charged not only with the necessity of proving himself, but also of satisfying his partner, a double burden that has become even more onerous now that female orgasm is considered as important as male orgasm in the sexual act.

Achieving orgasm is of equal importance for both male and female, but the means of achieving it, and even the quality of the orgasm itself, are different, and those differences affect their respective attitudes toward intercourse. Further, in maturity there are other physical differences between the sexes that influence not only their sexual behavior, but their social behavior as well. It is perhaps ironic that at no time in their lives is there greater need for the man and woman to come together as equals. It is assumed that they share the same human goals in marriage, child-rearing, and in the important work of the world. And yet at no time do they *look* less alike, and at no time do their biological differences exert a stronger influence over their behavior. Of course, society also plays a part in encouraging or discouraging, approving or disapproving, different patterns of behavior for each sex, based to a greater or lesser degree upon their biological differences; and again this combination of nature and nurture seems to follow patterns of internal diffusion for the woman and external concentration for the man.

First and foremost, the mature woman is subject to the physiological demands of her body in a way that the mature man is not. Her body passes through various cycles which include menstruation, pregnancy, parturition, lactation, and finally menopause, and this inner physical climate has decided effects upon both her sexual and social behavior. Man's inner climate is far less complex and variable; from adolescence through maturity to old age his body makes a single, consistent demand upon him, even given the inevitable decline in the physical energy necessary to satisfy it. The "male menopause" postulated by some writers seems to be largely a matter of individual psychology, as it is also largely psychological attitudes, healthy or unhealthy, that regulate his sexual performance. A woman's psychology influences her sexual performance, too, as it determines her attitude toward the physical demands her body makes upon her. Both men and women can also exert considerable conscious control over their expressions of sexuality, but the woman has no comparable control over menstruation and menopause, and if she becomes pregnant, by accident or choice, that physiological process runs its natural course unless it is terminated.

Curiously, investigations have just begun on the psychological effects of these physiological phenomena in normal, healthy women. Until quite recently, the emphasis in medical and psychiatric literature has been on the reverse process: physical dysfunction as a result of some psychological hang-up—irregular or extremely painful menstruation, "difficult" pregnancies and childbirth, postpartum depression, the "change of life" syndrome. No one denies the causative links to psychological problems in cases such as these, although the recommended cures vary widely. The new feminists have argued, convincingly, that many of these psychosexual difficulties are the direct result of society's overemphasis on the woman purely as a sexual being at the expense of her other human capabilities. Still it must be stated, speaking in the most general terms, that menstruation, pregnancy, and childbirth can be, per se, inconvenient and even painful. They, along with menopause, are physical facts of life for every woman, whatever her psychological attitude toward them.

The man has nothing comparable in his inner climate, and it is perhaps predictable that throughout the ages, male-dominated

societies have made of these female physiological functions everything from rituals of mystery and romance to objects of fear
and even repugnance. This same variety of reactions has also
characterized male attitudes toward the female genitalia. But
male reactions aside for the moment, how do these functions
affect even the woman who has made a satisfactory adjustment
to them and accepts them as no more or less than they really are?

Most researchers in this field agree that the endocrinological
changes that accompany menstruation, pregnancy, and
menopause do bring about behavioral changes.[21] These changes
are generally described in terms that imply they are somehow
detrimental to normal function—inability to concentrate, for
example, heightened emotionalism, or some other subtle or obvious behavioral variation. And perhaps they are. Clearly, a
woman in the last months of a pregnancy, whether it happens
only once in her lifetime or is a frequent occurrence, experiences
physical change and displays psychological characteristics that
may be quite normal in her condition, but pregnancy itself can be
considered abnormal in the sense that it is not an everyday
occurrence. Much or little may be made of the physical and
psychological changes that accompany pregnancy, or menstruation and menopause for that matter, depending upon the other
circumstances in the woman's life. How and what accommodations are made vary with each woman, but the fact that *some*
accommodation is necessary is unique among women; there is
nothing comparable in the male experience.

For women, again speaking in the most general terms, these
accommodations include a tolerance for whatever pain and inconvenience go along with these changes, a tolerance for whatever discontinuity they may cause, and an adjustment to the
perpetual reminders, at least during her child-bearing years, of
her physical functions. It has been well established that women
enjoy certain biological strengths that enable them to endure the
sometimes extremely rigorous demands of these functions; and,
it is assumed, this is all to the good if the species is to survive. But
by some quirk of logic it is also assumed that the psychological
accommodations that must be made to them are somehow dis-
advantageous or even debilitating to women, with the exception,
of course, of "mother love," whether it is instinctive or acquired,
which is generally considered to be a positive characteristic.

Thus, psychologists have postulated masochism as an inherent "feminine" gender trait, and use the discontinuity in physical function as a rationale for dependency, passivity, inconsistency, narcissism, and a host of supposedly typical traits. While such personality patterns are certainly possible under the circumstances, it is surely a mistake to consider them inevitable, just as it is a mistake to assume that "masculinity" implies sadism.

It can be said however that women may very well be profoundly and continually affected by the demands of their "inner climate" during their mature child-bearing years; still there is no reason why a woman need react negatively to these effects, to feel "cheated," deprived or unhappy because of them, any more than a man need feel deprived because his inner climate does not permit him to give birth. Further, a woman is not all womb any more than a man is all penis. While sexual function obviously influences social function, and the two shape individual identity, the whole is greater than the sum of its parts. The woman may indeed suffer some disadvantages because of her sexual function, perhaps the most significant of which are the short monthly interruptions of menstruation, and the long—sometimes lifelong—interruption of raising children. But this latter is more often a social requirement than a physical necessity. There are, however, compensating advantages: a tolerance for and an ability to withstand pain, a need for psychological continuity to offset the discontinuity of physical function, not to mention the satisfactions of giving birth, and the patience, compassion, understanding, intimacy, and love that accompany child care. By the same token, the man's comparative freedom from the demands of his inner climate can certainly be an advantage in terms of continuity; as Simone de Beauvoir says, "Man's biology is his work," while a woman's biology is only part of hers. But the external orientation of the male makes him excessively vulnerable to outside pressures which can lead to a compulsive desire to test and prove his "masculinity," and thus to aggression, impatience, and often a "hit-and-run" attitude toward sexual and social acts. It can also lead to an excessive dependence upon a woman for the care, approval, and internal continuity that he also requires, and as if to deny that dependence, in some cases, attitudes of denigration, hostility, and even fear toward the women in his life.

In a very real sense, then, the mature woman's biology is

complex and divisive, and it is by no means a coincidence that many are not able, or willing, to pursue goals outside of marriage and motherhood until their child-bearing and -raising days are over. But from this complexity and divisiveness many women are also able to achieve an "inner strength" that stands them in good stead, whatever goals they pursue. Neither the man's biology, nor the resulting sexual and social roles, are quite so complex, and both nature and nurture encourage the direct, uninterrupted pursuit of external goals which can result in an "outer strength." The roles of man, husband, and father are conceived as one role, while the roles of woman, wife, and mother entail several, sometimes contradictory, responsibilities. Ironically, the lack of complexity and potential divisiveness of what is conventionally considered to be the male role is made possible, in large measure, by the complexity of the female role and the success with which she is able to handle it, thus increasing male vulnerability and dependence. And statistics show that women—even women with children or who are still in their child-bearing years—survive the trials and master the responsibilities of divorce or widowhood far more easily, and in far greater numbers, than men.

It is not until middle age that woman's biology at last lets up. With menopause comes liberation from her body, and after an adjustment has been made to the physical and physiological changes that accompany menopause, many women report a feeling of new freedom—a freedom to enjoy sexual intercourse without the fear of an unwanted pregnancy and, if their children are old enough to start taking care of themselves, a freedom from the time-consuming responsibilities of being a housewife and mother. If she has invested all her talents and energies in these pursuits, she may, of course, feel that she no longer serves any useful purpose, particularly if her husband has by that time achieved a degree of success in his activities outside the home and no longer requires her support. But either way, the woman stands on the threshold of what amounts to a new and considerably less complex life. She now has more time to devote to herself and those aspects of her personality that are less intimately related to her physiology. If they have remained undeveloped in her formative years, or have been neglected or stunted during her years of housewifery, she is in trouble. If not, she may have many happy and creative years ahead.

The man experiences no such liberation. His biology does not give him a second chance, although he may wish wistfully that it did. He may elect, as many men do, to change jobs and even change wives and begin raising another family. But this is not a new life, it is merely a repetition or a re-creation of the old one under slightly different circumstances, usually undertaken in the hope of recapturing something he feels he lost the first time around. Paramount among the feared losses are his youth and physical vigor, which are gradually slipping away, his importance as a protector and provider and, of course, his sexual potency—all of which require some external verification in line with the conventional definitions of masculinity. The characteristics of external concentration have enabled him to master the demands of his relatively uncomplicated male role, just as the characteristics of diffusion have enabled the woman to stay on top of her complex role requirements. But while the woman's role changes in early middle age, the man's does not. And in an attempt to prove that he is still up to it, he may feel compelled to run a little harder merely to stay in the same place. His sexual needs remain urgent, although his abilities to attract a partner and to perform are definitely on the wane. The womb finally relinquishes its hold on the woman, but the power of the penis persists. And the man who has spent a disproportionate time satisfying its demands has the greatest difficulty adjusting to the physical and psychological changes that come with middle age.

It is not until late middle and old age that men and women come together again as physical equals. It has often been noted, in fact, that men and women who have been married for forty or so years even begin to look alike. Women outnumber men at this age and live on an average of seven years longer; so perhaps they do have a slight biological edge, but both usually share a preoccupation with their overall state of bodily health, rather than a concern about any particular physical function. The man, however, accustomed throughout his life to a greater degree of physical and mental activity in the outer world, may have greater difficulty adjusting to enforced retirement and the slackened pace of the inner world of old age. If the woman has a psychological edge, it is because she has usually had many more years to adjust to declining physical function and has, in most cases, been more at home in the inner world.

Thus for a few years at the beginning of their lives and a few years at the end, men and women enjoy something approximating equality—too soon and too late to offer much solace to those who advocate a lifetime of ongoing and complete similarity. Clearly, men and women *are* different throughout the various stages of their life cycles, and although both nature and nurture conspire to make them so, it is in nature's interest to take advantage of these differences.

It may very well be, then, that it is nurture or society that sees the differences between the sexes as disadvantages and has become the real divisive force in the battle of the sexes. It has been said often enough that the behavioral standards of any society are based not on what is, but what should be; and with that axiom in mind it should also be recognized that the standards of our particular society are white, middle-class, and male-oriented, and that these standards have in the past proved, and continue to prove, far from ideal, immutable, or, in some cases, even practical. The social body, however, which consists after all of the collective attitudes and actions of the individuals within it, is capable of growth and change, and therein lies the only hope for a reconciliation between the sexes.

Spokesmen for the women's liberation movement have been very quick to spot the deleterious effects that unrealistic social expectations, and the conditioning that always goes into their realization, have had on members of their own sex. It has been assumed that women's sex role is so important, so time-consuming, and so pervasive in their personal psychology that they are incapable of any other physical or mental activity. Thus the insistence that their gender roles parallel almost exactly the behavior that seems to characterize their sexual function. But by some curious inversion of logic, the gender, or culturally conditioned, role is considered to be the most important aspect of male psychology, perhaps because paternity is neither as time-consuming or as physically demanding as maternity, and the woman is almost always there to act as father as well as mother; or perhaps because with the woman bound so closely to the home and family unit, someone has to cope with the world outside its walls. The training that goes into that social expectation has also severely truncated the male personality, for the learned patterns of gender behavior that are thought to ensure success outside the home are all too seldom successful in dealing with personal problems, chiefly those associated with the male sex roles of husband and father.

By this unreal separation of sexual and social function in both men and women, society virtually guarantees that conflict will arise, conflict *within* each man and woman between two equally important parts of their personalities; conflict *between* men and women when one or the other strays across the boundaries of the prescribed patterns of behavior; and conflict between men and women with society itself if they are somehow unable to measure up to its rigid standards.

We have seen vivid evidence of this conflict in thousands upon thousands of replies to our Masculine and Feminine Inventories; we have seen it again and again in the sexual and social behavior of the men and women in our society; we have seen it in the generation gap and the rebellious and often rootless behavior of the young. Conflict is built into a system which insists there is something a little wrong with a woman who yearns to be more than just "feminine," and with a man who is afraid to be less than "masculine." And stating the problem in this way reveals another troublesome aspect of the situation.

Quite apart from its often arbitrary standards of gender behavior, society has also ascribed plus or minus values to each gender. Masculinity in men and femininity in women may be considered equally desirable, but clearly the characteristics of conventional masculinity are thought to be of greater social value. Conventional femininity is not only considered of inferior value, but one of its chief characteristics is ready and willing compliance to the demands of masculinity. Thus the man finds himself in a double bind: not only are conventional masculine standards extremely difficult to live up to in today's world, they depend, in large measure, upon the acquiescence and service of the woman who, it appears, is less and less willing to give them. But she also finds *herself* in a double bind, for even if she strictly complies with the tenets of "femininity," her rewards are in no way comparable to the man's; and if she defies them, or even bends the rules a little, she must act in opposition to the man and in the face of social disapproval.

Men and women both, of course, have been bending the rules for years, but social dos and don'ts are remarkably tenacious and often snap back with sharp and stinging results. Obviously the time has come to revise these conventional standards—but how? The fact is that they are not all wrong; they were not manufactured out of whole cloth. We have attempted to show, in answer to Henry Higgins' question, that men and women cannot ever be exactly alike; nature and nurture take them along different paths. But there is no need for those paths to be as widely divergent as they are; nor need they be parallel, separate but equal, whatever the distance between them. They should join if possible, and separate when necessary, in an effort to achieve mutually satisfactory goals. It is far too easy to assume that this is possible under the current system. Advocates of conventional gender behavior often state that even if masculinity and femininity are not quite equal, they are at least complementary, and the system would work beautifully if everyone knew his, or her, place and kept to it—the familiar and plaintive cry of traditionalists of every stripe. But the present system cannot work because the physical and social circumstances upon which it was originally based have changed, and because it never, even in its heyday, took into account the variety and complexity of human behavior, all within the range of normal.

Psychologists and psychiatrists have known for decades that aspects of masculinity and femininity exist side-by-side in men and women; that, in fact, masculinity and femininity may only be a matter of degree. They also know that if that degree is excessive, because of some genetic or hormonal imbalance, or because of some psychological overreaction, severe character disorder can result. A man who is too dominant, too aggressive, too active, too "masculine" is not a healthy man, and similarly the woman who is too submissive, too dependent, too passive, too "feminine." But then neither is the man who exhibits "feminine" traits to an excessive degree, or the woman who is excessively "masculine." Yet they know that these distinctive character traits occur, to some degree at least, among the members of both sexes often enough to be considered prevalent, typical, and normal—and that they stem not only from social conditioning; there are surely some inherent biological influences at work as well. Where the mental health professions have perhaps erred, at least in the recent past, is in their tacit or overt insistence that the individual, man or woman, at odds with his biology or at war with the social interpretation of his sex and gender roles, simply give up and "adjust." On the contrary, it is high time society adjusted to the needs of the individual.

We also believe that certain patterns of sex and gender behavior are prevalent in each sex, for a complex of physical and social reasons. We have tried to avoid using the conventional descriptive nouns wherever possible—aggression, independence, activity for the man, and submission, dependence, passivity for the woman—because not only are these terms too simplistic, they are also heavily weighted with social value judgments. We have chosen instead the terms external concentration for the man and internal diffusion for the woman, which are meant to include those characteristics that are inherent in sex role behavior and typical in male and female gender roles. Various commentators have used different terms and adjectives to describe them: Erik Erikson's inner and outer space; others, the characteristics implicit in "objectivity" and "subjectivity." But whatever it is called we believe that this external-internal distinction is, to use Erikson's phrase, the "rock-bottom of sexual differentiation," and revised standards of masculinity and femininity must be built upon it. Still it must be done with two important considerations in mind. First, that the characteristics implied in these terms are of equal sexual and social value; and second, that they are not the exclusive property of either a man or a woman, but rather exist side-by-side as complementary, not conflict-laden, aspects of the whole personality.

Traditional standards of sex and gender behavior fail to take into account both of these considerations. In the case of the latter, they insist that both the male and female repress any and all of the psychosexual characteristics that are supposed to typify the opposite sex, when, in fact, these characteristics are inherent in every personality, regardless of sex. Thus conflict and ambivalence are virtually inevitable; and the man is, in effect, cut off from the satisfactions of the inner world of intimacy and sensitivity which is thought to be feminine, while the woman who ventures into the outer world of achievement and independence, thought to be exclusively masculine, does so at her own peril. The error is further compounded by society's failure to provide suitable and constructive outlets for those psychosexual characteristics which predominate, as perhaps they must, among each sex. Masculine strivings for independence, activity, and achievement are severely curtailed by social pressures, not the least of which come from women, or are shackled in the service of some totally useless or even destructive social activity. And feminine strivings for intimacy, continuity, and peace are thwarted by social pressures that fail to provide suitable rewards, as well as by men themselves who pay them little more than lip service.

It is ironic that history offers countless examples of both men and women who have combined masculine and feminine characteristics thought to be incompatible into a single personality to achieve human goals that might otherwise have been impossible. Writers, painters, composers, and even architects are often thought to be "feminine," and yet the world would be vastly poorer without their contributions. The few women who have made lasting and significant cultural contributions also seem at least slightly "masculine," simply because it *is* masculine to dare to venture beyond the bounds of conventional thought and action. But women, given education, opportunity, and encouragement, are just as capable of innovative and creative activities as men, and the reason so few have aspired to them in the past is surely related to the relatively higher price they are forced to pay. The unconventional male has always had at least a tenuous place in society, and even if everyone else is against him, there is usually a woman, possibly several women, in the background ready to minister to his needs. The unconventional woman is almost invariably denied the satisfactions of both the outer and the inner world; her presence in the former is keenly resented, and viewed as irreconcilable with the latter.

It has been said that all achievement stems from unresolved conflict, either from within the individual or between the individual and the rest of the world. That may be a vast oversimplification, but certainly the man and woman content with themselves and the world rarely make waves. They do not grow, they vegetate; they do not challenge, they accept. Can it be assumed then, that the conflict and resulting ambivalence implicit in artificial distinctions between the sexes in their gender behavior is ultimately healthy? Certainly society feeds and encourages it. The fact is, however, that unresolved conflict is not in itself a guarantee of achievement; for every individual who is able to combine what society sees as the feminine sensitivity necessary to see to the very depths of the conflict with what is considered the masculine drive necessary to attempt a solution, there are thousands, perhaps millions, in whom no such combination is possible. The conflict remains unresolved, either because the individual is unable to effect such a resolution, or because he feels it is personally or socially unacceptable. Rigidly enforced sexual distinctions do indeed produce conflict, and while a few persons may effect a reconciliation, others are driven to extremes of rebellious or conformist behavior, and even, in some cases, to severe character disorder.

Revising traditional standards of masculinity and femininity will not in itself resolve every case of sex role conflict and ambivalence; there will always be, no doubt, those who are unhappy with themselves or the world around them. But broadening the avenues of acceptable expression for both men and women in their sexual and social behavior will likely alleviate some of that conflict, help avoid the extremes, and enable the individual to channel his psychosexual energies into potentially constructive, rather than self-destructive, pursuits.

It is easy enough to talk about revising behavioral standards, but just what are the new criteria that should replace the old? It is simply a question of taking a more realistic look at human behavior, male and female, and making the adjustments and accommodations necessary to allow an individual of whichever sex an opportunity to develop and function as a complete human being. Both bridge and water can be raised or lowered; there is no need to dam the river or dynamite the bridge. The present standards are not entirely wrong; they are based, to some degree at least, on differences and distinctions that actually do exist between the sexes. But they fall far short of perfection, as if the bridge were built only halfway across the river, and after that it is sink or swim. We must accept the fact that the sexes are different, and, although ideally they are headed hand-in-hand toward the same destination, they will cross the "bridge" in slightly different ways. Men and women are different because their biology is different, and to the degree that biology influences individual and social behavior, they will perhaps always remain different. But that is only one aspect of the total personality; viewed as complete human beings, men and women are much more similar than it is generally assumed.

We believe that women are biologically endowed, and later trained, to express the characteristics of internal diffusion both sexually and socially, while men are similarly endowed and trained to express the characteristics of external concentration. These characteristics, then, can form the basis for revised standards of sex and gender behavior not very much different from those that presently exist. The woman may perhaps always be more internally oriented than the man, and the man more externally oriented than the women, but no connotations of superiority or inferiority should be attached thereto. Both are equally valuable to the individual, to a relationship and to society where, indeed, both orientations act in complement. Beyond this point, however, conventional standards begin to break down, for it is erroneously assumed that, first, "normal" members of opposite sexes are endowed *only* with those characteristics deemed appropriate to their sex, and second, that they *must* display them, to the exclusion of any others, to be considered normally masculine and feminine.

It is much more complicated than that, for both men and women display the characteristics of the opposite sex in their personalities; they are composites of masculine and feminine traits, differing only in degree. In fact, it is a good thing they are. Masculinity or femininity may predominate, but it is wrong to assume, as conventional standards do, that this equips men and women only for precisely defined roles: the woman in the inner sphere of marriage and motherhood, and the man in the work of the outside world. Sensitivity, compassion, understanding, and a desire for continuity and peace, all of which may be considered internal or "feminine" characteristics, are no less valuable in business, the professions, and politics than they are in the home or the community; while independence, achievement, and activity serve family, community, nation, and world equally well. Again, they are complementary. Finally, there is nothing sexually exclusive about such personality traits: it is not only women who are capable of compassion and understanding; the man without them is not a whole man. Nor is it only men who are capable of independence and achievement; the woman can and should exhibit them if she is to be considered a whole woman. In short, both men and women are admirably equipped to function in both the inner and outer world. Their choices and their capabilities will vary, naturally, but as human beings not merely as sexual beings.

There are, of course, less desirable personality traits that can be said to go along with the external concentration typical of the man and the internal diffusion typical of the woman. For the man they are, chiefly, aggression and an excessive vulnerability to external and internal pressures, and for the woman, potentially excessive passivity and dependence. But again these are not sexually exclusive characteristics. They can exist in varying degrees in both sexes; and wherever a negative or a self- or socially destructive personality trait exists, whether in a man or a woman, it must be tempered, just as positive and constructive character traits must be encouraged, regardless of sex. Perhaps it is a mistake to consider these traits positive and negative, "masculine" or "feminine" at all, with the many connotations that those adjectives must inevitably bear. They are, primarily, *human* characteristics shared in varying degrees by both sexes; and here connotations are appropriate, for the adjective can be used to describe those extraordinary abilities, and regrettable fallibilities, that are part of human nature.

With the realization and acceptance of this duality in both men and women, the noise and smoke surrounding the battle of the sexes must inevitably subside. Neither man nor woman need deny or repress those psychosexual traits that might very well smooth off the rough edges, or fill in the rounded contours of their identities. A man need not be ashamed to "feel," nor a woman ashamed to "at," If a woman is psychologically equipped to function in the outer world, or the man better suited to inner pursuits, who is to say that they should not follow their inclinations? If work is fulfilling for a man, why should it not be so for a woman; if motherhood is important to a woman, why should not fatherhood be equally important to a man? Who is to say that men and women cannot function equally well together in both the inner and outer spheres?

It is, at present, the sexual preconceptions and prejudices not merely of an amorphous and ill-defined "society" that stand in the way, but the particular beliefs and behavior of the men and women conditioned by it. Paradoxically, then, men and women have stitched together a social fabric that they now find impossible to wear. They are in conflict with no one but themselves, and if change is to take place, it must come from within themselves. It is pointless to call for the radical overthrow of those institutions that seem to perpetuate sexual prejudice. Sexual anarchy is no less acceptable than political anarchy. Institutions are no more or less than the people they serve, and they, too, will inevitably change as the people within them change. The male-dominated organizations of the outer world are far from perfect; the female-dominated institutions of marriage and child-raising in the inner world are in equal jeopardy. And surely one of the reasons for this is the sexual exclusivity which merely intensifies and perpetuates the weaknesses and shortcomings of each sex. There is no need to pull down the churches, the statehouses, and the executive offices; there is no need to abandon the institutions of the monogamous marriage and the family. All that needs to be done is to participate in them not only as males and females, but as human beings; and constitute them to serve not only "masculine" and "feminine" needs, but human needs.

To become truly human in today's society may be the most difficult challenge we have yet faced, for it encompasses not only a realistic understanding of the nature and needs that all men and women have in common, but also those particular characteristics that they do not share. The goal based on such an understanding should, however, be the same for both sexes: to realize one's full potential as a male or female human being in sexual and social roles in both the inner and outer sphere; to find security, support, mutual satisfaction and a means of self-expression in relationships with other human beings, particularly one's mate; and to pass on to one's children and succeeding generations that same understanding. And in this undertaking men and women must be given equal opportunity and share equal responsibility. A large order, surely, but not impossible, for when one seeks to become a complete human being, given the full range of potentialities and limitations, the distinctions between "masculinity" and "femininity" can at last be viewed in their proper perspective.

NOTES

1. Bernard Shaw, *Pygmalion* in *Complete Plays with Prefaces*, Vol. I, New York: Dodd, Mead & Co., pp. 281 ff.

2. Kate Millet, *Sexual Politics*, Garden City, N.Y.: Doubleday & Co., 1970, p. 29.

3. Rene Dubos, "Humanistic Biology." *The American Scholar*, Spring 1965, p. 179.

4. Robert J. Stoller, *Sex and Gender*, New York: Jason Aronson, Inc., 1968, p. 10.

5. Stoller. *op citl.*, p.9.

6. Edmund W. Overstreet, "Biological Make-up of Woman," in *The Potential of Woman*, New York: McGraw-Hill Book Co., 1963, p. 15.

7. John Money, "The Spectrum of Femininity," in *The Potential of Woman*, New York: McGraw-Hill Book Co., 1963, p. 56-57.

8. Phillis Greenacre, *Trauma, Growth and Personality*, New York: W.W. Norton & Co., 1952. p. 149.

9. *Ibid.*, p. 152.

10. *Ibid.*,

11. *Ibid.*, p. 153 and 154.

12. Helen Thompson, "The Dynamics of Activity, Drive in Young Children," Psychology Bulletin, Vol. XXXIII, No. 9 (1936), p. 751.

13. Erik H. Erikson, "Inner and Outer Space: Reflections on Womanhood," *Daedalus*, Vol. XCIII (Spring 1964), pp. 582–606.

14. Erik Erikson, *Identity: Youth and Crisis*, New York: W.W. Norton & Co., 1968.

15. Peter Blos, *On Adolescence*, New York: The Free Press, 1962.

16. Douvan and J. Adelson, *The Adolescent Experience*, as cited in Hoffman and Hoffman (eds.), *Review of Child Development Research*, New York: Russell Sage, 1966, p. 494.

17. Eleanor Maccoby. "Women's Intellect," *The Potential of Women, op. cit.*, p. 30.

18. William H. Masters and Virginia E. Johnson, *Human Sexual Response*, Boston: Little, Brown & Co. 1966.

19. Robert Afhanasion and Philip Shaver, "Sex," *Psychology Today*, July 1970, pp. 39–47.

20. Recent unpublished studies on vasectomy show that some men have reduced their resistance. See Workshop: *Behavioral-Social Aspects of Contraceptive Sterilization: Research Approaches* by Center for Population Research, National Institute of Child Health and Human Development, Bethesda, Maryland, June 18-19, 1973. Unpublished.

21. K. Dalton, "Menstruation and Examinations," *Lancet*, Vol. II (1968) pp. 1386–1388; "Menstruation and Crime," *British Medical Journal*, Vol. II (1961), p. 752; F.A. Beach, *Hormones and Behavior*, New York: Paul B. Hoeber, 1948; S.C. Frees and W.S. Kruger, "Psychological Manifestations in the Menstrual Cycle," *Psychosomatic Medicine*, Vol. XII (1950), pp. 229–235; and *Time*, March 20, 1972, pp. 47 and 68.

CHAPTER 9

An Ounce of Prevention

$\mathbf{H}$ow do we rear a generation of males who can interact with females as equals without seeing what women do as threatening to their own status? How do we achieve a generation of females who can seek self-fulfillment without guilt or hostile defensiveness? First, the children have to be fortunate enough to be born to parents who are living out models of what fully satisfying interactive male and female adult lives can be. These parents would have to be people who have found their male and female identities by successfully working through the kinds of adaptations and modifications of behavior we shall discuss in the last chapter, and who, moreover, have done this with sufficient insight and awareness so that they are able to communicate their joy and satisfaction in being men or women to their children.

The second condition is that the parents have agreed that raising children free in feeling, thought and functioning will be one of the primary goals for child-rearing, indeed for family living. We say "primary" because to have a fighting chance of doing this will require such constant attention and such an expenditure of energy and time that it would be unacceptable to any parents other than those for whom this is a major goal. The breadth of the commitment must be sufficient for them to counter and anticipate the pressures which will operate on their infants and children once they set foot from the house into the larger culture, pressure which will operate to inculcate notions of sexual preferences and sexual prejudice.

The basic model must be that of rearing a healthy person. Parents must minimally have recognized what we have noted previously, that in the new definitions, masculinity and femininity are not defined in terms of behavioral or personality parameters unique to each gender, but rather in terms of personal and social parameters shared by both. Within such a model, the parent of a developing child concentrates on assuring that the child has a sense of human dignity and self-worth as an individual, not because roughness and aggression make him masculine, or docility and an affectionate nature feminine. The parents who value constructive aggression should accept, reward and value it from all their children of either gender and those who consider docility an important human trait should seek to inculcate it in boys and girls.

A quick test on the extent to which you are ready to move in this direction without further self-analysis can be gauged by the extent to which you reacted in the preceding sentence to the notions of reinforcing aggression in little girls and docility in little boys.

Again let us emphasize that we are not talking about bringing up all children alike, for we believe that it is ridiculous to maintain, as do some opponents of so-called "sexist" education and child-rearing practices, that boys and girls should be brought up alike. It would be impossible, just as it is impossible to bring up two children of the same sex in exactly the same way. Each child is different and the sex of the child is an important difference, for in childhood, as in later life, it is one of the factors that determines his preferences, his actions and reactions, his concept of self and means of self-expression. But to expect, or even to insist, that a child of either sex fit into some preconceived gender mould is to impose needless and possibly even harmful restrictions upon his personality at a time when it is not yet completely formed, restrictions that will, in all probability, become a permanent part of his emotional equipment. Physical, social and psychological imperatives are no less important in childhood than in later life, and each child, regardless of sex, should be allowed equal opportunity to express himself or herself on all levels of his being, to seek, to experiment and, finally, to integrate his knowledge and experience in shaping his own unique identity.

For some, this kind of equality and freedom may conjure up the specter of a degree of permissiveness even greater than that which we have discussed as characteristic of child-raising in this country in the fifties and sixties. Distorted permissiveness, however, stems from parental indifference or indecision. In contrast, when parents are intimately involved in this process of exploration and self-expression, serving both as models for the child in their own behavior, and teaching and guiding the child in his, then realistic, consistent and just standards can be set and maintained. Further, behavioral standards can, and should, be bent to fit the individual child, rather than the child bent to fit some preconceived notion of the way he is "supposed" to behave. If anything is more confusing to the child than being permitted to behave in any way he likes, it is being forced to conform to standards of behavior incomprehensible at his own level of experience. The little boy who is told that "men don't cry" will indeed hold back his tears, and may do so for the rest of his life, refusing to admit to any hurt or confess the need for any help because he has been taught that it is unmanly. In this way boys and girls are often separated from their real feelings at an early age, simply by not being allowed to express them, and that separation may last a lifetime. Parents who rely on these behavioral stereotypes in raising their children usually do so for their own convenience and gratification; it not only saves them the trouble of setting the proper example in their own behavior, it also spares them the necessity to understand their children's real feelings and needs.

And so when we consider how to head off future male dilemmas in tomorrow's children, we see as the initial step the acceptance of the goal of rearing a child who can accept the range of human behavior and reaction and a role as fully appropriate for him, and whose need satisfaction system is not tied to sexually oriented prerogatives, to gender-ordained superiority, or to antiquated notions of differentiated family roles and responsibilities. Thus when as an adult he selects specific behaviors and roles as those he prefers, he faces no conflict between the values internalized as a child, for these values say to him that any socially acceptable and personally rewarding role and response is good, is valid, and is fully compatible with his human personage and particularly with his maleness.

Obviously the same statements hold for the female child, and equally obviously unless this philosophy of child-rearing is adhered to for *both* male and female children it will not succeed in alleviating sexually oriented conflict in the next generation. For as we consider the specific dimensions of the Ounce of Prevention, it makes no sense to talk of solutions or suggestions for parents of male children as opposed to those for parents of female children. We can only talk of what to do in child-rearing.

Parents who want to raise their children to have different visceral reactions to situations and roles which are currently sex-linked must understand a few principles of how infants learn.

The first principle is that of modeling, learning which occurs almost indirectly by observation of others and what they do. Even the infant of a few months sees and, at some level, records in his conscious memory a response to what he sees. Just how much he sees and records is being debated currently in the experimental literature on infant development, but all schools of thought agree that the infant *does* see and *does* respond and all schools agree further that well before you can talk to a child and he can answer in words, he has seen and been impressed by immense amounts of behavior. It may well be that since the first behaviors seen are seen and recorded in the absence of impressions of other behavior and are unaffected by what is said to the infant, they form the foundation of the belief system which ultimately develops and so determines what we are calling visceral response to later, more complex situations.

But what are the kinds of things which get built into this system? What behaviors can an infant or young child see around him? Primarily human interactions, specifically the interaction of his mother and father with each other, with him, with other children, and the interaction of siblings with each other. Since the infant is unaware of sampling theory, he doesn't know how small and unrepresentative this sample is of the population and so we suggest that this is enough to form the basis of all later impressions of how adults interact, how males and females interact, how adults and children interact and by extension what kind of role differentiation there is on the basis of gender.

For, stripped of all its psychological and sociological trappings, parenthood boils down essentially to the important business of setting an example, the right example; and the mother-father-child relationship—i.e., the family—is the original and continuing site of that transaction. The child learns largely by perceiving that example and reacting to it, and every parent, indeed every couple before they become parents, would do well to consider just what kind of example they wish to provide. In broadest terms, that example includes every aspect of their lives; in particular, their concept of themselves, the nature of their relationship with each other, their commitment to the family and their place in society as a whole—all as an integral part of their roles as parents. Further, they should realize that the home is not merely a place. It is an atmosphere, an environment that is, in itself, a microcosm of the larger human world. In it the child should be able to acquire, with at least comparative security, the variety of experience that will eventually permit him to function fully in that larger world.

Described in this way, the prerequisites of parenthood and family life would seem to be virtually impossible for anyone to provide. And in a sense, that is true. No human being is perfect, no marriage is perfect, human society is itself riddled with imperfections. But that is precisely why parenthood cannot be left to accident or instinct, because instinctively many of the examples that parents set for their children are subconscious hangovers from the way they were brought up. Odds are that the man who was reared by an indifferent, non-communicative father will behave in much the same way with his own children, although on the conscious level he may be severely critical of his father's behavior. Odds are, too, that the woman brought up by a possessive, ever-present mother will pass that example on to her children. Parental patterns of behavior that may once have been appropriate or necessary in a given family situation are passed on in this way to the next generation where they are less applicable; similarly those patterns that were never appropriate whatever the situation. That is why the parents of each new generation must be careful not to perpetuate the mistakes of the past. They must examine their own present situation and set their goals for the future. And this task requires conscious thought and deliberate action.

It begins, of course, with the decision to have children in the first place, a decision that has so often been discussed in these pages that it is necessary to say here only that it must be made with the utmost care and with complete awareness of the long-term responsibilities that it entails. It is only within the last decade, with the advent of the Pill and other contraceptive devices, and legalized abortions that such a decision has become both possible and comparatively effortless, and it is hoped that one day soon the unwanted child will become a rarity. However, even today the emphasis remains on the physical aspects of parenthood—both as to prevention and preparation—and it is ironic that psychologically most parents are totally unprepared for one of the most demanding and complex roles they will ever perform. We would be justifiably horrified if a doctor tried to learn his profession as he went along; yet that is exactly what parents do, and human lives are just as surely at stake.

For the young men and women who are already, or about to become parents, taking a belated course in "Parenthood and Family Life" is hardly the answer; it is already too late. In many cases, they view their roles as parents with the same anachronistic unreality that characterizes their view of marriage. The man who imagines that his responsibilities end as a breadwinner and an occasional disciplinarian, while his wife is responsible for every other aspect of child-raising and domestic management, is living in the past. Even if his wife were willing to devote her full time to wifely and motherly duties, it would still be vitally important that the father amount to not merely a presence in the home, but a person. The mother, for her part, often finds herself torn between two conflicting and equally unrealistic views of her roles. It is not enough, as in the past, to be "just a mother" to her children; she, too, must be a person, an individual in her own right. But in her quest for that individuality, if it takes her outside the family circle, she cannot simply hand her children over to someone else. The fathers and mothers who are confronted with these conflicts are still operating under the old either/or assumptions, whether these are based on the traditional concepts of the "masculine" behavior of the father or the more modern interpretation of permissible "feminine" behavior. The parents who adhere rigidly to either view, and expect their partners to pick up the slack, can subject the marital relationship to an intolerable strain and, as bad if not worse, succeed only in providing their children with an example that will be just as unworkable in their own later lives.

And examples are important, since the second principle which guides this period of initial role learning is that behavior which is seen most often, when it is consistent, will be the behavior learned most effectively, the behavior most solidly built into the child's foundation of beliefs. Thus, when mother and father consistently allocate child care responsibility on the basis of gender, the infant from the moment at which he is first able to receive external impressions is receiving a consistent specific impression that mother feeds, mother cleans and diapers; father swings in the air and juggles mobile. If a continuous series of such reinforced impressions comes throughout infancy and early childhood—father leaves early in morning, mother stays home; mother plays during day, feeds, cleans, feeds, cleans, father comes back and roughhouses a bit . . . at some point the child generalizes that mothers and fathers do different things and/or are different kinds of people.

Interestingly enough, we are convinced that true sharing will not obscure the child's awareness of differences between his mother and father, for even when the role activity is the same —mother bathing the baby, father bathing the baby, the baby feels the difference. The mother's actions and father's actions are nonverbal communication of a difference. Watch mothers and fathers bathe infants. The father's movements are stronger and his hands larger. When the father puts the infant in his bath towel against his chest, the infant feels the difference in the male body, different from the soft breast feeling it gets from his mother's body. And of course sensing the difference is natural and appropriate. What is not sensed when responsibilities are shared is that "only the soft type bathes me."

A third principle which applies is that a child learns about other people in the context of his family. His first notions, at least the first notions he ever expresses, are that all women are "mommy" and all men are "daddy." Now we know that even a young child could pick his own mommy out of a police line-up from among all these other females he calls mommy. What he is saying simply is that all of these women represent one of the two kinds of people he has learned exist in the world, mommy-types and daddy-types.

We are convinced that the distinction is not exclusively a visual one, based on the fact that the mommy types look different and feel different than the daddy types, but is a distinction based on role and function in relationship to the infant. We are further convinced that once this role differentiation is learned by the

infant, he has a foundational notion of six-linked role differentiation which will be extremely difficult to undo at the conscious
level in later years.

Illustrative of this point is the experience of a couple with
three children. Throughout their children's lives both husband
and wife have worked. However, the two oldest were raised
during a period when because of the kinds of jobs each held and
the fact that the husband worked only a few blocks away from
where they lived, a total sharing of all infant and child care
responsibilities took place. Father was as likely to change a
diaper as mother, and mother as likely to swing as father. Both
fed the children, both bathed the children, both dressed the
children, and so on throughout the range of child care responsibilities and activities.

From the time of their earliest speech, the two children both
developed in the same way—almost interchanging the labels
"mommy" and "daddy," and expressing no consistent preference
for either parent doing either. They could be put to bed by either,
dressed by either, fed by either, and this continues to be true at
the age of seven and five, as this is written. Moreover, at this age
they still tend to integrate the two names, often looking at the
father and saying "mommy—daddy will you . . ." Or running to
the mother and asking "daddy—mommy can I . . ."

An interesting contrast occurred with the third child. Soon
after he was born the family moved so that the father was no
longer five minutes from work, but now followed the more traditional pattern of leaving in the morning and coming home at
night. Child care responsibilities were now split between mother
and a housekeeper, with only occasional involvement by the
father. At two and one-half, not only is there no mommy-daddy
equation in speech for this child, there is no mommy-daddy
equation in task preference. Mommy puts on pajamas, and
mommy puts this child to bed, or else the protest is heard halfway
across the city.

Now presumably mommy and daddy look and feel no less
alike to child three than they did to children one and two. In fact,
with jumpers, slacks and pants suits on mommy and longer hair
on daddy, they probably look *more* alike. But their behavior
toward the third child during infancy and early childhood was
very different from their behavior toward the first two, and this

we believe is clearly reflected in his sharp differentiation of roles, a differentiation not made by his siblings.

And so we urge parents interested in breaking the sex role differentiation cycle to recognize that their ultimate success is affected by the initial allocation and the extent of sharing of child care responsibility, and will continue to be affected by how they interact with each other and with the infant from birth throughout the first few years.

This means that parents who want to have children able to develop free of the confusions imposed by sexism must plan on how they will do this before the infant appears, and must be ready to live a more consciously structured life than they might otherwise prefer to do. They must consciously decide who is to do what kinds of chores, both those chores involving the infant and those other dimensions of family living which the infant will observe. They must consider the implications for sex role perceptions of all they do, considering what the act may imply to the infant observer.

For example, if mother and father are both working before the infant is born and they decide that one of them shall stop for the first several months, they should recognize how disparate their familial roles will become. They should consider alternative plans whereby the one who will have more responsibility for home and child continues to work part-, if not full-time, even if he or she nets nothing when the expense of travel and babysitters is added up. For while it may net nothing in terms of income, it may net immense gains in terms of the child's perception of both parents as mobile, active people with out-of-house responsibilities and purposes. It may add enormously to the child's view of both mother and father as people who have child responsibility but other responsitilities as well. And of course it will keep both parents alert and active with multi-faceted lives.

Needless to say there is a price to be paid for these gains in perception. And the price is not only the considerable expenditure of physical energy on the part of father and mother, but also the psychic energy eaten up by the child's unhappiness on those days when, failing to recognize how mother or father's leaving is important if he is to develop sound sex role perceptions, the infant howls hysterically when he or she begins to put on a coat. And the price is paid in the inability of the working parents to flop into the easy chair before the six o'clock news, replacing this with preparing supper, or giving the child a bath.

And that is why we stress the need for potential parents to reach a clear understanding of what it is they do want to teach their children, and what kinds of models they do wish to be *before* the children are born. As much of the conflict-resolution period as possible must be behind them, so that the model they present is that of two adults willingly and even joyfully going about their daily activities and carrying out their daily responsibilities. They would be dreadful models, defeating the purpose of what they have planned, if instead they come through to the child as conflicted, confused, and angry adults, reluctantly carrying out a series of behavioral charades because the other wants it or, worst of all, because of the arrival of "that brat, who I just changed for the fourteenth time today and isn't it about time you moved off *your* butt and changed him once?"

For another critical dimension of learning which parents often fail to understand is that children are sensitive to non-verbal cues and can sense the emotional tone of parental actions and reactions as deftly as they can respond to the words which their parents say. This means that the parent who does not truly believe what he says, or does not truly act in ways consistent with his beliefs, communicates ambivalence at best, and hypocrisy at worst to his children. He communicates a lack of certainty, a lack of value and a lack of strong conviction about just what is and is not important to him.

Because of this, the parent who has successfully worked through to where he understands his own feelings is far better advised to live in accord with those feelings *whatever* they might be, than to try and suppress those dimensions of his belief system which he feels are not socially acceptable or which connote a life style which intellectually he feels is not completely progressive. In other words, we are suggesting that it is better for a child to have parents living a consistent life, with homogeneous drives and actions, no matter what model those drives and actions present, than it is to have parents in a dilemma torn between what each wants to do and what each thinks or feels the other should do.

Obviously we are not talking about pathological behavior here, but within the generous bounds of normal behavior we do believe that children can cope more effectively with a consistent parent than with an inconsistent one. More important, the consistent parent provides the growing child with the freer atmosphere in which to learn and mature and decide for himself on a life-style and belief system. And so, if you cannot live a life-style with parallel or equally self-fulfilling roles, you and your spouse are better advised to work out some other way of living together. A family with sex role differences honestly accepted is preferable to a family where the parents try to pretend to be equals who happen to be of different genders.

But infants and infancy are not our only concern for obviously we cannot wait to do something for children until the yet unborn generation emerges. We are also concerned with those here now, i.e., those of nursery age, those of elementary school age who have not yet reached puberty, the early adolescent, and the late adolescent or young adult.

But what is needed if you are beginning with children rather than infants? The essential difference is that at all ages you must expect to have to re-educate and re-orient, as silly as that may seem in the young. But as we noted earlier, learning through observation and modeling has taken place for most of the years the child has lived, and if this was learning values and behaviors you now consider wrong, then they must be unlearned or extinguished and new values learned instead.

Unlearning and extinguishing are clumsy words, but there are no graceful substitutes. We are not talking about forgetting, in which over time a particular impression or belief slips into the unconscious levels of the mind because it is not reinforced or used. We are talking about directly seeking to remove an alive, active belief and impression in current use, a belief which has been learned and so must be unlearned; what psychologists call extinguishing a behavior.

And how do you foster unlearning? Just as psychologists extinguish animal behaviors and the behavioral therapists try to modify human behavior. One way is to begin to punish, rather than reward the behavior you want to extinguish. Another, which takes longer, but is more appropriate for the social behaviors we are considering, is to stop modeling and reinforcing what you want unlearned and start reinforcing and modeling what you want learned instead. You want your four-year-old to lose the

notion that only his mother can bathe him? Then let bathing be
done by father for a while and make the first few father baths
particularly desirable events complete with new bath toys, extra
special splashing privileges and an unheard-of five minutes of
free play. Then after a while start alternating bath time between
mother and father. The time line here is simple: the older the
child with whom you begin, the longer period of time over which
he has learned and lived with his impressions and therefore the
more difficult it will be for him to unlearn and replace his previous perceptions with an alternate set of perceptions.

Are little boys, then, to be allowed to play with dolls and little
girls allowed to climb trees? Why not? The father who finds it
difficult or even distasteful to play with his own baby was probably forbidden to play with dolls when he was a child. The
mother who insists that her daughter "act like a lady" was probably told the same thing when she was growing up. Similarly,
and as we noted earlier in this chapter, aggression and competition are to be encouraged in little girls as well as boys, if they
represent constructive self-expression and are considered
necessary means toward the goal of self achievement. Perhaps
labeling aggression as drive would ease the transition. Encouraging, or condoning, aggression and competition in boys, simply
because they are boys, is to confuse the means with the ends. The
result, in the man, may be an aggressive and competitive drive
which is considered an acceptable form of "masculine" behavior
even if it is patently self-destructive or destructive of others. In
other men who do not, cannot, or prefer not to employ these
particular means to achieve their ends, the result may be a deep-
seated sense that somehow their achievements are less worthy
because they are less "masculine," or that they themselves have
somehow failed to measure up. For girls, at least until quite
recently, aggression and competition were considered inappropriate because achievement outside the home itself was considered inappropriate for females, a serious psychological and
social error which may take a generation or more to correct. It
can only be remedied by giving girls equal freedom and opportunity to pursue their preferences and realize their abilities in
constructive achievement, and if aggression, drive, and competition are necessary to that end, they should be encouraged in girls
as well as boys.

Play during these early years provides a particularly fertile field for this retraining by providing opportunities for teaching young children the notion that the full range of human emotions and behavior is appropriate for all persons. Traditionally, we make use of play to develop and then continually reinforce the most stereotyped notions of sex-oriented actions and responses, but it could be used as simply and effectively to develop and reinforce the kinds of notions we are discussing.

Consider dolls. They can be used for the obvious teaching of mothering. Why not also for teaching fathering or for teaching both future mothers and fathers how to express affection, concern for another, how to take responsibility for the care of a less self-reliant person, and a variety of expressive dimensions of personality which have no sex link, and which would be equally appropriate for the male child as for the female child. In fact, in a culture such as ours, where men are not sufficiently verbally self-expressive, the kind of verbalizations emphasized through doll play are more important to male than to female development.

For play situations to become non-sex stereotyped giant steps toward adult development parents must rid themselves of the notion that unisex play in childhood will lead to a confused sense of sexual identity in adults. There is no evidence or reason to believe that a generation of boys who play with dolls and of girls who play with cars will produce a generation of male and female homosexuals to any greater extent than current play practices. And if there is no evidence that in today's world of sex oriented play, a child's preference is anything but a symptomatic reflection of sex role stereotypes, it would cease also to be a pressure point in parent-child sexual confusions and concerns. Then the father whose sexual identity as a male is more fragile than he admits to himself would not flip should his male toddler cuddle a doll, nor would the ambivalent maternal feminist grow hysterical with guilt should her daughter spend her hours building forts with Lincoln Logs.

Once again let us note that we are not talking about an identity of activities for boys and girls. We have discussed at length basic physiological differences between males and females and these will obviously be expressed for most boys and girls in preference for different play activities, particularly in athletics.

When these differences are naturally expressed, we would accept and encourage them as fully as we would accept the child who does not fit into the average physical pattern of his or her sex.

Children, as every parent knows, are incessant role-players, and role playing, if carefully structured, can provide another opportunity to reinforce the values and behavior stressed at home. Beginning in kindergarten, and even toward the end of nursery school, children, if permitted and encouraged, can and will deal with those aspects of human relationships which have most meaning for them and which best express their concerns and problems. Obviously any age group will do this at levels appropriate to their development. Given the guidance of a sensitive and skilled teacher, even three- and four-year-olds can be helped through role play to move to a fuller understanding of the very values involving human dignity which the parents too should be seeking to teach. Moreover children of both sexes should be allowed full freedom of self-expression in order to sort out for themselves those patterns of behavior—or roles, if you will—that provide them with the greatest measure of self-satisfaction. That kind of freedom does not, however, imply license, for it must be contained within the framework of parental authority, and setting limits is a parental obligation. Not only must parents provide living examples of the kind of behavior they wish their children to emulate and then encourage that behavior, they must stand ready to discourage behavior that is potentially destructive or inappropriate to the child's level of physical, intellectual or emotional development. Parental approval or disapproval is perhaps the most important factor in reshaping the child's development, but it must not be confused in either the child's or the parents' mind with love. Parents who withhold their love as a form of disapproval, or bestow it as a reward, undermine not only the child's security but also their own authority. Yet parental authority, and the importance of the family unit, must be firmly established if the family is to serve its function successfully, and clearly it must be based, not on giving love and taking it away, nor on fear of punishment, but on the mutual realization that the parents are older and wiser than the child; and because they love him, and respect him as an individual in his own right, not merely as a reflection of themselves, certain standards of behavior are both necessary and just.

Assuming, sharing and exercising this kind of authority will go a long way toward revitalizing the family unit, for it implies mutual commitment and mutual responsibility. No one child or adult can be permitted to tyrannize the family, or shirk his obligations to other family members. This kind of solidarity does not, however, imply a return to the old cliché of "togetherness." There, it was assumed, the family was the *only* significant social unit, and that locking the doors, pulling down the blinds and "playing," "praying," or just "staying" together was the only sure road to happiness. But such self-imposed isolation, such idyllic irrelevance, is the exact opposite of the function the family is supposed to serve. If it is to have any efficacy as a training and testing ground for youth, if it is to have enduring importance in the lives of adults, the family must be a very active part of the larger social community.

Not only has the family circle been called "the seedbed" of society, it is generally given credit for instilling and perpetuating those ideals and standards of behavior that are of value to civilization. As we have discussed, it is there that the child first shapes his opinion of himself and begins to act on that opinion; there that he learns to relate to those older and younger than himself, both male and female; there that he has his first taste of responsibility to himself and others. The family is, perhaps inevitably, conservative and slow to change, for its dominant influence is the parent brought up by a generation twice removed from his or her children. The phrase that sums up this kind of conservatism most succinctly is the familiar "What was good enough for me is good enough for my kids."

But the simple fact is that this is no longer true. The real or imagined virtues of the way parents were brought up may *not* be good for their kids; they may not have been very good even for them. The notion of male superiority and female inferiority, and the rigid sex role distinctions and expectations that characterized the previous generation's upbringing, is only one case in point. As we have seen in previous chapters, the sex role hang-ups that plague today's adult generation can be traced directly to the conflict between the expectations of their early years and the realities of their later ones. For that reason, the family must not only be flexible, open to change, and in tune with a part of today's world, it must work actively to avert those forces that have contributed to our sexual dilemma in that world. Conservative, yes, but reactionary, no.

Change must, of course, begin from within, and parents who are secure within themselves and with each other in their sexual and social roles will pass that security on to their children. But the parents who have decided to put an end to the sexual prejudices and preferences of traditional marriage and child-raising are faced with other equally difficult hurdles, for many of the institutions of society perpetuate those prejudices. The worlds of business and of education, to name only two, are, if anything, even more conservative than the family; and if they are to change, again the impetus must come from within—from the individuals and families that they are designed to serve.

Parents isolated from, or indifferent to, the concerns of their community, or any of the wide range of social factors that so profoundly influence child-raising and family life, have no recourse when they discover that the values and standards that govern their lives, and which they wish to pass on to their children, are being subverted or even contradicted as soon as they leave the house. It is crucial, then, that parents make their voices heard and work actively for change where change is necessary. At the very least, their efforts will focus new attention on the importance of the family, and will force consideration of the options and alternatives that should be open to every family if it is to function effectively.

One basic change a revitalized family could accomplish would be to restore childhood, meaning that parents make a conscious effort to re-establish a sequential life-style for their children, consisting of relatively discrete periods with finite terminal points. The stages should have different privileges, different responsibilities and age appropriate demands. The stages should be graduated so that as the child grows older, he sees himself moving upward toward ever-increasing levels of maturity, levels which should be increasingly attractive.

Remember, we need only return to the America of the nineteen thirties to find a culture which had reasonably well-defined structures for establishing the boundaries of childhood and adolescence. At that time, nursery schools were rare and the child spent his first six years dependently within the family. Going to school was a sharply delineated developmental step. His first school was an eight year elementary school and graduation to high school was another clear developmental step, a sign that childhood was behind and he was now an adolescent. Clothes provided other signs of a clearly defined boundary between childhood and adolescence. Any male older than forty will remember the triumph which came from putting on that first pair of long pants, an event which was a sign that childhood was behind you.

In contrast, in the forties and even more so in the fifties, sixties and seventies, the child remained a child for very few years. Little boys were clothed in long pants long before they could walk in them. Little girls had bras before they could fill them. Before a child was fully aware of his status, he was in nursery school and so by three or four, he was spending time independently apart from his family. Both in these schools and in the family, even the youngest child was considered a participant in decision-making, a free soul who had the right of participation.

This combination of early transitions to higher stages of development, often accompanied by complex ceremonies of too early and meaningless *rites de passage* and the early assumption of responsibility and participation, all amount to the loss of childhood. Instead of a slow, sequestered period to explore, to learn, to identify, and to develop, to test and see what worked and what failed, there was involvement in social situations and in actions with social consequences.

But decision-making and social consequences are incompatible with our notion of childhood. For in a genuine childhood, the early levels should be free of premature adult responsibility. They should have only limited structure so that the child begins his life in an atmosphere permitting growth and exploration in any direction. It should be a period where, except for physical danger to himself or others and damage to his surroundings, the child learns the consequences of his actions by trial and error, a primitive but effective first way of direct learning. Parents must permit activity during childhood in terms of the child's definitions of "activity." Thus what to an adult may seem aimless or pointless, or simply doing "nothing" must be acceptable if the child wishes to do it. The adults must make a special effort to free themselves of the prevailing notion in American middle-class culture that every activity of the child must be achievement oriented and that the future success of the adolescent or adult depends on the level of accomplishment reached by the age of three. We would not want to see remedial work for the two-year-old in distinguishing up from down!

Hence we emphasize the need for a period of childhood in which the infant and toddler can unfold and develop with stimulation he can handle but without pressure and without standards and norms for development. The child's entrance into formal school is soon enough for his entrance into the competitive world in which he is measured against other children and abstract notions of what he should be learning, doing and saying at his chronological age and maturity level.

And childhood is a critical period too, in that it is the period when attitude formation is affected by outside influences as well as family situations. For while the battle to erase the old masculine-feminine stereotypes begins within the family circle, with parents serving both as models and teachers, their example is not the only influence that will shape their children's perceptions of themselves, and of their sexual and social roles. Words and pictures—books and television—make an early and lasting impression, and that is as it should be, for both are inseparable from the educational process. But that impression should be the *right* impression. In the case of books, for example, the nursery stories and fairy tales that the child customarily hears first are bristling with sexual and social implications, and we should not underestimate the ability of children to generalize and abstract. Once they can understand speech, they can generalize to some level, and a verbal three-year-old begins to abstract. Thus the women's liberation groups who, in 1971, attacked Snow White's spending her days in the forest cleaning and cooking for seven dirty little men and her ultimate rescue through Prince Charming's bestowal of "love's first kiss" were not as ludicrous as the media made them out to be. In and of itself, Snow White will not teach any child different sex role values, but if to Snow White you add Sleeping Beauty and throw in Cinderella for good measure, you get a well-reinforced foundation from which to abstract a notion of male and female roles totally inappropriate for the kind of belief system we are considering.

Not only does the child learn that wolves and stepmothers are universal evils, but also the little girl may be led to believe that her life will consist solely of lying around in a trance until she is brought to life by "love's first kiss," or of being rescued at last from the kitchen by an invitation to a ball. And the boy, for his part, may derive the notion that his sexual role will consist solely of waking up a sleeping beauty who will then stay put in the castle while he spends his time slaying dragons.

We are particularly concerned with these stories the child first hears, well before he enters any formal school setting, because it is from these stories that the toddler secures his first impressions of sex-linked roles and behaviors. And once a role abstraction is made, then all future efforts at teaching must first overcome the already existing precepts, and we face the extinguishing problem again. Try to convince a six-year-old who has read Cinderella and Snow White that stepmothers are not cruel, hostile and rejecting.

It is easy to poke fun at these stories, and their implicit and explicit connotations have been criticized many times before. But the fact remains that they are not all bad; they teach the virtues of love, honesty, bravery, fidelity and a host of other useful lessons; and they both stimulate and satisfy the child's powers of imagination. It would be a foolish overreaction to ban them; equally foolish to insist that they be censored or rewritten. They are "classics," and it is to be hoped that we have outgrown the impulse to bowdlerize books—juvenile or adult—to conform to some more "moral" or simply more modern standard. But what, then, can the parent do who is concerned about the sexual and social stereotypes that they convey? It is quite simple. Just as a parent would never think of leaving a child with the impression that every apple he may eat will be poisoned, or that a wolf lurks around every corner, ready to devour him, so these other erroneous impressions can, and should, be the subject of questions, answers and discussions—all at the child's level of understanding and awareness. It is the difference between fact and fiction that is the issue here, and the child can be guided to an understanding of that difference by stimulating him to relate the products of his own, or others' imaginations to the realities of his everyday experience.

As for those books that are not classics and that, under the guise of fact or fiction, perpetuate sexual stereotypes, parents should take an active stand against them, whether they happen to be reading primers or slightly more sophisticated descriptions of "masculine" or "feminine" behavior written for juvenile instruction. Criticism of the sexist book is as important as criticism of the books which ignore or present distorted views of blacks, Indians or any other aspect of human experience. It is ironic that, in recent years, far more attention has been paid to how early or how well a child reads, rather than what he reads or how well he understands it. Naturally, parents should take an active interest in their child's reading abilities, but if it is not their prerogative to teach reading, it is certainly their responsibility to know what their children are learning from the books they do read. Again, it is not a question of banning, censoring or editing any book, or of demanding perceptions of the child far beyond his years. Books are meant to convey ideas, and parents familiar with the books their children read, and the ideas they contain, can discuss them, thus stimulating the child's perceptions and guiding his understanding. This kind of exchange should be a part of the open and honest communication between family members, whatever the age of the child, whatever the books he reads or the complexity of the ideas they contain.

The other dimension of books and other communication media is that they can all be a vital force in effecting the cultural changes we have discussed. The speed with which the media can be mastered, and the thoroughness with which they can move was demonstrated between 1965 and 1970 when they were committed to assisting in the civil rights movement. From total lack of visibility in all of the media, black men and women suddenly joined American life. They entered television with programs of their own, became members of news teams, and were pictured in commercials as living regular middle-class lives. From total absence in school texts and history books in 1960, the current book market is filled with revised texts which devote attention to minority representations and with special materials devoted exclusively to black Americans in our historical past. And from children's books which were completely white, we have in a few years reached a point where one can easily stock a child's library with books of multi-ethnic populations.

And so we suggest that the media embark upon a new social campaign to unsell the false notions of gender-oriented behaviors which contribute to the male dilemma. And we suggest that while all media have this responsibility, television has a special responsibility to enter this movement, since so much of what television now does strongly reinforces the concept of a society in which the women are sexual objects of little intellect whose main concern is staying slim enough to elicit whistles. Men don't come through much better, for their main concern seems to be finding enough cold beer. And two-parent families hardly exist, with bachelor fathers and mothers raising various combinations of children with the aid of ethnically atypical housekeepers whom no agency for domestics seems able to produce in real life.

Publishers aren't helping as they might either, for although black men and women have finally entered the world of children's literature, the effective father hasn't. Nor has the professional woman. A respectable publishing company, for example, in 1971 published two books for children on what "you can be" when you grow up. The book for boys suggests to the little boy that he can enter a wide variety of active fields beginning with fireman on page 1, going on through policeman, cowboy, doctor and pilot, and culminating on the last pages with astronaut and President. No family roles are noted, no aspiration to be husband and father is listed. But little girls? Instead of doctors they can aspire to being nurses, and instead of pilots they can aim to be stewardesses, and other mild positions such as secretary or teacher in a nursery school. And their highest aspirations? The last three pages list these as bride, housewife and mother. Obviously, everything is no longer "up-to-date in Kansas City," where the company publishes.

It is difficult to believe that two archaic books could be published in the midst of a profound revolution and redefinition of roles. But imagine how books like these contribute to the solidification of false notions of what it is to be a man or a woman in America in the 1970's and 80's. Here is the continued foundation for the false expectations which doom many little boys to seeing themselves and to being seen as inadequate males if they don't have aspirations for leadership and domination within the circumscribed "male" occupations, and here is the continued foundation for the view that the woman who doesn't see motherhood as her prime destiny or nursing as the highest expression of her intellectual potential is some strange unfeminine beast.

And since publishers and media men have done so much to

sell these notions, we believe they have a responsibility to unsell them. Let them develop the advertisements and posters and the radio and television spots which stress the egalitarian view of men and women developing as individuals to whatever end their talents and abilities lead them. Let them publish the books which suggest to children that women work at varied jobs and that not all boys have to want to be President but may, with perfect sense and respectability, become nurses and teachers. Let them try and portray families with both mothers and fathers who face problems which are real, who love each other yet have conflicts, who have problems not always solved in 30 minutes, and who also enjoy life and each other without slapstick, ridicule, or debasing each other.

Parental participation, and close and continuing interactions between parent and child, remain important when the process of the child's formal education begins, particularly because now, for the first time, the child will undergo formative experiences outside the family circle and thus beyond parental supervision and control. The present-day trend toward greater parental and community involvement in the administration and operation of the public schools is long overdue, and even in those cases where parents band together to oppose an educational innovation, it is an indication that the classroom can neither be isolated from nor irrelevant to wider social concerns. Parents should, of course, know who is teaching their child, and how and what he is being taught, and by keeping the lines of communication open with the child and with his teacher, parents can and should keep a close watch on the child's progress throughout his school years. But apart from these broad and common-sense concerns, parents should be no less insistent that the school complement and reinforce—not contradict—the free and full development of the child as a unique and individual human being, whatever his shape, color or size, whatever his sex.

For while parents with these goals can expect conflict more than reinforcement from many institutions of the larger society, one institution which must reinforce their goals is the school. And it must be changed to do this. Fortunately, it is one societal institution which can readily be changed to accommodate a new social order and prepare children to live within it. Consider now despite reluctance, resistance, and both subtle and violent physical opposition, in the 1970's large numbers of children in the South were attending integrated schools where almost none had been a decade earlier. And in addition to organizational changes, the school materials of the 1970's changed to reinforce the notion of an integrated society with a history which included minorities, and a science to which contributions had been made by scholars and scientists who were not white.

Why not a similar use of the schools to help the next generation develop a mutual self-respect for each other as individuals without the knee-jerk response to roles and activities as "boys don't ... girls do ...."

Just as the school approach to the question of racial relationships involved organization, curriculum and materials, so would the use of the schools in the area of sexual relationships. We would begin with the teacher, making every effort to move men into the early childhood and lower elementary grades and women into the secondary level subject fields. Children should, by observation, see no sex role connotation to "teacher." For just as we want to equalize the dignity of both male and female in the family, so in the school.

At present, the model is poor, for where the children are learning basic skills, including how to play and socialize, the teacher is an out-of-house "mommy," while in the upper grades where serious learning and teaching of advanced skills and complex ideas takes place, the teacher is a man, i.e., the traditional daddy who goes to work and deals with the problem of the real world and making a living.

More than just a factor, the school can be the leader in presenting to children the model of a sub-stratum of society in which common human characteristics take precedence over those unique to each sex. To the extent that sufficient male staff are available, the school can also provide more varied models of male-female interaction than the home, and can assure that all children are exposed to such models and behaviors.

The pivotal questions on school organization relate to segregation by sex and by age or developmental levels. When you consider the relative merits of sexually segregated as opposed to sexually integrated educational activities for young people, you can find social, psychological and practical arguments to support either position. But we believe that the most compelling argument is the sex-role analogy to the point made by the Supreme Court in its decision on school segregation. This was that enforced separation in and of itself has such a strong connotation of superiority-inferiority, that it is socially evil no matter how "equal" the separate facilities are.

And so it is with sexual segregation. No matter how carefully it is handled, once you separate boys and girls and channel them into different classes, separate rooms and different subjects or activities, you are implying that one sex is able to handle certain materials and the other is not, or at least that one sex is able to function at different levels than the other. This subtle communication has historically been used to underline the superiority of males, and we believe it must stop, for it has been one of the key contributors to the development of weakly-founded notions of superiority which not only inculcate spurious notions among males, but also develop into spurious standards to be met. Thus we have schools in which all the male students are mortified and humiliated when a girl becomes valedictorian, and the comparable educational and personal loss when girls refuse to participate at the levels of their full ability for fear of damage to their social popularity.

Segregation by developmental levels is a more complex issue. Today's schools continue to treat chronological age as the basic variable by which to organize a school system and through which to assign children to classes. It is ironic that the larger culture and the specific institution of the school, which have reacted to so much bad psychology and pseudo-psychology, have paid little attention to the sound psychological notions of varying rates of psychological and social maturity. Ironically, the little attention they pay occurs at the young end of the continuum, with some school systems making an effort to estimate the psychological and social maturity of four and five year olds about to enter the school system.

But none, to our knowledge, pays attention to psychological maturity in adolescence, and none does anything to alleviate the psychosexual damage which comes from the differential onset of puberty and sexual-social maturity in males and females.

The closest we come to considering maturational levels is the ungraded concept slowly entering the educational patterns, a concept that children should proceed through subject levels at a pace appropriate to their intellectual and cognitive development. Why not a parallel notion of ungraded social activity, not segregated by sex, but rather a relatively natural segregation by social development and maturity. This might mean 13-year-old girls going to dances at which were boys not only of 13, but of 15 or 16 years, while other 13-year-old boys were down the hall watching films of the last World Series with those 13-year-old girls and boys of other ages who had this as a primary interest, or who simply didn't feel ready to attend a dance. It would avoid the beautifully apt description of the typical junior high school dance as a function attended by young ladies and male children.

Some day we may progress to the point where children are grouped together according to their psychological and developmental ages, rather than by the date of their birth and their sex. Their instruction will proceed as rapidly or as slowly as they themselves can take it, and given the time and guidance necessary to explore and develop their individual potential, it will be much easier to determine what practical goal their education should seek to achieve, and just when it should stop. But until that day arrives, and as assembly-line education remains the exception rather than the rule, parents must perform a dual role. First, they must exert their influence to prevent any kind of separation or segregation within the school system, except on the grounds of the proved abilities or preferences of the individual child. And second, if the child's special needs cannot be met within the school system, parents must do what they can to help the child explore his preferences and encourage his abilities in other ways.

Fortunately, segregation by sex is gradually giving way in many, if not most, public and private schools due to a combination of pressures from parents and students alike. The belief that boys and girls should take different subjects, and that their performance even in the same subjects should be measured by different standards, has been revealed as a social anachronism and a psychological deprivation. Yet it is still extremely difficult for both boys and girls, from kindergarten through graduate school, to cross sexual barriers in either subject matter or standards of performance. And that difficulty can usually be traced to the expectations of their teachers—and of their parents.

Admittedly, it may take a kind of course for some parents to face up to the possibility that their girl child might prefer, and excel at, physics and shop, and their boy child may prefer home economics and poetry. If they have been unable to buck the sexual stereotypes in their own role behavior, there is little hope that their children will be spared the guilt and frustrations of either conformity or rebellion. But if they have, or at least have achieved sufficient self- and social-awareness to realize that these stereotypes are arbitrary and possibly even dangerous limitations of full human function, they can then encourage and support their children in whatever form of self-expression they choose, and insist that their teachers do the same.

Parental and educational expectations should be governed primarily by a single consideration—the preferences and abilities of the individual child. This does not imply, however, that the forms of self-expression that the child chooses and at which he excels will be, can be, or even should be completely asexual. To some extent, the sex of the child will influence the choice, not only of the subjects he or she will prefer, but also of forms of play and recreation and of the peer group associations in which he or she will participate. But child, adolescent or adult should not be barred from any activity because of sex. Heretofore, the educational system has directed the bulk of its attention to the usual rather than the exceptional, bending the child to fit the system. It is time we insist that the system bend to fit the child, that it give individual children of both sexes a wider choice of alternatives based upon their similar needs and abilities, rather than their dissimilar sexual characteristics.

As to the curriculum for the schools, it has to move into the real world and begin to deal with the complex problems and situations which people face, if it is to serve the function of preparation for life, which we have discussed. One necessary addition to the curriculum of the schools is direct teaching of the history of sex roles and the sex orientation of all the previous generations. The alternative would be an ostrich-like effort to act as if the past never happened, an unreal denial since many influences from the past will continue on through the formative years of the generations with whom we are now concerned. These courses of study should include consideration of what happened in the area of roles, but also consideration of the moral issues involved in differentiation of role and right on the basis of gender.

We believe that moral considerations are critical, for unless the dimension of feeling is added to the intellectual dimension, we doubt that children will be equipped to judge the actions of the adults around them. And children must judge, or else the efforts of the family and schools to teach will be thwarted by the traditional conflict between life in and out of school, the conflict in which the child hears one notion at school but sees a different notion reflected in the behavior he sees at home and in his neighborhood.

However, if the child can recognize behaviors as left over from an earlier age, but inappropriate by the standards of the new generations, then he can incorporate the discrepant behaviors into the value system taught in school and at home. Thus, for these families consciously seeking to teach the new sexual values and concepts within the home, the work in school will serve as an active reinforcer of what they are trying to accomplish.

A specific set of materials to put back in the curriculum is a literature that emphasizes heroes, heroines, and courage, courage of every kind, not only physical courage, but courage of a moral and spiritual nature. Pre-adolescence is a good age at which to stress the moral and spiritual concept of male and female heroism. Children at this time are ready for and need the concept of the true hero for their emotional maturation. Moreover, the hero and heroine provide vivid examples of the human values we see as essential in education, not gender values—but human values.

From the earliest years, the schools should also consider the realm of family living to be a basic part of the instructional repertoire it is responsible for. Not the narrow physiological view of sex education, but the broader view of family life education.

But this would be of use to the redirectional effort we are discussing only if these educational efforts were done in a sense and a spirit far different from the pathetic efforts which characterize most programs devoted to family living and sex education today. The cliché-ridden advice about how to live and how to carry out family roles and responsibilities was inappropriate even for the 1930's when it was created. Family living education which is the psychosocial equivalent of Dick and Jane is not going to move us forward one inch, since it totally reinforces the out-

dated notions of sex-linked family roles, and nonviable relationships which are the very ones we seek to change. Only when real
emotions of love and lust, jealousy, rivalry, satisfaction, pride
and real situations move into these programs, will they serve any
function in the re-educational effort.

Since young people are marrying at a younger age than they
have for many years, we suggest that as we move to secondary
school, direct training and experience for marriage and parenthood itself be included at some point in the high school curriculum, since this type of training rarely is obtained by young
people at home. As a matter of fact, training for marriage is rare
and, as we noted earlier, training for parenthood is practically
nonexistent. As far as possible, both young males and females
should be formally confronted with the realities of marriage, the
sexual realities, the money realities, the parenting realities. It
certainly might be stressed that marriage is for men and women,
not for boys and girls.

Now that sex is gradually beginning to peek around the cur-
tains of romance and taboo that have surrounded it for so many
centuries, perhaps it, too, may one day soon become a topic of
open and honest communication between family members. If it
did, an increasing proportion of sexual education could happen
at home. But it is not only the physiology of sex that needs greater
illumination and understanding than most parents seem able to
give their children; it is the psychology of sex and the sexual roles
that must at last be brought out in the open. And this, we believe,
should be the province of the schools.

But it belongs in the school only if the school can provide a
teacher to give the instruction effectively, without embarrass-
ment and without communicating that there are areas which he
or she would prefer not to discuss and about which questions are
unwelcome.

Bad instruction in school only reinforces bad or absent instruction at home. When reinforced, the notion of sex as something difficult, dangerous, mysterious and dirty becomes the
dominant notion.

It is ironic that teen-agers undergoing the trials of puberty are
required to study the reproductive apparatus of the frog in the
minutest detail, but remain largely ignorant of their own. But
that is not the real issue here; most parents and teachers have no

difficulty explaining where babies come from, or answering the fundamental questions about anatomy of the sexes when they arise. What they do not realize, however, is that when they talk about what boys do, or what girls do, or what their children will do and be when they grow up, they are also talking about sex education. Many, if not most of the pressures and proscriptions of both childhood and adolescence are directly related to adult concepts of sexual roles, and the maturing boy and girl has every right to know where these concepts came from, and what applicability and validity they have in their own lives. It is not until college that the young are exposed to the study of sexual and social mores, and there the focus is usually on abnormal sexual psychology or the anthropological study of some remote South Seas society which may only indirectly illumine our own sexual and social situation.

The study of the physiology of sex should begin, as it now does in some schools, as soon as the child begins to express an interest in his own body, and should be geared in complexity to the child's increasing intelligence and awareness. Why not a similar study of the psychology of sex and the sexual roles? In the lower grades, it might consist simply of study and reading materials that illustrate past and present sexual attitudes and roles. Just as black studies and a new emphasis on women's roles have recently been introduced into school curricula, so male-female relationships and the changing concepts of masculinity and femininity should be included as an area of study and discussion. The fact is that they exist, implicitly, in the study of history, literature, current events; it would be necessary to do little more than simply bring them out in the open.

For teen-agers, who for the first time are beginning to think of themselves as adults and consider the alternatives in role behavior that will be available to them, the study of sexual psychology could be conducted on a much deeper level, but it should also be geared to the practical consideration of what being a man or a woman will mean in their own lives, including an attempt to illumine the similarities as well as the differences between the sexes and their future roles as husbands and wives, fathers and mothers.

One of our recent sub-studies[1] presents an interesting example of how such school-based programs can have an effect on developing sexual self concepts. This study measured the self and ideal concepts of adolescent males and females before and after they participated in an eight week, four-hour-a-week sex education course in a public junior high school in Connecticut. While the course had no measurable effect on the role perceptions of the females, it did move the males toward a more self-oriented, self-achieving perception of themselves. We felt that more important than the change was the indication that even a brief eight week, 32 hour exposure to structured materials on sex roles and attitudes could generate a measurable change. This strengthened our conviction that should there ever be a community-wide consensus on socially appropriate roles the schools could effectively communicate this.

In the past, studies for boys have customarily been career-oriented, while girls took the courses in marriage, child-raising and family life, under the assumption that that would be their career. Now that girls are being motivated to pursue career goals too, there is the danger that neither the boy nor the girl will have anything but an intuitive understanding of their adult sexual roles, burdened by the still prevalent sex and social prejudices and misconceptions. Family life is coeducational; it is only common sense that courses in family life should be coeducational as well. Further, coeducation in those courses directed toward career goals would provide additional insight into working relationships between men and women, and with that new dimension, it would also be possible to consider any career not as the province of one sex or another, not as a pursuit that exists completely apart from other sex and social roles, but as an activity that must be integrated with every other aspect of adult life.

We are, and the schools must be, alert to the danger that this new emphasis on communicating to boys and girls that as adolescents and as men and women they are capable of the same range of reaction, response and ability can easily lead to a misemphasis that they therefore *must* function in the same way. We can easily see such courses subtly or directly denigrating the female student whose own needs and drives are toward marriage and motherhood without work or career, and this is socially as unproductive and unsound as current practices which suggest that this is the preferred adult life. In short, we are advocating the free and full development of each child in whatever direction that child finds most compatible with his or her needs . . . We are not suggesting a new set of proscriptions to replace those we believe need change.

If the free and full development of the individual child, male and female, is the goal of the educational process, the school, like the nuclear family, must begin to chart wider spheres of activity and concern. The school, like the home, is an environment for students of all ages; teachers, like parents, must realize that their attitudes, behavior and achievements serve as adult models for the child. That is why sexual segregation and discrimination among teachers must also be brought to an end.

Teachers must also be concerned with developing the broadest possible range of human behavior among their students. A simple mastery of skills is no longer enough; the educational process is incomplete if it does not aim for mastery of self. Here again, the physical, social and psychological imperatives serve as the frame of reference. Self-mastery consists of the constructive integration of these three aspects of the personality, yet most schools pointedly ignore the developing sexual and social awareness of their students, perhaps on the assumption that it is more properly a parental responsibility. In fact, it should be a shared responsibility. A comprehensive program of sex education is only a single step in the right direction, for in many ways, in adolescence in particular, sexual and social roles are inseparable. Their exploration and expression should begin in the classroom, where the student may first learn something of himself and his abilities, and undergo the experience of relating to his peers of both sexes. But this rather abstract and intellectualized experience should be expanded and reinforced outside the classroom, not only in school yards and on street corners, but in constructive, coeducational extracurricular activities.

Unfortunately, the extracurricular activities that receive the greatest attention in many schools serve to separate the sexes and reinforce the stereotypes of sexual and social role behavior. Athletics of almost every kind are for boys, while the girls are confined to the sidelines as passive watchers and admirers or with their major activity leading cheers in sexually provocative costumes. Seldom, if ever, do both sexes participate in the same sport, and many states actually forbid it at the secondary level. The adulation showered on a boy of more than usual athletic ability can, and often does, lead to the belief that life consists solely of playing games, a belief that is extremely hard to sustain in later years. The shoe is on the other foot when it comes to dances, proms and other school-supervised social get-togethers. It is the pretty girls, the "prom queens," who are the center of attention, while the less attractive girls—and most of the boys —sit sulking in the shadows. Both organized sports and dances undoubtedly serve some useful purpose, but it is not difficult to question their overemphasis in the schools. In fact, in recent years, adolescents themselves have questioned their utility, preferring to spend the time, and the money, allocated for these activities in some other way.

In our view, singling out physical prowess in boys and sexual attraction in girls as the criteria for popularity and success is not only questionable, it is downright dangerous. It not only perpetuates the sexual stereotypes, it sets up unreal standards of achievement that are quickly found to be irrelevant in the real world. It is time that the real world was introduced not only into school curricula, but into extracurricular activities as well. Adolescence and immaturity are merely prolonged if young boys and girls are allowed to continue to exist in idle and self-centered isolation from the concerns of their communities. Youth would not be wasted on the young if they themselves were not permitted to waste it.

The Peace Corps and the eighteen-year-old vote are recent innovations that have stemmed from the realization that the young are capable of something more than dribbling balls and sipping Cokes. To those few colleges that have always included work or social service in their curricula, there have recently been added several more conservative institutions that now permit their students to live off-campus and integrate study and work programs toward a degree. Youth gangs in some of our major cities have been seen to attack constructively a social project with the same zeal that they once attacked each other. But why wait until the young have left high school, or have left home? The concept of service should be instilled in both boys and girls, first in the home, then in school and then in the community. A child of any age can, and should, be asked to contribute to the functions of the home: what better preparation for the day when he will have a home of his own? In school, why should pride and cooperation be channeled solely toward cheering a football team to victory? Why not teams of older students to help the young; why not teams of students working together with adults in some useful community project? Work and service programs could also be integrated with classroom studies as they are on the college level.

The isolation, the indifference and the irrelevance that so many young people have complained of, and that have been at the root of the drop-out problem, would thus be avoided, and in assuming their share of responsibility for others, the young would learn to assume responsibility for themselves. Further, in working with adults, the young would be exposed to a wider variety of adult models on which to pattern their own lives. "Education" and "experience" would not be an either/or choice for the young. The generation gap could be at least partially breached, and in working together toward common goals, according to their individual preferences and abilities, the young would come to know each other as human beings, and would not so easily fall into the trap of stereotypical "masculine" and "feminine" behavior.

In fact we would institutionalize the process of service in late adolescence by providing a wide variety of social service real-life experiences away from and unprotected by family, but also away from and without the achievement anxiety of academic studies. In these settings with something real to "do," the adolescent male and female could find out who and what he or she is and in what direction they wish to go. We are tempted to suggest that colleges should mandate such service before admitting anyone to the freshman year. Fewer might ever get to college, but we also believe far fewer would drop out or flunk out than the 50 percent or more who do now, for those who would enter college under this plan would be there because they want to learn, strengthened by the maturity of independent life experience. And for all, whether they go on to college or to work, social service would add to self esteem by providing the opportunity to understand early in life that there are things you *can* do, and moreover an immense variety of things to be done.

There will, of course, always be differences—physical, social and psychological—between men and women, and between boys and girls. There is no system of child-raising, no system of education that can completely eliminate those differences. But by precept and example, at home, in school and in society, the young of this and future generations can be given a wider range of acceptable alternatives and greater freedom in choosing the kind of lives they will lead. They will learn to accept realistically the necessary limitations of their sexual and social roles, the necessary responsibilities in love, marriage, and family life, and given those limitations and responsibilities move on from there to the realization of their potentialities as complete human beings. It is, in most cases, simply a question of opening up—our society, our schools, our families, our marriages and our minds.

Let's get Utopian for a moment. Let's assume that husbands and wives in their thirties and forties face the reality of their conflicts and dilemmas openly and frankly and talk to each other sufficiently to reach understanding and some accommodation. The major social institutions change too, so that schools become places where children can learn and develop as individuals.

And so a generation is reared relatively free of the confusions of the generations which preceded it. And that free generation matures and has children of its own, which are raised in an atmosphere even more completely free of the sex-linked prejudices of our own.

Were that ever to happen, that Utopia would be a fascinating place to be in many respects, but in one of particular relevance for the areas we have discussed. For that second generation would be reasonably free of the cultural overlay of notions about sex-linked behaviors and attitudes. And if free, then it would be reasonable to assume that whatever differences existed then between the sexes were attributable to the kinds of physiological, hormonal and endocrinal differences we now know about, but whose behavioral and attitudinal implications we cannot now differentiate from culture.

Would there be any differences then between men and women? Would the variations within each sex outweigh the differences between them? We don't know, and until we rear that generation, we won't know. For now, we aspire to the understanding which is the first step toward cure, prevention, learning and, ultimately, harmony.

NOTES

1. The sex role perceptions of junior high school boys and girls in relation to a sex education course. Presented by D.J. Fox, A. Steinmann, and S. Losen at the 42nd Annual Meeting of Eastern Psychological Association, New York, New York, April 16, 1971.

CHAPTER 10

A Pound of Cure

What of the adults we have studied? Is role confusion and the resulting conflict between the sexes somehow an inherent part of being a man or a woman born in the decades between nineteen thirty and nineteen fifty? Does everyone come down with it, like chicken pox, which cannot be prevented or even diagnosed until the rash appears? Or is it an acquired ailment, engendered by our particular culture, which cannot only be prevented but cured? All the evidence seems to point to the latter. There is no natural law that segregates the sexes; in fact, nature conspires ingeniously to do just the opposite. It is the customs and traditions of their culture, sometimes accident, sometimes intention, that have driven these men and women apart.

What society has done, society can undo. A recent example is the concerted attempt to eliminate racial prejudice in this country. The progress, however painful and slow-moving, that has been made so far has been the result of a complex of social, legal, political, educational and economic efforts, and it will take a combination of the same forces to eliminate the outmoded attitudes and beliefs that underlie sexual prejudice. But perhaps the most potent force in both the racial and the sexual revolutions, a force that is often overlooked, is the power of personal example. It is virtually impossible to legislate change in the psychological attitudes that result in prejudicial behavior. Such change must come from within the individual, often through the painful process of reappraising.

The most recent example is the concerted effort to eliminate racial prejudice in this country. The progress that has been made so far has taken a complex of social, legal, political, educational, and economic efforts, and it will take a combination of the same forces to eliminate the outmoded attitudes and beliefs that underlie sexual prejudice. But perhaps the most potent force in both the racial and the sexual revolutions, a force that is often overlooked, is the power of personal example. It is virtually impossible to legislate change in the psychological attitudes that result in prejudicial behavior. That change must come from within the individual, often through the painful process of reappraising values and beliefs once taken for granted, shedding the old and trying on the new, opening a closed mind, if only a crack.

It is this kind of change that is the essential first step in seeking a final truce in the battle between the sexes. But *is* it possible to shed the cumbersome baggage of outmoded beliefs and unreal expectations? Is it possible to experiment with new self-perceptions and life-styles? Of course it is not easy to look at one's self, one's marriage and family, one's place in society from new perspectives; it is not easy to buck the behavioral stereotypes. But why should men and women continue to subscribe to,aand be devoured by, a body of outmoded beliefs that has no validity for them? Why should they take behavioral cues either from what used to be, or even from what many still consider ought to be? Every man and woman must be concerned with what is, here, now, even if it runs counter to the way in which they were brought up, or the way others of their own generation choose to lead their lives. The psychological and social pressures of both past and present are extremely difficult to ignore, and the man or woman who attempts to move in new directions will almost inevitably suffer some doubt, insecurity, guilt, and ambivalance. Today's adults can probably never hope for a sudden and miraculous cure for their sexual ailments. But they can examine the symptoms, identify the causes, and work toward preventing the increasingly serious consequences. They can learn to live with themselves, and with each other.

Speaking realistically, a cure is probably less important than diagnosing the disease. Both men and women must face up to the fact that sex role confusion and conflict are very real problems in our society. The causes are not difficult to discover, but it serves very little purpose to waste time trying to fix blame. It is probably too easy to say that society is the villian. Of course society is guilty of perpetuating obsolete standards of sex and gender behavior, but, what, or who, is society: a top-secret government board, the Chamber of Commerce, a group of religious elders, the Board of Education, a suburban coffee klatch? It is all—and none—of these. *We* are society and, in the final analysis, we have no one to blame but ourselves for the social and sexual dilemmas that mar our lives. Granted, in a country as large and diverse as ours, society, or rather social consensus, tends to be conservative, old-fashioned, slow to adapt to change, and often hypocritical. But we cannot look to society to correct its own ills. It is we who must change as individual men and women, and such changes taken all together will be felt in an ever-widening circle until social consensus itself has changed. In short, in seeking both the causes and the resolution of our sexual conflicts, we need look no further than ourselves. "We have met the enemy, and they are us."

It is also too easy to speak of sexual confusion and conflict in high-sounding generalities, as if the victim of chicken pox were to be treated by his doctor with a long-winded discussion of the nature of virus infections, when what he really needs is something to stop the itching. Just how, then, can men and women, within themselves, within a relationship, and within society as well, stop the itch of sex role confusion? The key words are, quite simply, understanding and accommodation; and the goal, again quite simply, a search for some middle ground between the sexes where both male and female can function fully and equally within the physical, social, and psychological needs of their own personalities and of their relationships.

By talking about a middle ground, however, we are not arguing for a unisex world, with undifferentiated sexes. In preceding chapters we discussed at length the kinds of sexual distinctions related to psychological differences which we believe are reflected in emotional patterns of response, and we considered need patterns which may be so deeply rooted in Western culture and American mores as to be impossible to manipulate significantly in a generation or two. And even if these did not exist, we would consider a unisex world relatively pallid and unexciting in comparison to a duosex world.

We believe that the human animal will always behave as other animals do, with one sex having as its basic rationale for life the attraction of, and sexual relations with, the other. And for those behaviors related to sexual attraction, we see no need for a blurring of distinctions. We would continue to dress female children in dresses and male children in pants, and we endorse bras and makeup for those women who consider they add to their sexual appeal and attractiveness, just as we would beards for those men who find this a satisfying overt expression of masculinity which women cannot match.

We see no social virtue in women knocking down the doors of McSorley's Saloon any more than we would see men demanding the right of access to Elizabeth Arden's Miracle Morning. In fact, as we have noted before, we regret the steady attrition of social opportunities for men to meet with other men without business or familial pressures. We consider the development of social interactions with the same sex just as much a part of healthy development as interactions with the opposite sex, and would argue against the notion that all social institutions and all social practices must or should be sexually integrated, either in the adult world or in the new world we would want to create for the children yet to come.

Rather, what we would hope to eliminate are the behaviors and responses which have nothing to do with sexual attraction and interaction, but which over the years have culturally been tied to gender. And moreover, if this were accomplished, and these reactions and responses ceased to differentiate men from women, those sexually relevant characteristics which remained would be immensely heightened in their importance and thus in their impact and effectiveness. The more you take away, the greater the importance of what remains.

In considering how to "cure" the male dilemma for those who are already adult, we have used as a base four of the basic findings of the research which motivated this book. First, is the ambivalence expressed by so many of our respondents—ambivalence not only about what they want to do with their own lives and their own behaviors, but ambivalence as well about how they want their spouse and others of the opposite sex to react to, and behave toward, them. Second is the fact that both men and women express little understanding of each other's expectations, and neither sex believes that the other sex really understands, or sincerely wishes to accommodate to the needs of the other. To this we add the finding that both our male and female respondents consider "companionship" the primary human characteristic to seek in a spouse. Finally we have considered the finding that despite the ambivalence and disbelief, there was extremely close correspondence between the self perception of each sex and the ideal image of the other . . . for example, the kind of man that men described in saying how they thought and felt about themselves was remarkably close to the kind of man women described as their ideal.

We believe that this last finding suggests that it is possible to bring the sexes together, accepting and allowing for the profound changes which have occurred and undoubtedly will continue to occur in sexual roles. Our other findings suggest that this process must involve rebuilding the relationship between couples, the basic social unit, in a new climate of candor and with new processes for effective communication. Simple logic adds that for this to occur, certain social adaptions and changes must be made. Let us consider each area in turn.

Many recent writers on male-female relationships and marriage, in urging the necessity of individual self-expression and self-fulfillment, speak as if a man or a woman could pursue these elusive goals alone, unencumbered, unimpeded, full speed ahead. But most men have wives and children, most women have husbands and children, and the male-female and parent-child relationship must be integral parts of that pursuit. These relationships are, of course, shaped by the personalities of their participants, but they also make their own demands and impose their own restrictions. In other words, sex and gender behavior do not exist in a vacuum; they must be regarded not only in an individual context, but also in the context of the male-female relationship, the family group, and society itself.

Every individual, male or female, exists at three levels: as a physical organism, as a psychological personality, and as a social being, and it is the integration and expression of these three levels of being that constitute human identity. To emphasize one level at the expense of another, or to forbid self-expression on one level or another, is to truncate the identity, as if a car were forced to operate on only two cylinders or two wheels.

The same integration is necessary in a male-female relationship. It, too, must find mutually satisfactory means of expression on the physical, psychological, and social levels if the relationship is to be considered whole and constructive. Obviously the problem is difficult when two people, two separate identities, are involved, and it becomes increasingly difficult as the relationship expands to constitute a family. Compounding the problem is the fact that the participants are different people and will not have the same physical, psychological, and social needs, or may express similar needs in different ways. This is particularly true in the realm of sexual relationships, usually the foundation upon which marital and family relationships, at least at first, are built.

If in a sexual relationship the needs of both partners were the same, and were expressed in the same ways, intercourse might very well be like making love to yourself. That is not to say, however, that these different needs and the means necessary to express and gratify them are consistently or even predictably dissimilar. Obviously, they vary with the sex of the individual, his or her age, the length of the relationship, and an incredible complex of other internal and external factors.

It is, of course, completely impossible to separate sex from psychology; it is not merely a physical act but an expression of the total personality. Nevertheless, sex itself, both as a reflection and an expression of physical and psychological needs, must be seen for exactly what it is: as only *one* of the three levels of human function. It is a very important one, true, but no more important than other forms of individual and social self-expression and psychological satisfaction.

Yet it is shockingly apparent, from only a cursory view, that our culture is completely preoccupied with sex. It pervades politics, where a candidate must have "sex appeal" to woo the voter; business uses it to manipulate and motivate the buyer; it saturates books, music, plays, movies. This preoccupation may be little more than an overreaction to the secrecy and repression of previous generations, a wide swing of the pendulum that may eventually subside. But it has brought with it a view of sex that is as distorted as the Victorian, for it is still shrouded with the unrealistic expectations and outmoded standards of gender behavior of the past. Fantasy rather than reality is its keynote; hostility, anxiety, and guilt are aggravated rather than alleviated; and this physical drive becomes nothing short of a neurotic compulsion. Surely even more damaging to mature, healthy sexuality in a relationship is the archaic notion that sex is somehow a separate human function, so important to the woman that it, and the roles of housewife and mother related to it, make it impossible for her to function on any other level, and so important to the man that complete submission and quick compliance are necessary to enable him to get on with his other work.

Sex *is* important, and mutually gratifying patterns of sexual behavior are essential if a relationship is to survive. The surest way to disrupt that relationship is to consider sex as an end in itself, rather than as a means to an end, and to separate sexual function, either by glorification or denigration, from the other equally essential means of self-expression. There need not be any hard-and-fast rules for behavior in bed divided along traditional "masculine" and "feminine" lines, or any other lines, as long as that behavior is mutually satisfactory. Sex is complicated enough, both physically and psychologically, without approaching it with preconceived platitudes about who should do what to whom and how often. Rather it should be approached with understanding, both of one's own needs and the needs of the other.

In discussing these sexual aspects, "understanding" is emphasized reluctantly because it would seem to put the discussion within the context of the overintellectualized approach to sexual relationships which has inhibited the achievement of sexual satisfaction for many of the adults we have studied. For, in many respects, the generations we have studied may be considered brainwashed generations . . . generations which have been bombarded with research and psuedo research and with theory and expert opinion to such an extent and so continuously that they have accepted and adopted expectations and viewpoints from the outside. Rather than thinking through their own needs and expressing these in their own goals and satisfactions, these generations accepted the notion that sexual satisfaction was, if not the only, clearly the primary way of expressing the relationship between men and women.

Seeking companionship, they accepted instead the notion that social interaction is primarily measured by the frequency, intensity and timing of their sexual relationships; seeking reaffirmation of their sexual identity they instead accept the notion that most of the behaviors inculcated into their psychosocial belief system were anachronistic ways of seeing women as sex objects and serfs. Seeking affirmation of self and self identity, they evaluated themselves and each other by the standards others set, which had no relevance to their individual identities or to their special identity as a couple.

And so they approach a physical relationship with another person loaded down with expectations for what they *should* do, what *should* be done to them, how they *should* feel and respond, as well as how the sexual partner *should* react.

As a befuddled man says to the woman in bed with him in a 1973 *Playboy* * cartoon as he lies inactive, "But how can *I* enjoy it when I know *you're* not fully enjoying it because you're concentrating so much on doing what you think I enjoy?"

The sexual education and indoctrination of the decades of the forties through the sixties gave men and women a psychic checklist for evaluating each sexual interaction ranging from whether or not their foreplay was sufficiently varied, through communicating the proper mixture of excitement and affection, and culminating with the achievement of orgasm by both at reasonably close to the same time. And the seventies have complicated this even more by adding new items to the list, so now the degree of creativity and the effective use of audio-visual and mechanical aids are included.

This is not the realization and actualization of sexual needs. Satisfactory sexual relationships are not achieved within the same model which would be appropriate for evaluating the quality of an arithmetic lesson in the third grade, where we might appropriately ask if the prelesson activities motivated well, if the lesson was varied and creative and used aids well. Neither is it the same as evaluating the effectiveness of two tunnel-digging teams who ideally come together under the middle of the river.

Nor is it the other extreme, the simple expression and release of sexual energy in contact with the body of another person. Rather what we mean by a satisfactory sexual relationship is the achievement of satisfaction of one's sexual needs and drives through a physical interaction with another, giving and receiving pleasure and joy through a natural expression of the internal psychological states. It is not only a sexual interaction but a physical expression of delight with self and delight in sharing this intimate expression of self with another.

The history of the last century has been characterized by

---

* *Playboy*, July 1973, p. 105

dramatic changes involving satisfaction of the sexual needs of men and women, but unfortunately the change has involved a swing from one extreme to the other. Where the late nineteenth century might be described as living by a standard which involved men being satisfied and women providing satisfaction, the current climate could be described as requiring both being satisfied all of the time, and ideally always at the same time.

The problem with this egalitarian and overintellectualized approach to sexual satisfaction is that it creates what social psychologists call a dissonance reduction situation; that is, a situation with expectations so emotionally charged that, if they are not realized, the persons involved must develop some explanation which satisfies his or her emotional and psychological needs. Given the differing climates of men and women in general and of any two individuals at any one point in time, equal interest in, or need for, sexual interaction and release is less likely than unequal interest or need. As an isolated fact this is neither threatening nor damaging, nor a necessary precursor to sexual frustration or conflict. One disinterested partner and one interested partner can relate and have intercourse which is richly satisfying to the interested partner without being either demeaning or damaging to the disinterested one provided there is no double satisfaction criterion to be met, and provided both are willing.

The notion of giving pleasure to another has apparently been buried, particularly for women, beneath the overraction to the "sexual object" role, historically female. The overreaction is understandable, for by current views of human dignity the role was, and is, intolerable, and totally incompatible with a relationship between two mature adults. There is no need to look back to it longingly as the answer to the male dilemma, nor to suggest that women should contribute to the solution of that dilemma by resuming their traditional roles as passive partners in male sexual release and realization. Given today's values, this is not only demeaning; it also would not work, for men too have gone past that point.

What is suggested is that both men and women relax, and try to forget all the judgment-loaded so-called sexual advice of the last several decades. Forget the contrived ways to be sensuous, forget the stopwatch approach to simultaneous climax. And after all of that is forgotten, remember instead what it is *you* want from a physical relationship, not what you think your partner wants, or what you think you *should* want, but what you *actually* want. If the two people involved in a sexual relationship both do this and express their needs and desires with thorough candor in action as well as speech and if they respect each other and respond to each other's needs, as well as their own, then physical momentum should take them the rest of the way.

Ironically, the factors that interfere most often with this kind of sexual parity are seldom physical at all; rather they are psychological. Although a great body of myth and legend has grown up around the "magic" or the "electricity" of the original sexual encounter between a man and a woman, most couples will testify that achieving a mutually satisfactory sexual relationship is hardly an instantaneous, instinctual event. It is, instead, a learned experience, a matter of time, and if there is a magic ingredient, it is the love that both partners have for each other that enables them to be patient, to learn, to understand, to trust, and to feel free to express their needs and to seek mutual satisfaction. In a new relationship, this ingredient is usually strong enough to see the couple through the initial difficulties of adjusting to each other, but in too many cases lines are drawn to correspond to the conventional standards of male and female sexual behavior. Each partner acts and reacts in ways that are thought to be appropriately "masculine" or "feminine" and the exploration of their relationship stops there, far short of the full expression of their unique and individual human needs. Thus the man who has been taught to believe that it is up to him to initiate the sexual advance feels it is his masculine prerogative and, further, exactly what the truly feminine woman has been taught to expect. Similarly the woman may imagine that it is her feminine prerogative to be coy, passive, or even very sparing of her sexual gifts, simply because that is the way she has been taught to behave and that is what she believes the man expects. Secretly the man may wish that, just once, his wife would come to him and stop making him jump through so many hoops; and the woman may wish, just once, that she could behave as she really feels, not as she is supposed to feel. But is is extremely difficult to alter the preconceptions and prejudices of sexual behavior, even in a marital relationship, and more often the man actually does feel that his "masculinity" has been compromised if his wife takes the sexual initiative, and the woman feels that her "femininity" is threatened by any unladylike response. The truth is, however, that notions of masculinity and femininity that depend upon these, and other equally shaky behavioral props, are usually reflections of sexual ambivalence and a concept of self that is far from secure.

But we believe that they also reflect the gradual preoccupation with the pseudopsychology of sex that has so pervaded our culture that at all levels people have been conditioned to believe the false and simplistic notion of the primacy of intense sexual satisfaction as the necessary condition for relationships and marriage.

And so relationships flounder, and marriages dissolve at frightening rates, and not always because of the social and psychological incompatibility of the husband and wife. We suggest that many fail because either husband or wife or both have accepted these culturally pervasive expectations of unreal levels of sexual bliss and excitement which neither their psychosocial nor physical realities can produce or maintain. Thus they are misfits; the marriage is a failure and so they dissolve it and search for a partner with whom they can try again to reach the fantasy summit.

It would be more sensible if the culture imparted the notion that in sexual satisfaction and social relationships, as in every other phase of human behavior, there are wide ranges in response. What is satisfaction for one may be bliss for another, frustration for a third. Far more important than accepting without thought the false notions of the marital marketeers is that couples talk through their expectations and needs so that they understand themselves and each other.

But this understanding will not come easily, for the adults we're writing about are consumed by the pressures of these conflicts they have not been able to understand, in part because their involvement is so complete and constant. They never have the luxury of standing off and observing and so have neither seen nor understood the pressures pushing them to carry out actions they don't fully believe in and to accept false goals, leaving them with failure and unrealized ambitions.

Sexual relationships comprise only one part of the complex of relationships which each couple must resolve to arrive at their own solution, and that can only be done through open and honest communication. How can a husband understand what his wife wants if she does not tell him, or if she does tell him and he does not listen? How can a wife be expected to accommodate her husband's needs if she does not know what they are?

It seems absurd to think that a man and wife do not, and even worse, cannot talk to each other, but our Inventories and Surveys have proved beyond a doubt that this is usually the case. When they do talk, their actions often belie their words and whatever communication there is between them is effectively short-circuited. It goes without saying that establishing intimate contact with one's partner, on both the verbal and non-verbal levels, is one of the most important, if not *the* most important aspect of marriage, for only in this way is the sharing complete. Mutually gratifying sexual relations are part of that sharing, as are the shared responsibilities and rewards of marriage, but thoughts and ideas, attitudes and beliefs, feelings and emotions must also be shared. Just talk, however, is not enough; both partners must also listen. Only then can they hope to understand each other and make themselves understood. Only then can they express their changing needs and explore the changing needs of their relationship to arrive at those patterns of behavior that will satisfy both. And then, as a final step, they must do as they say; words and deeds must correspond.

The specific techniques of this kind of communication are beyond the province of this book, but one point is clear: if understanding and accommodation are to be achieved, couples must talk. They must talk about their dreams, their hopes, what their relationship really is all about. Each should seek to identify and express his or her aims and goals, and what each one wants and needs from the other. The female should verbalize her feelings about whether or not she wants to achieve on her own, outside of the family. The male should verbalize his feelings about whether or not he wants her to achieve, as well as verbalize his feelings and attitudes toward his own self-achieving role and what he feels about a woman's drive toward self-achievement and home and family needs.

However, if during the coming years talking is to be at all useful, there will have to be a reversal of what we have found to be the current hypocritical and inhibited pattern of verbal interactions between the sexes. In fact, our research indicates that the adults we have studied might well be considered the inhibited generation, who for a variety of psychosocial pressures have developed a pattern of suppressing what they consider expressions of hostility, anger, contempt—replacing these with bland noncommittal statements, devoid of feeling and to which there is little opportunity to respond. This is a pattern which seldom permits discussion, and what little there is lacks candor and reality. The majority of men and women we studied know this, and freely admit that they have little belief in what their spouse says to them, whenever the discussion involves a topic which has any degree of emotional charge.

Instead of sensitive candor, the adults we have studied enter into a complex combination of guessing, role playing, and assumption-making which as often as not leaves both frustratedly committed to a point of view or a pattern of behavior they neither believe nor want.

As we have learned the sequence from our respondents, it goes something like this. Some matter of importance comes up which requires decision and action. And the game begins. Each spouse now begins to think not only about what he or she would like to do, but also about what the other would want each to do, and what each would want the other to do. And each then debates between saying what they actually believe or what they think their spouse wants to hear.

And in recent years a third element enters, as each considers what their idealized sex image would want and say. Men wonder what an enlightened man should think and want in the situation, particularly if he wants to think he is at least reinforcing, and hopefully expediting, the continued liberation of his wife. In the same vein his wife considers what the liberated woman should do, or what the sensuous woman would do, or most confusing of all, what the liberated sensuous woman would do!

We believe that the truth would be simpler to live with for men and women of all ages, than this complex of half-truth and assumed truth, half lie and half pretend. We hesitate to go to the extreme exemplified by Elwood P. Dowd in *Harvey* who speaks with perfect candor and who assumes that even social clichés such as "We must get together sometime soon" are completely sincere and so replies that he is completely free next Tuesday. But we would go close enough to that extreme to suggest that any conflict within a relationship can best be handled if both parties first think through to what they want for themselves and from each other and say so.

We believe it would be an immense relief for the adult generation to be able to say what it thinks and believes, after decades of inhibited reactions. We see the appeal of Archie Bunker and *All in the Family* tied in part to the delight at being in the company of a candid person who says what many others think but stifle.

In short, communication is critical to a successful relationship. Thoughts, words and deeds are the sum total of the individual personality, and if a marriage does not allow for their free expression, it cannot hope to be a successful marriage. With communication, couples may discover, as did many of our Survey subjects, that they are in much closer agreement than they thought, and with that reassurance they can begin to behave in ways that will reflect their shared needs and goals. If they discover that they do disagree, however, and their disagreements stem from real and valid needs, a more profound change of behavior may be required to solve the conflict and save the relationship.

The most obvious example of this kind of conflict is the problem of the active wife. A man can certainly be inconvenienced, and may feel genuinely threatened by a wife who does not conform to the traditional patterns of feminine behavior. His feelings, although anachronistic, are nevertheless real, and the wife who disparages or ignores them merely compounds the conflict. Complete capitulation on one side or the other can be even more destructive; the conflict is merely repressed, not resolved. The only solution can come in compromise, a compromise based on an understanding of their separate as well as their similar needs. The behavior necessary to effect such a compromise may be grudging at first, but a shared goal is worth shared sacrifice, and the only way to evolve patterns of behavior that will satisfy both partners in a relationship is to try them.

Even the man who feels put upon by the need to assume more than what he sees as a traditional degree of family responsibility because of his wife's activity in the community, can nevertheless volunteer to be baby-sitter to free her for an evening political meeting, can volunteer to be one of the poll-watchers she is recruiting, and can offer to drive one of the cars chauffeuring people to the polls under her supervision. He may feel like a damn fool taking orders from his wife, and he may feel that everyone will look upon him as a Caspar Milquetoast, but he can still do it. If he waits to stop feeling like a damn fool he will never move and so will lose the opportunity for positive personal and social feedback which could come from a grateful wife and from others within the situation who understand the nature of the accommodation he is attempting.

For the adult male who wants to "cure" his dilemma will set out about the job of social reconstruction, rather than sit, like the southern plantation owner of 1865 and live out his life thinking back to the "good old days" and passing that nostalgic fantasy notion on to the next generation. He will find satisfaction in the self-fulfilling activities of his wife and in the new and deeper kinds of male-female relationships possible with a fully functioning woman. He will be one who can enjoy, and incorporate into a broadened male image, the interactions with his children and the emotional interchanges with other men and women possible with less restrictive standards of masculine behavior.

In fact, the areas of emotional expression and free verbal expression of thought and feeling are particularly significant in the development of self and in the resolution of the psychological aspects of the male dilemma. Their significance lies in the fact that these are areas in which men will be achieving greater opportunity and a broader behavioral sphere. Most other areas represent men's acceptance of a narrower world, with the previously undefined limits now sharply delineated by the protests and reactions of the women in his life. But if a man rejects as nonsense the notion that masculinity is linked to or expressed in restricting or inhibiting his levels of verbal and emotional expression, this simple act of rejection makes available to him the full range of human emotional response. Moreover, if he moves on to decide to express himself as fully and freely as "women" do, he will learn that not only is it simpler to say what you think when you think it, but this frees you from the internal churnings and furies which come from the endless repetitions to yourself of those arguments you never argued and those complaints you never complained. And the benefits proliferate, for he will also discover that the women with whom he interacts can respond in kind, and understanding will increase almost immediately and continually deepen. He will also learn that people will not crumble either in astonishment or fear when he expresses his thoughts and feelings, and that there is no personal or social gain achieved from internalizing them.

A different aspect of the "cure" lies in recognizing that a man has physical needs other than sex which need expression just as his psychosocial needs do. Society has greater use for his brain than his brawn; yet the need to express himself physically remains. From childhood, males exhibit a greater degree of movement and activity, and the need for external verification of their masculinity in some form of physical competition, usually with other men.

Granted, this kind of activity represents only one level of male function and an excessive preoccupation with it, as a child or as an adult, can lead to a number of problems. The boy who is unable to compete physically for one reason or another, may come to consider himself a permanent outsider; and the boy who is successful in physical competition may neglect other aspects of his personal development to his later regret. There is something a little sad about the first-rate professional athlete who is "washed up" at thirty-five; something equally sad about the middle-aged man who tried to act like a college football hero. However, it cannot be disputed that some form of activity, appropriate to their ages and physical condition, is essential to the health of both sexes, and for a man it can also be an important means of self-expression and, with the added dash of competition, it can contribute to his sense of self and his security as a man.

Finding a suitable avenue of physical self-expression is not easy for a man, given the circumstances of urban or even suburban life in this country. His job seldom requires it; even around his own house do-it-yourself repairs or maintenance are more in the way of necessities than means of self-expression. Further, many wives are suspicious of adult "games," or think them "childish" or "selfish," particularly if they are played outside the home apart from other members of the family and in the company of other men. As a result, many men, confined to the house by their wives, or by their own torpor, spend endless wasted hours in front of the television set watching football or some other sport, satisfying their need for male companionship and physical achievement vicariously. It is often men like this, too, who insist upon "masculinity" in their sons, again to satisfy their own needs vicariously, thus perpetuating standards of behavior that the next male generation will find equally difficult to express when they grow up, marry, and lead no less sedentary lives.

The adults whom this chapter is considering need to recognize this and provide physical outlets. A basket nailed to the garage door will do, or a night at the gym of the neighborhood high school. Deciding to walk rather than take a bus or drive will provide at least a modicum of physical activity, as will deciding to attend a ball game, with its opportunities to yell and cheer and boo real people and to jump up at every exciting play rather than sit sunk in a couch, dozing off watching six inch animated figures act out the game.

Developing outlets to express man's need for physical activity and movement will require the understanding and accommodation noted earlier. Both men and women need to understand that these are legitimate needs for the adult male. He is not seeking to retain or recapture his childhood when he goes out to play golf on Saturday; he is expressing and seeking to fulfill a physiological need for expressive physical movement. And he should be able to do it without guilt, which requires that his wife understand and accommodate to this need as well.

An example of man's biological need and expression of physical movement in "horsing around," and incidentally his need to enjoy this physical expression with members of his own sex, is seen in John Cassavetes' *Faces*. In this film, two groups of men, strangers to each other, visit the home of two call girls. They arrive almost simultaneously because of a mix-up in time. After initial anger and frustration, the four sex-eager men start in rather embarrassed fashion to drink and talk among themselves. They find that they have a common interest in football. Almost immediately, all four men completely ignore the costly women and, with noisy relish, play touch football in the girls' living room.

The fad appeal during the past decades of anything which provides bodily movement for men demonstrates the male need for physical outlets. Whether expressed as an interest in golf and tennis, a willingness of city dwellers to arise at six in the morning to jog through mugger-infested parks, or the do-it-yourself approach to household improvements, the evidence is ample that urban man needs to use his body to maintain a sense of physical well-being.

As a society we have recognized that the end product when motorized and mechanized homelives combine with sedentary work roles are bodies which dissatisfy us. But we only deal with the result and try to modify the result when it is too weak or too fat. And so, just as in the nineteen thirties when our parents were attracted by Charles Atlas' promises to transform 97-pound weaklings into men who could defend themselves on a beach, we were attracted by isometric exercises which can build you up with five minutes a day of flexing fingers against a desk drawer, or by the Canadian Air Force exercises which used structured jumping to build up the body. Weight Watchers and endless dieting reduce bodies in bulk if not in significance. But society has not dealt with the basic conflict between a male childhood which ties masculinity to activity and movement and participation and a sedate adult life of limited physical activity.

Vicarious participation is, for physical activity, an unsatisfactory substitute, as are repression and fantasy representations. Rather we suggest that this desire for physical self-expression and external verification be turned into more useful and constructive social channels. In other words, why not encourage men, not just boys, to do something with their bodies as well as their brains, or better yet, to seek ways to integrate their functions wherever possible?

Society, with few exceptions, does just the opposite, and women in particular, seem bent on "domesticating" their men. In so doing, they often invite a secret or open rebellion which can severely strain their relationship. Ultimately it is up to the man to choose and pursue the kind of physical activity that gives him the greatest satisfaction, when he requires that form of self-expression, but it is up to the woman to support him in such a pursuit. If other members of the family can derive equal pleasure from participating in it, all the better. But a man should not be denied the pleasure of testing and proving himself in this way, even if it is done in the company of other men. The myth of togetherness for a family has long since been exploded. Children are encouraged to test their wings outside the nest; women are clamoring for the opportunity to express themselves in other than domestic roles. Why should not men have this avenue of self-expression open to them, both as an occasional escape from the pressures of their jobs and family responsibilities, and as an additional source of personal satisfaction? The boredom, frustrations, and tensions of marriage, and even the incidence of infidelity, might be considerably lessened if the man's pent-up or repressed physical energies could find an outlet that contributed to his sense of himself and his own identity. Male resistance to women's liberation might also diminish if it became apparent that in this sphere, at least, a vestige of former privilege could be preserved.

The extent of that privilege must, of course, depend upon the other circumstances of a man's personal, professional, and family life. And it must depend upon the nature of the activity he chooses and its importance to his sense of self. Obviously, nights spent at the corner bar, or at stag movies at the club, may satisfy the need for male companionship, even if they are more forms of escape than constructive forms of self-expression. Any activity with a purpose and a goal can be just that, whether it happens to be handball at the gym, golf, leading a Boy Scout troop, or coaching a Little League team. And when it is pursued for the genuine satisfactions it offers, the need for escape and vicarious participation diminish. Nor should those activities that are not purely physical be excluded, particularly as the need for physical expression declines in later years. A hobby of any kind can serve a rewarding personal purpose, and participation in community activities and projects can be both personally and socially constructive at any age.

It might seem to some men that sports, outside interests, or an occasional night out with the boys are mere crumbs and small consolation indeed for their decreasing freedoms and increasing responsibilities. But if the man is to understand and accommodate the woman's needs for self-expression on the social level, surely it is up to the woman to understand and accommodate the man's needs for physical self-expression.

This is not in any way to deprecate woman's need for physical self-expression. Of course, she as well as man has a need for motility and physical activity, a need more structured than the actual physical activity which is included in her role as mother and wife. For her as well as man, technology has reduced natural outlets for release of her physical energy. And for her too, outlets and resources for her thwarted physical needs have sprung up in the environment. Establishments featuring gymnastics and body movement exercises for women have arisen all over the United States. Also, the organization of intramural and international gymnastic exercises in which girls and women, young and old are now taking part establishes the recognition of women's physical needs and skills.

In the context of this chapter "A Pound of Cure," it is not the game, nor the physical activity which we are emphasizing. Both men and women need fulfillment of their motility pulls. What we are emphasizing is that the male has a need for physical activity and engagement with his own sex. It is the same need that women have to be with their own sex for whatever mutual activities they wish to enjoy. However women have easier access to each other. Man's lot is not that simple.

While the responsibility to achieve mutually satisfactory means of sexual expression can and must be shared, for it involves both partners in a relationship, there is no rule that says that a man and a woman must always be a team in whatever they do. Nor is there any rule that says they must always share the same interests and activities outside the shared goals of their relationship. Each should be allowed, and allow each other, to pursue whatever avenues of self-expression are deemed necessary for a sense of personal achievement and worth. If that pursuit is impeded or resented by either partner, the relationship will, of course, suffer. But if it is encouraged through the understanding and accommodation of both partners, it can only be strengthened by the love and respect that come from that kind of support, and from the participation of two partners who are secure in their identities as a man and a woman as well as husband and wife.

The complaints most often heard from the husband of a newly "liberated" wife, or a wife who seems to be moving in that direction, are, to be frank, primarily selfish. As the replies to our Masculine and Feminine Inventories indicated, many men agree in principle that "liberation" is a good thing, that a woman should be given an opportunity to express herself in roles other than those of wife and mother. Yet when she attempts to do just that, as the replies to the Behavioral Survey indicated, complications and conflict are generated, chiefly by the fact that it may be inconvenient for the husband. It is true that a late supper or the few added domestic chores necessary to accommodate a working wife may indeed be inconvenient or an intrusion upon the period of rest and relaxation after a hard day at the office that is usually considered a husband's prerogative. But is that really what bothers men? Most men have for years suffered any number of inconveniences for the sake of their children; irregular hours and domestic chaos are almost an inevitable part of parenthood and society approves of the considerate or even indulgent father. In other words, this kind of accommodation is considered suitably masculine by the members of this generation of parents. Why then are men suddenly objecting so strenuously?

Clearly, they are concerned not only with inconvenience or with giving up time that could be better spent, but with appearances—the visible signs of masculinity. Women are no less concerned with appearances, it is true; many are indifferent or apprehensive about expanding their usual roles for fear of losing that precious commodity, femininity. Such a concern, whether on the part of a man or a woman, stems from extremely complex causes, but certainly one of the most powerful of these is that body of beliefs that labels certain patterns of thought and behavior as appropriately masculine or feminine. They are the standards that underlie the education and training of the individual, and later they provide the criteria by which society measures the behavior of the individual, and by which the latter measures his own behavior. Further, they have a particularly profound effect in a male-female relationship, and, in what could be called a vicious circle, they also have a profound influence on the strictures and institutions of society itself.

For some, rigid role restrictions result in outward displays of supermasculinity or superfemininity designed as a defense against the anxiety of inner uncertainty. In most, however, the result is simply a preoccupation with the appearances of masculinity or femininity, again a hypocritical external disguise that may mask an internal ambivalence but cannot resolve it. A relatively harmless form of compensation, perhaps, but when those appearances are threatened, the personality itself is threatened. The same is inevitably true in a relationship; a man concerned with the appearances of masculinity requires the support of the appearances of femininity in his partner to reinforce his self- and social image, and the woman concerned with the appearances of femininity requires similar masculine support. If these appearances are threatened, the relationship is threatened.

To avoid that threat, to protect themselves and their relationships, many men and women "go through the motions" of masculinity and femininity. In essence, they cast themselves and each other in sex and gender roles that ultimately permit expression of only a part of their personalities and result in a relationship that can only be maintained through the hypocrisy and mutual self-deception revealed in our research data. It is this kind of hypocrisy, this kind of self-deception, that is at the very core of our sexual dilemma. The confusion and conflict that characterize the relationships between the sexes today can be traced directly to the social standards that dictate rigid, artificial, and anachronistic standards of masculine and feminine behavior without regard to the real difference between the sexes, the real needs of the individual, whether male or female, to their combined needs in a relationship, and indeed to the changing needs of society itself.

Upon closer examination, those pressures that compel a man to seek exclusively external verification for his prowess often cut him off from the rich rewards that stem from no less important inner recognition of accomplishment. The man whose whole life revolves around demonstrations of his "masculinity," whether it is in some form of physical activity, in sexual conquests, or even in hard-driving business competition, seldom has time for the less visible, but nonetheless masculine, pleasures of intellectual pursuits, for a truly shared sexual relationship, and for the very real joys of fatherhood. His personality and human function are as severely limited as the woman who feels she must demonstrate her "femininity" in sexual and social passivity and dependence.

Directly relevant in this discussion is one of the more intriguing findings of the research. The reader may remember that while men were not as strong and self-assertive as they would like to be, they felt that they were more self-assertive than their wives would want them to be. But if one believes what the wives said, the men were wrong. True the wives wanted husbands who accepted and understood their (the women's) needs, and who had strong family orientations, but they nevertheless wanted their husbands to be strong, self-assertive men. Both our clinical experience and data have convinced us that the women were telling the truth, and have also convinced us that the combination they ask for is possible within the psyche of one human male. Given the variety of changes and adaptations we have discussed earlier, particularly the expansion of the affective repertoire available to men, we believe that many men can achieve this combination without diminished masculinity.

For one of the most serious instances of noncommunication is that men have apparently heard women saying, "for me to become more of a person, you must become less of a man." We see no evidence that women are in fact saying this, either in our research data or in our clinical interviews, and certainly nothing in our social analyses to suggest that it is true. In contrast we see a great deal of evidence that women are troubled and dismayed to learn that for every step they take toward a more developed stage of personhood, the man in their life thinks he takes one back from "manhood."

At this particular moment in our history, it is women who are the most active in expanding their social roles, and surely this is inevitable, since they have much farther to go. But why should men resent that? Are they truly content with what they have achieved, and unwilling to share it because they believe that they themselves can go no farther? If so, progress must come to a halt. Is it an unrealistically Utopian vision to see men and women working together in the future, each contributing their separate or similar talents toward a common goal? If it is, it is primarily because both men and women, quite mistakenly, still see their "masculinity" and "femininity" threatened by role restrictions when, in fact, *more* will be demanded of them, not less. Again, it seems to be appearances that matter, but it is ridiculous to assume that a more equitable redistribution of opportunity and responsibility in the outer world of work, where men are now dominant, and in the inner world of personal and family relationships where women now exercise powerful control—would significantly alter gender behavior. It would, rather, enhance it, for only men and women secure in their own identities, a security achieved through meaningful and fulfilling sexual and social roles, can be called truly masculine or feminine.

And so a critical dimension of the "cure" lies in the redefinition of these social standards, for if they are not redefined we must continue to suffer the disastrous consequences of trying to live up to unreal images and, when we fall short, as we must, of insisting upon equally unreal appearances. The battle in the early nineteen seventies over the Equal Rights Amendment is a good illustration. It was and is folly to claim that there is a "man's world" and a "woman's world" and never the twain shall meet. The world has become far too small and complex for the luxury of that kind of segregation. It is, first and foremost, a human world, populated by both men and women who must be given equal opportunity to share in its pleasures and equal responsibility for helping to solve its problems, not necessarily according to their sex, but according to their individual preferences and abilities. It is equally foolish to continue to insist that "masculinity" and "femininity" are somehow mutually exclusive, that an individual must be either one or the other, educated and trained to conform at least outwardly to certain standards of behavior, and forever confined to roles specific to that sex. Again the world has already become too specialized to afford the luxury of that particularly spurious kind of specialization.

But the battle over the E.R.A., under way in state legislatures as this is written, provides a simple example of how men (and some women) can see increasing the spectrum of human interaction as a threat rather than an opportunity. With some exceptions it has been women's groups who have fought the battle to pass this amendment, first in Congress and now in state legislatures. But it should have been a fight fought by men as well as women, for achieving the equality of right and opportunity is one of the critical first steps in the redefinition of standards.

There is an ever-widening sphere of social functions that can be appropriately performed by members of both sexes, and performed in ways that will prove of incalculable benefit to the individual as well as to society. The first step, then, in redefining the social standards and realigning priorities lies in the recognition that some form of constructive social action or self-expression is equally important in both sexes; it is a level of human function, not merely a sexual prerogative. Second, whatever form this kind of action or self-expression may take must depend upon the interests and capabilities of the individual, not only some preordained notions of appropriate behavior. There is no form of social self-expression that comes with "masculine" and "feminine" labels already attached, nor should either a man or a woman assume that a gender identity is automatically guaranteed, or automatically sacrificed, in the performance of a particular social function. That again depends upon the interests and capabilities of the individual, and just how well he or she is able to integrate the equally important physical and psychological aspects of the personality with the social function. Jobs, like other forms of social self-expression are in themselves sexless; it is the individual who performs the job that gives it both its sexual and wider human dimensions. Referring to a woman doctor, a woman jockey, a male nurse or a male secretary tells you the sex of the job holder but nothing about the quality of the job function.

It would seem ironic in this day and age, when there are fewer and fewer forms of social function that permit any degree of individual self-expression, that we still insist upon sexual segregation and outmoded notions of "man's work" and "woman's work." Men jealously guard jobs that require little or nothing of them, in the realization, perhaps, that women could perform them equally well and, in addition to the dullness and depersonalization of the job itself, such an arrangement is a final insult to their male pride. Women, for their part, and in particular those women who exhort their sisters to leave domestic drudgery behind and move out into the world of work, often assert that a job, any job, is the answer to all of life's problems, only to find that in competing for jobs, they earn the resentment of men, and in landing them, they are often still drudges. The moral is obvious for both sexes: no job in itself is a guarantee of human, let alone sexual, identity. Again, it is only one level of function that can, and often does, contribute to individual fulfillment. But then it can also thwart it, depending upon what kind of job it is, what the individual, male or female, brings to it, and what satisfactions he or she is able to derive from it.

It is probably safe to say that the majority of jobs in today's automated, assembly-line world offer little in the way of personal satisfaction. As forms of employment, they must serve some useful or profitable purpose or they would not exist, and they will undoubtedly become more and more depersonalized until an army of robots is trained to take over. Viewed in this light, then, what difference does it make if it is a man's or a woman's finger that tightens the bolt or touches the button? A man who is dehumanized by his job, and demasculinized by the presence of a woman performing the same job, can find no real solace in sexual exclusivity, segregation, or discrimination. He is defending an arid turf. Obviously, both men and women must be given equal access to jobs, equal pay for equal work, and equal opportunity for advancement. Further, those situations that do require individual skills and do offer an opportunity for individual self-expression—the professions, for example—should also be open to both sexes. They are of incalculable social value, and because they generally feature people rather than products, they require a full range of human talents and abilities, male and female; they cannot be the special province of one sex, one race, or even one class.

And finally, because it seems unlikely that the working world will ever renounce the assembly line and the computer and return to the good old days of the craftsman or artisan who could take real pride in his work, both men and women who of necessity earn their livings in this way must look elsewhere in society for opportunities to make an individual contribution and find individual satisfaction—in community projects or politics, for example, and in other constructive leisure-time activities. In short, it is a waste of time and talent to complain about a dehumanized society. If it is the individual who still counts—and we believe it is—then it is up to the individual to make his or her presence and importance felt, first by opposing the discrimination that is very much a part of dehumanization, and then by expanding social roles in ways that will be of personal benefit as well as of benefit to society.

The individual can make his presence felt not only through joining in the fight for legislated social change, as in the Equal Rights Amendment, but also through demanding the social adaptations neeeed to make a world with new social structures work. Individual accommodation and adaptation will not be enough, for we must also create new institutions and develop new kinds of occupational models to allow for the major changes in the status of women and the chain reaction effects on marital relationships, the structure of the family and child-rearing practices.

The absence of such adaptation is particularly striking in a culture which has a history of almost instant occupational and career adaptation to other kinds of social and economic change. Consider for example, the speed with which the infusion of computers into American life created instant new careers as programmers, card punchers and data processors. With the careers came the educational programs and institutions to prepare personnel for the new industries as well as courses in other fields to prepare nurses, teachers, physicians, and businessmen in the use of the new techniques. Or in a different vein, consider the speed with which black students began to appear on college campuses, and black workers in banks, offices and public agencies, once there was social consensus that their exclusion should cease.

The closest we have come to social adaptation to expedite sexual role revision is the increasing availability of day care facilities. Originally developed to provide a custodial service for the children of the working poor, the day care concept is being broadened somewhat to allow for the children of the more middle levels of affluence. But even this broadening began only in the early nineteen seventies and then at the insistence of women's groups. Much more needs to be done if all adults are to have a full opportunity to realize their potential while simultaneously assuring that children are reared under optimal psychosocial conditions.

But this recognition is delayed and confounded by the resistance to change of the more basic attitude that essentially women should *not* work outside the home, but should stay home and care for their children. And accompanying this is the attitude that when they do work, this is a public sign that the husband is an inadequate provider. We believe from our research that these attitudes persevere and continue to characterize large majorities of the population.

This is a social attitude in Western culture which has a long history, beginning with the urbanization and industrialization movements when women went to work outside the home primarily because their husbands did not earn enough. In the United States the attitude was reinforced in the nineteen thirties when the entry of many women into the work force was directly attributable to the inability of men to find jobs to earn enough during the Depression.

That situation no longer exists but the attitude lingers on, and so must be countered directly by public education efforts to develop the counter-notion of productive couples contributing their abilities individually and fully, supplemented by sound resources to assist them with child-rearing.

There are simple social changes which, if implemented, would contribute to the alleviation of some of the psychological components of the male dilemma by removing some of the burden for supporting social change from men. For example, if day care centers were routinely available for the children of working parents (not working "mothers," but working *parents*) of all social and income levels, then child care would be much less a mother-father conflict situation. If the center was well staffed, the parents would know that their children were being well cared for and, for example, much of the ambivalence the mother feels because of role conflicts, would not appear. Relieved of this ambivalence, the concern she communicates to her husband would be lessened and his reactive mixture of anger and an anachronistic guilt over not providing well enough so that his wife can stay home to care for the children would also be less likely to appear.

Since a broadened day care program was defeated in Congress as recently as nineteen seventy-two, it apparently will have to be private industry which will support expanded facilities, if they are to appear. The practice one sees in Denmark of factories with attached day care facilities for working parents may well be one answer to American needs. Area facilities, supported by the local business community may be another.

Other adaptations as well would help. The resurrection of the English nanny, a respected professional child care specialist, would provide a new resource that current family and role structures could easily absorb, even if she lacked the special skills of Mary Poppins. We offer neither dignity nor preparation to those interested in spending their days devoted to in-home child care. And so we have innumerable families faced with a dilemma: the unacceptable alternative of one parent staying home to care for the children, or the equally unacceptable alternative of transferring child care to an untrained and unprepared domestic worker.

But why not a specialization in infant and child care? Knowing the American motivational scheme, we would probably have to concoct an impressive role title along the lines of "culture transmission specialist" and put the training program at least at the community college level, but these would be small prices to pay to develop a pool of men and women directly trained in child development, child psychology, play and expressive techniques for children, pre-school readiness skills and other specific skills and knowledges needed to be an effective parent surrogate.

It is interesting to note that creative thinking here could resolve two social problems in one action. Develop the notion of parent or grandparent surrogate and establish training programs for older men and women to fill these responsibilities and you have an ideal job for the active retired person or couple. Working, say, from two through seven in the evening, they arrive, shop, care for the children when they come home from school, prepare dinner, clean up and leave. They have a continued feeling of social value and self worth and earn valuable supplementary income in an inflationary age. The jointly functioning couple come home to a dinner prepared and can leave the table free to move to interactions and activities with their children, and the children have the advantages of something like an extended family and the presence, now too rare, of grandparent figures.

These and other social innovations and adaptations would do much to make it more feasible to restructure marital responsibility, for the need for change there surprisingly is an area which few recent writers on the sexual changes in American society discuss. Yet how couples willing to attempt restructuring their social and familial roles are to allocate family responsibilities is usually the ground on which the first serious battles are fought—first, often insurmountable area of conflict. Dishes need to be washed and children need breakfast and someone has to be in the house when pre-schoolers are there, for the responsibilities remain even when the roles change. Just as we believe that the over-intellectualized approach to sexual relationships has destroyed spontaneity and diminished the potential for joy, so do we believe that over-planning can institutionalize and deaden the allocation of household responsibility. Rather we have seen greatest success in this area with those couples who combine a philosophy of "as something needs doing, whoever is most available does it ... " with sufficient advance planning to be certain that they both don't walk out the front door on Tuesday morning without any one left to care for the two toddlers.

One key adaptation in marital responsibility is a conscious shift from the child-centered emphasis of the nineteen sixties back toward the emphasis on adults of the nineteen twenties and before. Not all the way back, for the family in which children were all but ignored was as psychologically unhealthy for children as the child-centered family is for adults. But the need for adaptation stems not only from this psychological consideration. It is simply impossible for parents living a child-centered family life pattern to simultaneously seek active rounded lives with intra- and extra-family dimensions for both husband and wife. To seek such lives one must accept the fact that the needs of adults have equal claims on family time and energy as the needs of the children. The precise balance of these separate needs in any one family must of course be resolved by each couple in the context of their own situation.

Our clinical experience and research interviews have convinced us that it is possible to find some middle level in which there is sufficient parent-child interaction for children to develop secure senses of self as loved members of a family, and sufficient time for the parents, separately and together, to be free from family responsibilities to undertake career and avocational interests. But parents must work at it steadily, and the something which has "gotta give" in achieving this balance may turn out to be sleep. However, we have found that a week-end away can do wonders to restore energy levels and send the parents back into the family refreshed and ready to resume the multi-faceted lives which we see as becoming increasingly characteristic of the liberated family.

The development of adult lives independent of children is also acutely important if there is to be a strength to the marriage and to the identities of the adults at that point when the children are grown and ready to leave home. For only if the marriage is strong and the parents do have separate identities and interests of their own can they handle this critical maturational stage with grace, and provide the support, guidance and encouragement the young adult needs when he leaves home. Parents who make their children and child-rearing the entire focus of their lives find themselves existing in a socio-personal vacuum when the children leave.

The parent for whom child-rearing was the raison d'être of

marriage, or even the primary motivation for living with a person of the opposite sex with whom little else was shared and discussed, is inevitably devastated when faced with the realization that the children are moving out. The loss of the children means to them the end of the useful, productive portion of their lives, and so these parents cling, they fight to maintain their usefulness even if it means infantalizing their children well past adolescence and making them dependent on into what would be normally adult life. Thus in the nineteen sixties and nineteen seventies we saw young couples living together, some married, some not, physically separate from their parents but tied dependently by the fact that it was the parents who provided the money for rent, for food, and for tuition.

Those who wondered why parents put up with this, particularly those whose children were living under conditions which only a decade earlier would have been labeled living in sin, simply failed to recognize that financial dependence perpetuated the parental role and continued to provide the parent who needed it with the reinforcement of his or her own social significance. For many parents, their own needs motivated their reactions to their children's behavior. In contrast, parents with lives of their own as individuals, and as an adult couple, see children reaching maturity as the successful culmination of one phase of their lives that does not threaten other dimensions.

In areas of social change involving reactions and responses as deeply rooted in the developmental process as are role responses and reactions we do not expect reform and change to come in one step. Rather, it will be achieved in stages and to understand the cure we must know the stages.

First comes insight, when adult men and women sufficiently analyze the patterns of the larger society and their own places within it to identify the nature of their problem and the behavior which is symptomatic of it. When insight is followed by the desire to change, it leads to the second stage, behavioral modification. Here, by sheer strength of will, the individuals involved in the situation decide to change their behavior, even if their reactions and responses have not been affected at all. The Marlboro Man husband who has reached this stage puts the TV dinner in the oven when he learns his wife is tied up in traffic on her way home from the office. And even if his stomach is churning at the nature of this imposition, and his sense of masculinity is offended, his *behavior* has changed, since prior to insight and determination to change he would have sat before the 6 o'clock news on TV growing more furious every second as supper was delayed. And he would have continued to seethe as his wife hurriedly prepared dinner, seething on her part at the injustice of it all.

A reader may well wonder if this is progress. Instead of facing fury and anger the wife comes home to a husband feeling imposed upon and with a damaged male ego, and she may have a portion of guilt herself. Progress? Yes. For one thing dinner will be ready and so that pressure is removed from the situation. For another, the husband's action will have contributed a positive, perceivable step on his part to changing the psychosocial dynamics of the relationship. He will feel that he did something nice; so will his wife. For a third, her feeling that there is an unfair division of responsibility, that too much is expected of her, is alleviated. And if they can open up enough to discuss their feelings about the situation, they move to the third stage, shared feelings.

We believe that after a few repetitions of this sequence of behavioral change and shared feelings many couples will move on to the fourth stage of changed emotional response. This comes when the new or modified behavior is, for the first time, not deliberate but spontaneous and not accompanied by anger but by a positive feeling which may be of self-righteous virtue or may be just feeling good. And ultimately the new behavior becomes sufficiently routine to be accompanied by no particular affective state at all. In brief, we are arguing that the process can begin consciously and deliberately and that it need not wait until feelings change and until insight brings new emotional responses. Change the behavior and there is a good chance that ultimately the emotional response will change.

The sexual revolution of the nineteen sixties and nineteen seventies will have been little more than a tempest in a teapot unless this kind of change can be effected. We have made a few tentative steps in that direction, but for the present-day adult generation the road has been rough and will become even rougher yet until they realize that masculinity is not all there is to being a man and femininity not all there is to being a woman. The itch of sex role confusion may take a generation to fully subside but even today men and women, if aware of its causes, can work together to prevent its most serious consequences, and can help each other achieve these two most vital human goals, a secure individual identity, and a loving companionable relationship.

Inventory of Masculine Values

Appendix A contains the thirty-four statements of the Inventory of Masculine Values, followed by the answer and scoring form and instructions for completing and scoring each of the four versions of the Inventory: (1) Man's Self-Perception, (2) Man's Ideal Man, (3) Woman's Ideal Man (to be completed by men only), and (4) Woman's Ideal Man (to be completed by women only). To avoid marking in the book, it is suggested that the answer and scoring form be copied on a separate piece of paper. You will need four of them, one for each of the four versions.

When you have completed and scored the forms, read the interpretations that follow to obtain an idea of where you stand in relation to our other respondents.

Inventory of Masculine Values

1. I worry about what people think of me.
2. An ambitious and responsible husband does not like his wife to work.
3. A father's place is in the home when he is not at work.
4. I am not sure that the joys of fatherhood make up for the sacrifices.
5. To be successful, a man needs his wife's encouragement.
6. To be fully satisfied, a man needs interests besides his job and family.
7. My main interest is to raise normal, well-behaved children.
8. I argue with people who try to give me orders.

9. Married men should not be personally ambitious if it interferes with their families.

10. A man should not give up his personal goals and ideas in order to have a good marriage.

11. I can put myself in the background and work hard for a person I admire.

12. I would like to do something everybody knows is important.

13. A man needs the responsibilities of marriage to develop fully.

14. When a man has a conflict between what he wants to do for himself and what he has to do as a husband, his ambitions should come first.

15. I try to do what I think people want me to do.

16. I sometimes feel that I must do everything myself, that I can accept nothing from others.

17. A man should get married even if the woman does not measure up to all his hopes.

18. I express my ideas strongly.

19. The needs of a family come before a man's personal ambitions.

20. wwhen I am with a group of people, I usually become the leader.

21. I like listening to people better than talking.

22. A husband's opinion should be more important than his wife's opinion.

23. If we disagree, I should give in to my wife more often than I would expect her to give in to me.

24. The greatest satisfactions in life come from what you do yourself.

25. Marriage and children should come first in a man's life.

26. I usually pay no attention to other people's feelings.

27. If a woman is as smart as her husband, the marriage will not work.

28. A father with active interests outside of his job can be as close to his children as a stay-at-home father.

29. I am sure that what a man gains from marriage makes up for sacrifices.

30. I would rather be famous, admired, and popular throughout the nation than have the constant affection of just one woman.

31. A father who spends his free time away from home cannot possibly be as good a father as the one who is home a great deal.

32. How I develop as a person is more important to me than what others think of me.

33. Modern fathers should bring up their boys and girls to believe in absolute equal rights and freedoms for both sexes.

34. I would not get married if I had to give up what I really believe in to get along with another person.

Inventory of Masculine Values
Answer and Scoring Form

Column
A   B

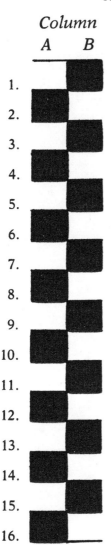

1.
2.
3.
4.
5.
6.
7.
8.
9.
10.
11.
12.
13.
14.
15.
16.

17.

18.

19.

20.

21.

22.

23.

24.

25.

26.

27.

28.

29.

30.

31.

32.

33.

34.

Your Score
(Subtract Column B total from Column A total)

Totals

A   B

Instructions for Completing and Scoring

1.   Man's Self-Perception
Read the Inventory of Masculine Values carefully and think how *you personally* would answer each statement. Then in Columns A and B of the answer and scoring form indicate the extent to which you agree or disagree with each statement by entering the appropriate number in the proper space. Use the following scale:

> 1 = strongly agree
> 2 = agree
> 3 = no opinion or not sure
> 4 = disagree
> 5 = strongly disagree

Please note that the answer and scoring form is numbered to correspond to the statements of the Inventory. Take care to enter your responses to the odd-numbered statements in the proper space in Column A and to the even-numbered statements in the proper space in Column B. When you have completed the form, to obtain your score simply add up all the numbers you have put in Column A and enter that total in the box provided. Repeat this for Column B and enter that total in the box provided. Then subtract the total for Column B from the total for Column A. This will leave you with a plus score if your Column A total was higher, and a minus score if your Column B total was higher.

2.   Man's Ideal Man*
Read the Inventory of Masculine Values again. This time, however, think of your *ideal man* and respond to the statements as you believe *he* would respond. Use the same form for your responses as before, and also use the same 1 to 5 scale to indicate the extent of your agreement or disagreement with each statement. Take care to enter your responses to the odd-numbered statements in the proper space in Column A and the even-numbered statements in the proper space in Column B. When you have completed the form, obtain your score by adding up the figures in Columns A and B, and then subtracting the Column B total from the Column A total as before.

3.   Woman's Ideal Man (for men only)*
Read the Inventory of Masculine Values again. This time, think of *woman's ideal man* and respond to each statement as you think *he* would respond. Use the same form and the same scale to indicate

the extent of your agreement or disagreement, again taking care to enter your responses to the odd-numbered statements in the proper space in Column A and the even-numbered statements in Column B. To obtain your score, subtract the total of the figures in Column B from the total of the figures in Column A as before.

4. *Woman's Ideal Man (for women only)*

Read the Inventory of Masculine Values carefully and think how your *ideal man* would respond to each statement. Use the same form and the same scale to indicate the extent of your agreement or disagreement with each statement. Take care to enter your responses to the odd-numbered statements in the proper space in Column A and the even-numbered statements in the proper space in Column B. To obtain your score, subtract the total of the figures in Column B from the total of the figures in Column A.

*Scoring Interpretations**

The statements on the Masculine Inventory, as with the Feminine Inventory, are arranged in such a way that a plus score indicates an orientation toward self-realization and independent activities and achievement for a man, while a minus score indicates an orientation toward family-centered interests, goals, and satisfactions. In scoring the Inventory in this way, we did not mean to ascribe either positive or negative values to these attributes. It might just as easily have been scored the other way.

1. Man's Self-Perception

The results of the Self-Perception version of the Masculine Inventory were very similar to the results of the feminine version. Two out of every five men we studied had a self-perception score between +4 and −4, while one-third had scores above +4 and one-fourth had scores below −4. If your score was in the +4 to −4 range, your self-perception is that of a man with strong family-oriented interests, but with equally strong needs for self-realization and a life independent of your home and family.

If you had a score higher than +4, you are among the third of those men whose self-orientation overbalances their family orientation. Most men who held this view of themselves had scores between +5 to +12, clearly self-oriented while still retaining a clear-cut family commitment. Only one man in nine had a score of +13 or higher and if your score went above +21, you were in exclusive company, for only one man in thirty-three had that clear and relatively consistent orientation to self with a corresponding decrease in family-oriented interests.

If you had a minus score below −4, most likely it is in the range from −5 to −12, for only one man in twelve dipped below this. A score in the −5 to −12 range clearly indicates a strong family-oriented view, which, however, still retains some of the components of self-realization. It is when you get into scores of −13 to −20 (where we found only one man in fourteen) and especially when you go below −20 (where we found only one man in thirty-three) that the family orientation begins to overwhelm self-realization needs and drives rather completely.

2. Man's Ideal Man

If you are like our typical respondent, your score on this version of the Inventory corresponded very closely to your self-perception score. Sixty percent of the men we tested had scores on these two forms within four points of each other. For these men, and for you if you fell within this group, your view of yourself and your view of how you would like to be are reasonably homogeneous. You are about what you would like to be.

If your scores on these two forms were further apart, consider which is higher. Here the mathematics can get a bit tricky. If you had two plus scores there is no problem, but if you had two minus scores the higher one in this case is the one closer to zero, so that a −7 would be "higher" than a −14. If your self-perception score is higher than your ideal score by more than four points, you are, like 20 percent of the men we studied, more concerned with your self and your activities outside the home than you would like to be. The larger the discrepancy the larger the gap between you and your ideal. Only one man in seven or eight had a gap of more than ten points, with only a rare one in fifty more than sixteen points apart; 15 percent had a gap of twenty points or more.

If, in contrast, your ideal score is higher than your self-perception score by more than four points, you, like 20 percent of our respondents, are not as self-oriented as you would like to be. Here large gaps were less frequent, for only one man in twelve (8 percent) had a gap larger than ten points and only one in one hundred a gap larger than sixteen points.

3. Woman's Ideal Man (for men only)

If you held views similar to two men out of every three that we tested, you had a plus score on this version of the Inventory; that is, you thought that women's ideal man is slightly more on the self-oriented than the family-oriented side. Only one man in fourteen, however, with a score higher than +20, believed that women want an extremely self-oriented man. If you were among the one man in three who had a minus score, most likely between −1 and −8, you believed that a woman prefers a man with a stronger family orientation than self-orientation. Only one man in twelve, however, had a score below −10.

4.   Woman's Ideal Man (for women only)

Three out of four women we tested had a male ideal who was on the self-oriented side. Their ideal was not too strongly self-oriented, however, for only one woman in twenty had a score higher than +20, while one in three had scores between +10 and +20. If you had a minus score, your ideal man is on the family-oriented side and you hold views like one woman in four. Almost all the women tested who had a male ideal on this family-oriented side had scores between −1 and −10. Only one in twenty-five had a score below −10.

*In our research, we scrambled the order of the statements of the Inventory in each of its versions so the respondent might not readily remember how he or she had answered previously. If you wish to duplicate this procedure, read the Inventory and fill in the answer form in reverse numerical order or at random. But be sure to enter your responses in the proper space and column.

Inventory of Feminine Values

The most direct way to obtain an understanding of the research on masculine and feminine values and behavior which is the basis for this book is to complete some or all of the Inventories and Surveys, just as our respondents did. Appendix B contains the thirty-four basic statements of the Inventory of Feminine Values. Following these statements is the answer and scoring form which can be used in all four versions of this Inventory: (1) Woman's Self-Perception, (2) Woman's Ideal Woman, (3) Man's Ideal Woman (to be completed by women only), and (4) Man's Ideal Woman (to be completed by men only). Instructions for completing and scoring each version follow. To avoid marking in the book, it is suggested that the answer and scoring form be copied on a separate piece of paper. You will need four of them; one for each of the four versions of the Inventory.

Once you have completed and scored the forms, read the interpretation of our findings which follows to obtain an idea of where you stand in relation to our other respondents. Obviously, if you want to use the Inventory for this kind of self-appraisal, it is better to complete it before you read the interpretations.

Inventory of Feminine Values

1. An ambitious and responsible husband does not like his wife to work.
2. I usually pay no attention to other people's feelings.
3. A woman who works cannot possibly be as good a mother as the one who stays home.

4. I would like to do something that everybody knows is important.
5. I try to do what I think people want me to do.
6. A woman has a conflict in what she has to do as a woman and what she wishes to do for herself.
7. A woman should get married even if the man does not measure up to all her hopes.
8. I sometimes feel that I must do everything myself, that I can accept nothing from others.
9. The needs of a family come before a woman's personal ambitions.
10. ii am not sure that the joys of motherhood make up for the sacrifices.
11. I like listening to people better than talking.
12. I argue with people who try to give me orders.
13. Marriage and children should come first in a woman's life.
14. When I am with a group of people, I usually become the leader.
15. I worry about what people think of me.
16. I express my ideas strongly.
17. Single women need personal success, but all a married woman needs is her husband's success.
18. I would not get married if I had to give up what I really believe in order to get along with another person.
19. It is up to the woman to make a marriage work.
20. A working mother can get along as well with her children as can a mother who stays at home.
21. The greatest help a wife can give her husband is to encourage his progress.
22. It is unfair that women have to give up more than men in order to have a good marriage.
23. I can put myself in the background and work hard for a person I admire.
24. A wife's opinion should be as important as the husband's opinion.
25. My main interest is to raise normal, well-behaved children.
26. How I develop as a person is more important to me than what others think of me.
27. If we disagree, I would give in to my husband more often than I would expect him to give in to me.

28. The greatest satisfactions in life come from what you do yourself.
29. I would like to marry a man whom I could really look up to.
30. A woman should have interests outside the home.
31. I am sure that what a woman gains from marriage makes up for sacrifices.
32. Modern mothers should bring up their boys and girls to believe in absolute equal rights and freedoms for both sexes.
33. A woman's place is in the home.
34. I would rather be famous, admired, and popular throughout the nation than have the constant affection of just one man.

Inventory of Feminine Values
Answer and Scoring Forms

Column

A   B

1.
2.
3.
4.
5.
6.
7.
8.
9.
10.
11.
12.
13.

14.

15.

16.

17.

18.

19.

20.

21.

22.

23.

24.

25.

26.

27.

28.

29.

30.

31.

32.

33.

34.

Your Score
(Subtract Column B total from Column A total)

$$+$$

Totals

$$+$$

A   B

Instructions for Completing and Scoring

1. Woman's Self-Perception

Read the Inventory of Feminine Values carefully and think how *you personally* would answer each statement. Then in Columns A and B of the answer and scoring form indicate the extent to which you agree or disagree with each statement by entering the appropriate number in the proper space. Use the following scale:

1 = strongly agree
2 = agree
3 = no opinion or not sure
4 = disagree
5 = strongly disagree

Please note that the answer and scoring form is numbered to correspond to the statements of the Inventory. Take care to enter your responses to the odd-numbered statements in the proper space in Column A and to the even-numbered statements in the proper space in Column B. When you have completed the form, to obtain your score simply add up all the numbers you have put in Column A and enter that total in the box provided. Then subtract the total for Column B from the total for Column A. This will leave you with a plus score if your Column A total was higher, and a minus score if your Column B total was higher.

2. Woman's Ideal Woman*

Read the Inventory of Feminine Values again. This time, however, think of *your ideal woman* and respond to the statements as you believe *she* would respond. Use the same form for your responses as before, and also use the same 1 to 5 scale to indicate the extent of your agreement or disagreement with each statement. Take care to enter your responses to the odd-numbered statements in the proper space in Column A and the even-numbered statements in the proper space in Column B. When you have completed the form, obtain your score by adding up the figures in Columns A and B, and then subtracting the Column B total from the Column A total as before.

3. Man's Ideal Woman (for women only)*

Read the Inventory of Feminine Values again. This time, think of *man's ideal woman* and respond to each statement as you think *she* would respond. Use the same form and the same scale to indicate the extent of your agreement or disagreement, again taking care to enter your responses to the odd-numbered statements in the proper space in Column A and the even-numbered statements in the proper spaces in Column B. To obtain your score, subtract the total of the figures in Column B from the total of the figures in Column A as before.

4. *Man's Ideal Woman (for men only)*
Read the Inventory of Feminine Values carefully and think how *your ideal woman* would respond to each statement. Use the same form and the same scale to indicate the extent of your agreement or disagreement with each statement. Take care to enter your responses to the odd-numbered statements in the proper space in Column A and the even-numbered statements in the proper space in Column B. To obtain your score, subtract the total of the figures in Column B from the total of the figures in Column A.

Scoring Interpretations*

The statements on this Inventory are arranged in such a way that a plus score indicates an orientation toward self-realization and independent achievement for a woman, while a minus score indicates an orientation toward family-centered interests, goals, and satisfactions. In scoring the Inventory in this way, we did not mean to ascribe either positive or negative values to these attributes. It might just as easily have been scored the other way and, at one time, actually was.

1 Woman's Self-Perception
If you had a self-perception score between +4 and −4, you are among the one-third of the women we studied who had similar scores. A score in this range means, in essence, that you are a woman with strong family-oriented interests, but you also have equally strong needs for self-realization and a life independent of your home and family.

If you had a score higher than a4, you are among the one-third of the women we tested whose self-orientation overbalanced their family orientation. Most women who held this view of themselves had scores between +5 and +12, which indicate a strong drive toward self-realization and independent achievement, while still retaining a clear-cut family commitment. Only one woman in nine had a score of +13 or higher; and if your score went above +21, your self-perception corresponds to only one woman in fifty of our research. Scores in this range indicate an extremely strong drive toward self-realization with a corresponding decrease in family-oriented interests.

Interestingly enough, much the same things can be said about the size of the company in which you find yourself if you had scores below −4. One-third of our respondents also fell into this range, most of them with scores from −3 to −12, with only one in seven going below this. A score in the −5 to −12 range clearly indicates a strong family-oriented view which, however, retains some of the components of self-realization. It is when you get into scores of −13 to −20 (where we found only one woman in eight) and especially when you go below −20 (where we found only one woman in fifty) that the family orientation begins to overwhelm self-realization needs and drives rather completely.

2. Woman's Ideal Woman

If you are like our typical respondent, your score on this version of the Inventory corresponded very closely to your self-perception score. Fifty percent of the women we tested had scores on these two forms within four points of each other. For these women, and for you if you fell within this group, your view of yourself and your view of how you would like to be are reasonably homogeneous. You are just about what you would like to be.

If your scores on these two forms were further apart, consider which is higher. Here the mathematics can get a bit tricky. If you had two plus scores there is no problem; but if you had two minus scores, the higher one in this case is the one closer to zero, so that a −7 would be "higher" than a −19. If your self-perception score was higher than your ideal score by more than four points, you are, like 30 percent of the women we studied, more concerned with your self and your activities outside the home than you would like to be. The larger the discrepancy the larger the gap between you and your ideal. Twenty-four percent of our respondents had a gap of more than ten points; 15 percent had a gap of twenty points or more.

If, in contrast, your ideal score was higher than your self-perception score by more than four points, you, like 20 percent of our respondents, are not as self-oriented as you would like to be. Here large gaps were less frequent, for only one woman in eight (12 percent) had a gap larger than ten points and one in fourteen (7 percent) a gap larger than twenty points.

3. Man's Ideal Woman (for women only)

If you answered this version of the Inventory like most of the women we studied, your score came out a minus; that is, you saw man's ideal woman as more concerned with family responsibilities than self-realization. Eighty-seven percent of the women in our research answered this way. If you came out with a plus score, you agreed with one woman in eight who saw man's ideal woman as oriented the other way: more concerned with self than with family. And if you had a score of exactly zero, you were another of that rare group, one woman in a hundred, who saw men as wanting a woman whose self-orientation exactly balanced her family concerns.

If you belong with the large majority of women who obtained minus scores, the size of that score enables us to place you more precisely. One woman in four (27 percent) saw men as wanting an extremely family-oriented, socially passive woman. This extreme was occupied by those with scores in the minus thirties, forties, fifties, and sixties. Another one in four saw a strong, but not an extreme, family orientation. To fall into this group your score would be between −17 and −29.

4. Man's Ideal Woman (for men only)

Most of the men who answered this version of the Inventory described a reasonably well-balanced woman as their ideal, in dramatic contrast to the women who answered it and saw man's ideal woman as definitely oriented to family concerns. One in three (35 percent) of the men had a score between −4 and +4 for their ideal woman. The other two men in every three divided in opposite directions: one saw their ideal woman as somewhat, but not excessively, more self- than family-oriented; the other saw her as somewhat, but not excessively, more family- than self-oriented.

You are a man with unusual views about women if you had a score beyond either +13 or −13. In either case, only one man in seven (if you were higher than +13) or one in nine (if you were lower than −13) had views like yours. If your score went beyond 20 at either end of the scale, then you are out there with the one man in twenty-five who wants a woman strongly oriented to one kind of value system or the other.

*In our research, we scrambled the order of the statements of the Inventory in each of its versions so the respondent might not readily remember how he or she had answered previously. If you wish to duplicate this procedure, read the Inventory and fill in the answer form in reverse numerical order or at random. But be sure to enter your responses in the proper space and column.

Decision-Making and Behavioral Surveys

Both the Decision-Making Survey and the Behavioral Survey are included in Appendix C in the form in which they were given to our respondents. Since both surveys are relatively long, it would be difficult to copy them out so that each reader could complete the forms. However, we recommend that you read the surveys through carefully, first, to understand the nature of our research in this field, and second, to test your own reactions to the questions asked. Even if you do not complete the forms, we think you will find that each situation will stimulate considerable thought and some lively discussions.

Decision Making Survey

(Circle one)   1.   Male   Female
(Circle one)   2.   Single   Married or Widowed   Divorced or Separated
(Circle one)   3.   Under 21   21-24   25-29   30-39   40-50   Over 50

Listed below are several specific situations which involve a decision. In each instance you should decide whether husband and wife should have an equal voice in making the decision or whether one's opinion should have greater weight. In the columns headed "SHOULD BE" indicate how YOU believe the decision should be made. In the columns headed "TRUE TODAY" indicate how the decision is made in your community among your friends and neighbors. Indicate your choice each time by placing a check in the appropriate column, using the following scale:

the number "1" means "Completely husband's decision"
the number "2" means "Both should be involved but husband's opinion should count more"
the number "3" means "They should have equal weight"
the number "4" means "Both should be involved but wife's opinion should count more"
the number "5" means "Completely wife's decision"

A. Assume Mr. & Mrs. Jones are a young married couple. Mrs. Jones is a housewife who does not work. Mr. Jones has a good job and they live comfortably. They have no children.

	SHOULD BE					TRUE TODAY				
	HUSBAND		Equal	WIFE		HUSBAND		Equal	WIFE	
	Complete	Mainly		Mainly	Complete	Complete	Mainly		Mainly	Complete
Decision Making Situation	1	2	3	4	5	1	2	3	4	5
1. Deciding what to do for an evening together.										
2. Deciding which news magazine to subscribe to.										
3. Deciding what the husband should do with his spare time.										
4. Deciding whether or not to have a baby.										
5. Deciding whether or not wife should buy a new dress she "doesn't really need."										
6. Deciding whether to buy a car or not.										
7. Deciding where to go on vacation.										
8. Deciding whether or not to get needed space by moving into larger, more expensive living quarters.										
9. Deciding what color to paint the living room.										
10. Deciding how the wife should vote in political elections.										
11. Deciding whether they can afford a color television.										
12. Deciding whether husband should accept offer of new job which will involve moving to a new community.										
13. Deciding how much to spend on gifts at appropriate occasions.										
14. Deciding how the husband should vote in political elections.										
15. Deciding sexual pattern of marriage.										
16. Deciding what to do with some money they have saved.										

	SHOULD		BE			TRUE		TODAY		
	HUSBAND		Equal	WIFE			HUSBAND		Equal	WIFE	
	Com-plete	Mainly		Mainly	Com-plete		Com-plete	Mainly		Mainly	Com-plete
	1	2	3	4	5		1	2	3	4	5
17. Deciding what wife should do with her spare time.											
18. Deciding how often to visit in-laws.											
19. Deciding whom to invite to a party.											
20. Deciding what to do with money received as a gift.											
21. Deciding best living arrangements for a dependent surviving parent.											
22. Deciding about husband's change of occupation.											

B. Now assume that both Mr. and Mrs. Jones work, as Mr. Jones' income is not enough for them to do all they would like to do. Consider the situations again, and indicate the Jones' relative role in decision making by a check in the appropriate column.

	1	2	3	4	5		1	2	3	4	5
1. Deciding what to do for an evening together.											
2. Deciding whether husband should accept offer of new job which will involve moving to a new community.											
3. Deciding which news magazine to subscribe to.											
4. Deciding whether or not to have a baby.											
5. Deciding what the husband should do in his spare time.											
6. Deciding whether they can afford a color television.											
7. Deciding sexual pattern of marriage.											
8. Deciding whether or not to get needed space by moving into larger, more expensive living quarters.											
9. Deciding how the wife should vote in political elections.											
10. Deciding where to go on vacation.											
11. Deciding whether to buy a car or not.											
12. Deciding what wife should do with her spare time.											
13. Deciding about husband's change of occupation.											
14. Deciding what color to paint the living room.											
15. Deciding how the husband should vote in political elections.											
16. Deciding how much to spend on gifts at appropriate occasions.											

	SHOULD BE					TRUE TODAY				
	HUSBAND		Equal	WIFE		HUSBAND		Equal	WIFE	
	Com-plete	Mainly		Mainly	Com-plete	Com-plete	Mainly		Mainly	Com-plete
	1	2	3	4	5	1	2	3	4	5
17. Deciding whether or not wife should buy a new dress she "doesn't really need."										
18. Deciding best living arrangements for a dependent surviving parent.										
19. Deciding what to do with some money they have saved.										
20. Deciding how often to visit in-laws.										
21. Deciding whom to invite to a party.										
22. Deciding what to do with money received as a gift.										

BEHAVIORAL SURVEY

Described below are a number of situations. Please answer the questions relating to each situation. In the yes-no questions, circle your choice of answers.

1. Mr. and Mrs. X are both employed. One evening, Mr. X arrives home and finds that his wife is not yet at home. She comes in shortly and says, "I'm sorry I was delayed at work. Dinner will be late tonight."
A. What does Mr. X think?_____

_____

B. What does Mr. X reply?_____

_____

2. Mr. and Mrs. X are reading the Sunday paper. She reads an article about the increasing number of married women going back to school. She thinks she would like to go back and complete her education and says to her husband, "What would you think of my going back to school?"
A. What does he think?_____

_____

B. What does he reply?_____

_____

3. At a community meeting, an issue about which both Mr. and Mrs. A feel rather strongly is being discussed. If they hold the same point of view, who should speak? (circle one)
                    Mrs. A only   Mr. A only   Both

4. Assuming they hold opposite points of view, who should speak? (circle one)
                    Mrs. A only   Mr. A only   Both

5. Mr. and Mrs. X have two young children. Mrs. X is a housewife and does not work. Mr. X is beginning a new career. His job keeps him at work several evenings a week and weekends. He often brings work home with him. In a discussion with friends, he is asked if he ever feels guilty about the time his work takes away from his family.

A. What does he think? _____

B. What does he say? _____

C. If his wife were asked if she feels any resentment about the time her husband's work takes away from his family, what would she think? _____

D. What does she say? _____

E. If the children were asked how they feel about their father's spending so much time away from them, what would they say? _____

6. Mr. and Mrs. X have lived in a very fine suburban community for 10 years. They own their own home and have many friends in the neighborhood. The children enjoy school and are active in extracurricular activities. One evening, Mr. X arrives home and tells his family that he has just been presented with an opportunity for a position at a considerable increase in salary, and a considerable rise in status. However, this change will entail the family's moving to another state.

A. If Mrs. X has opinions like most young women you know, what is her first thought on hearing this news? _____

B. What does she say? _____

C. If Mr. X has opinions like most men you know, what is his first thought on being offered the new position? _____

7. A married couple in their early thirties have one young child, too young to attend school. The wife does not work, but she devotes a considerable amount of time to voluntary community activities. One evening, in a discussion with friends, the topic of marriage and volunteer work is brought up. The wife is asked if she ever feels any guilt about the time that her volunteer work takes away from her marriage.

A. If she has ideas like most young women you know, what does she say? _____

B. Do you think this is what she believes   (circle one)   YES   NO

C. If no, what is her real belief? _____

Her husband is then asked if he feels any resentment about his wife's volunteer work.

D. If he has opinions like most men you know, what does he say? _____

E. Do you think this is what he really believes?   (circle one)   YES   NO

F. If no, what does he really believe? _____

G. If the child were asked how he feels about his mother being away from home, what would he say? _____

8. Both husband and wife are employed. The wife has been offered a promotion which would raise her salary and job status above that of her husband.
A. If the wife has opinions like most women you know, would she tell her husband about the offer?   (circle one)   YES   NO
B. If she decides to discuss the offer with her husband, if he has opinions like most men you know, what would he think when she asks his advice? _____

_____

C. What would he say? _____

_____

_____

D. If the wife has opinions like most women you know, would she accept the position? (circle one)   YES   NO
E. Why? _____

9. A couple is celebrating their 40th wedding anniversary. In recalling their life together, it is evident that they have achieved personal contentment and satisfaction and have accumulated considerable wordly goods and social status living together. They have a son, daughter and grandchildren, who are apparently satisfied and happy in their adjustment to life. The couple are both highly respected as leaders in the social, political, and philanthropic life of the community. At a dinner given in their honor, each is asked to respond to the following question: "What is the accomplishment of which you are most proud?"
A. What does the husband think of first? _____

_____

B. What does the wife think of first? _____

_____

C. What does the husband say? _____

_____

D. What does the wife say? _____

_____

10. A married couple in their early thirties have no children. They both work at full-time jobs. In a discussion with friends one evening, the topic of marriage and work is brought up. The wife is asked if she ever feels any guilt about the time that her job takes away from her marriage.
A. If she has opinions like most young women you know, what does she say? _____

_____

B. Do you think this is what she believes?   (circle one)   YES   NO
C. If no, what is her real belief? _____

_____

Her husband is then asked if he feels any resentment about his wife working.
D. If he has opinions like most young men you know, what does he say? _____

_____

E. Do you think this is what he really believes?   (circle one)   YES   NO
F. If no, what does he really believe? _____

_____

11. Now assume that this couple has one child, too young to attend school. The mother still works, with the child cared for by a competent and interested housekeeper. Again, the mother is asked if she experiences any guilt about working interfering with her marriage.

A. If she has opinions like most young women, what would she say? _____

B. Do you think this is what she believes?   (circle one)   YES   NO

C. If no, what is her real belief? _____

Her husband is then asked if he feels any resentment about his wife working.

D. If he has opinions like most young men you know, what does he say? _____

E. Do you think this is what he really believes?   (circle one)   YES   NO

F. If no, what does he really believe? _____

12. Listed below are several popular notions about men and women. Indicate if you agree with each by circling the "yes" or "no."

A. Providing equal educational opportunities for women has not resulted in equal intellectual achievements.   YES   NO

Why? _____

B. Girls who go into masculine careers like science will have difficulty getting a husband.
                                                                          YES   NO

Why? _____

C. Women best express their intelligence intuitively.   YES   NO
D. Teenage boys do not like girls who do well in school   YES   NO
E. Men who go into careers like nursing are not really masculine.   YES   NO
F. When with men, women often deliberately speak less intelligently
than they might.   YES   NO
G. Men do not like very intelligent women.   YES   NO

Why? _____

H. Equal educational opportunities should be provided for women.   YES   NO
Why? _____

13. You are a member of a college admissions committee. The college can accept only 3 of the following 6 candidates who have applied for admission. All have average I.Q.'s. The differences below are the only ones regarding these prospective candidates. Place a 1, 2, or 3 in front of the candidates to indicate your first, second and third choices.

____ A. Young man, average scholastic achievement, average attractiveness.

____ B. Young woman, average scholastic achievement, average attractiveness.

____ C. Young man, average scholastic achievement, physically unattractive.

____ D. Young woman, average scholastic achievement, physically unattractive.

____ E. Young woman, poor scholastic achievement, unusually attractive.

____ F. Middle-aged woman, average scholastic achievement, who married after high school and wants to begin college now that her children are in school.

14. Mr. and Mrs. X have three children, two in ₁ementary school and one too young for school. They have their own home in a nice community. Mr. X is making a good salary, but he feels he cannot take full advantage of his potentialities and ambitions in his present job. He is seriously thinking about a different line of work. However, he does not know how long it would take him to find a satisfactory job. Mr. and Mrs. X are discussing this with friends. In the discussion, someone says that married men are trapped in jobs by family responsibilities.

A. What does Mr. X think when he hears this statement?_____

B. What does he say?
_____

C. What does his wife think when she hears this statement?_____

D. What does she say?
_____

15. Imagine you are an employer with several women in executive and managerial positions in your employ. Your personnel manager wishes to discuss two of these women with you, since he has applications from qualified replacements. All are excellent employees except for the specific problems noted below.

A. The first is an unmarried woman who periodically misses two or three days from work a month. She claims that she feels very ill at that time of the month.
Would you advise him to retain this woman?   (circle one)   YES   NO
Why?_____

B. The second woman is married, with small children. She is absent on the average of two or three times a month because her children have colds or other minor ailments.
Would you advise him to retain this woman?   (circle one)   YES   NO
Why?_____

16. Below are qualities attributed to wives. Place a 1, 2, or 3 in the appropriate column next to the quality that you consider first, second, and third choices to a man considering marriage, and to a man married 15 years.

	Considering Marriage	After 15 Years
A. Ability to be a good mother.	____	____
B. Ability to earn money.	____	____
C. Good looking.	____	____
D. Good education.	____	____
E. Ability to be a good companion.	____	____
F. Intelligence.	____	____
G. Sexual competence.	____	____
H. Ability to help him socially.	____	____

17. Number the following functions in a married woman's life according to their order of importance to a woman (column 1), and to a man (column 2).

	Woman	Man
A. Bringing up children.	____	____
B. Contributing to community affairs.	____	____
C. Developing her husband's potentialities.	____	____
D. Making the home comfortable for her husband and family.	____	____
E. Contributing to the financial suppor' of the home.	____	____
F. Developing her own potentialities.	____	____

18. Below are qualities attributed to husbands. Place a 1, 2, or 3 in the appropriate column, next to the quality that you consider first second and third choices to a woman considering marriage and to a woman married 15 years.

	Considering Marriage	After 15 Years
A. Ability to be a good wage earner.	___	___
B. Ability to be a good father.	___	___
C. Good education.	___	___
D. Good looking.	___	___
E. Willingness to help around the house.	___	___
F. Sexual competence.	___	___
G. Intelligence.	___	___
H. Ability to be a good companion.	___	___
I. Ability to help her socially.	___	___

19. If it is a question of staying single, or marrying below one's ideal, on what qualities listed below should a person compromise? In the column headed Man Should Compromise circle the word "yes" next to each characteristic on which you think a man should compromise. Do the same in the woman's column.

	Man Should Compromise	Woman Should Compromise
A. Education.	YES	YES
B. Social Position.	YES	YES
C. Intelligence.	YES	YES
D. Financial Position.	YES	YES
E. Physical Appearance.	YES	YES
F. Emotional Stability.	YES	YES
G. Sexual Competence.	YES	YES

20. Five couples (A,B,C,D, and E) are contemplating marriage. In discussing their plans with a marriage counselor, each couple finds that they are compatible in most areas, except one of those noted below. In each case, indicate how serious you think the difficulty is according to the following code: 1-extremely serious, 2-serious, 3-not serious.

____A. The man, although he had dropped out of school, has achieved success in business. The woman is a college graduate.

____B. The lone parent of the man will live with the couple.

____C. The man can well support a family, and wishes one as soon as possible. The woman does not wish to have a family right away. She wishes to work until she has furthered her career.

____D. The woman had dropped out of high school at the end of her second year. The man works in one of the professions.

____E. The lone parent of the woman will live with the couple.

Companionship Questionaire

In a recent study, several thousand men and women throughout the United States were asked to indicate the attributes most important to a man or woman considering marriage, and to a man or woman married 15 years. In answering men and women alike selected "ability to be a good companion" as the first choice both for men and women considering marriage and also after 15 years. What characteristics, skills and behaviors would *you* include in the concept "ability to be a good companion," for a wife for husband?

A. For a wife, the ability to be a good companion includes:

B. For a husband, the ability to be a good companion includes:

Index